D1432780

PRODUCTION FUNCTIONS

CONTRIBUTIONS
TO
ECONOMIC ANALYSIS

75

Honorary Editor

J. TINBERGEN

Editors

D. W. JORGENSON

J. WAELBROECK

NORTH-HOLLAND PUBLISHING COMPANY
AMSTERDAM - LONDON

PRODUCTION FUNCTIONS

An Integration of Micro and Macro,
Short Run and Long Run Aspects

LEIF JOHANSEN

Institute of Economics,
University of Oslo, Norway

1972

NORTH-HOLLAND PUBLISHING COMPANY

AMSTERDAM - LONDON

Library of Congress Catalog Card Number: 70-157030
ISBN: 0 7204 3175 1

Publishers:

NORTH-HOLLAND PUBLISHING COMPANY – AMSTERDAM

NORTH-HOLLAND PUBLISHING COMPANY, LTD. – LONDON

Printed in The Netherlands

Introduction to the series

This series consists of a number of hitherto unpublished studies, which are introduced by the editors in the belief that they represent fresh contributions to economic science.

The term *economic analysis* as used in the title of the series has been adopted because it covers both the activities of the theoretical economist and the research worker.

Although the analytical methods used by the various contributors are not the same, they are nevertheless conditioned by the common origin of their studies, namely theoretical problems encountered in practical research. Since for this reason, business cycle research and national accounting, research work on behalf of economic policy, and problems of planning are the main sources of the subjects dealt with, they necessarily determine the manner of approach adopted by the authors. Their methods tend to be "practical" in the sense of not being too far remote from application to actual economic conditions. In addition they are quantitative rather than qualitative.

It is the hope of the editors that the publication of these studies will help to stimulate the exchange of scientific information and to reinforce international cooperation in the field of economics.

THE EDITORS

Preface

I have used some rudiments of the theory (or theories) presented in this book in teaching at the University of Oslo for a number of years. The more systematic work started during a stay of a few weeks at the University of Essex in 1967. Since then I have had the opportunity to discuss the main ideas with colleagues at seminars in Belgium and Sweden and at the Second World Congress of the Econometric Society in Cambridge 1970 besides, of course, at the University of Oslo. I have received many interesting and useful comments, which have influenced the final form of the work as presented on the following pages. They are too many to be mentioned individually, and I can only express my gratitude in general terms.

Most of the research has been carried out at the Institute of Economics at the University of Oslo, where a number of research assistants have been more or less involved in special parts of the work. Their contributions have appeared in part in research reports from the Institute of Economics. In this preface I want to thank them all for their very valuable contributions and wholehearted collaboration; in the text I have tried to individualize my indebtedness by giving more specific references.

Work is still going on along various lines suggested by the following chapters. By delaying the book even more behind the original time schedule I might have included more material. However, I hope the book will convey the impression of a reasonably complete structure as it stands.

The research work has been partly supported by *Norges Almenvitenskapelige Forskningsråd*, and some special expenses in connection with the preparation of the final manuscript were covered by *Professor Wilhelm Keilhaus Minnefond*. To both institutions I want to express my gratitude.

LEIF JOHANSEN

Table of contents

CHAPTER 1

Introduction

Econometric research on production functions is growing ever more sophisticated as far as functional forms and statistical methodology are concerned. Nevertheless the results of this research are not very comforting. The increasing degree of sophistication has, by producing many widely diverging results, served to reveal and expose our ignorance in this field rather than to produce firmly established knowledge.

My feeling is that this may be due to the fact that, in spite of the sophistication in other respects, the basic notion of production functions has remained almost untouched. The crudeness of the concept of the production function, as it is being used in most econometric research, is accordingly out of proportion with the sophistication of the theories and methods by which it is surrounded. Perhaps further progress might therefore best be made by subjecting the very notion of a production function to a critical examination and reformulation. This is the main aim of the present study.

The point may be illustrated by reference to a recent study of estimations of the elasticity of substitution in Constant Elasticity of Substitution functions – Mayor (1969).[1] The author sums up previous research by asserting that studies based upon time-series have produced results clustering around the value of one-half, whereas cross section studies have typically yielded estimates close to unity. He then goes on to consider the question of "which of these estimates, if any, approximate the actual elasticities". The question is tackled by considering specification problems which may lead to biases in estimation. The approach taken by the present study is rather to ask if it is at all meaningful to talk about "the actual elasticities" in this way as something unique which we could try to reveal by various types of data. It may well be that we *should* get different estimates by different types of data, these different estimates reflecting different aspects of a more complex technological structure than that described by traditional production functions.

It should be said right at the outset that I do not claim any general validity for the approach to be pursued in this study. It will mainly be con-

---

[1] See the bibliography at the end of the book.

cerned with sectors of production where there are many micro units (enterprises or smaller units, e.g. machines) producing a fairly homogeneous type of output. For such a sector we shall study various concepts of production functions, in relation to the micro/macro and short run/long run distinctions, and their interconnections. A by-product will be some thoughts on the classification of types of technological progress. Some new ideas on the economic growth process will also emerge from the discussion of the production functions.

The assumptions about substitution possibilities are crucial to the whole approach. As I have already pointed out I do not believe the assumptions which will be adopted here to be of general validity, but I believe that they are more realistic than the traditional assumptions for many branches of manufacturing industry and also for some transport and other service industries.

The main ideas incorporated in the present approach were proposed already in my 1959 paper with its distinction between substitution possibilities "ex ante" and "ex post" and its emphasis on the embodiment of technological progress. Closely related is the theoretical part of Salter's book (1960) with the distinction between "best practice productivity" and "average practice productivity". Furthermore a very important source is Houthakker's paper (1955–56), which has not yet had much impact upon theory and practice of production studies, but which fits in in a very natural way as a main building block in the approach which is to be outlined here. The present work had been carried some way already when I read Solow's plea[2] that Houthakker's idea ought to be followed up, but his remarks were of course stimulating.

The emphasis of the present study will be on theory. It is hoped, however, that the study will be useful also for clarifying the question of what sorts of production functions one really gets (if any at all) by the various types of data and econometric methods commonly used in empirical work, as well as for suggesting new approaches for empirical work. Some simple illustrations, mainly based on data from the Norwegian tanker fleet, will be provided.

In the following the basic production units at the micro level will be referred to simply as "production units". In practice these may be identified as enterprises, departments within enterprises or individual pieces of production equipment, according to practical circumstances. The aggregated level

---

[2] See Solow (1967), pp. 46–48.

will be referred to as the "sector" level or the "macro" level. In practice this could best be conceived as a branch of an economy with a reasonably homogeneous output. In the main empirical illustrations which will be reported the production units are tanker ships and the sector is the tanker branch of Norwegian shipping.

CHAPTER 2

Different concepts of production functions and their interconnections

2.1. *General considerations*

The fundamental assumption underlying the following approach is that the essential technological choice with respect to factor proportions and exploitation of new production techniques has to be made at the stage when investment in new production equipment takes place. At later stages choice is restricted to deciding to what extent the equipment is to be operated within bounds set by its capacity, operation requiring current inputs in fixed proportions as between themselves and in proportion to output. Disembodied technological progress modifies this scheme to some extent, and it will also be argued further on that somewhat more general interpretations can be placed on the model. However, most of the time we shall think of the model as representing the simple structure suggested above.

The case for such assumptions is straight-forward: Direct inspections of production processes indicate that such assumptions give a better approximation than the traditional assumption of smooth substitution possibilities at all moments of time. Now there is of course much talk about short-run and long-run production functions in connection with traditional theory. Presumably this is meant to take care of similar aspects, e.g. when the elasticity of substitution is thought of as being different in the short run and in the long run. However, these considerations are rather obscure and not easy to identify operationally with actual production processes as visualized in physical or technical terms. In other words, I think it is, in very many cases, easier to communicate with technicians and production managers on the basis of the theory to be outlined here than on the basis of traditional theory.

There are two stumbling-blocks which may render the present study irrelevant.

(A) There may be such wide substitution possibilities between inputs by operating existing equipment that the present theory does not yield a reasonable approximation. This is the main point to be considered in each individual case when there is a question of what type of theory to adopt as a basis for study of a branch of production. However, even for sectors where the present approach is somewhat unrealistic, I think that exercises along the lines suggested by this study may be a good starting-point for developing more general models with some more flexible assumptions about the operation of existing equipment.[1]

(B) There may be various types of interactions between different vintages of capital equipment, e.g. in the form that certain basic structures already acquired may facilitate the instalment of new pieces of equipment, or that modernization or reconstruction of old equipment may be more profitable than either operating the equipment in its old shape or acquiring new equipment. We would then get equipment of mixed vintages which are different from equipment of any well defined vintage, and it might be necessary to trace the whole history of individual pieces of equipment.[2] However, even where such effects are important it leaves much of the following analysis (those parts which refer to the short run) unaffected. It would mainly affect the study of the dynamic aspects.

The degree to which the difficulties raised by these two points will make themselves felt may depend on the definitions of inputs and output and on the delimitation of the micro units of production. E.g., if we have some basic inputs which are used in the production of intermediate goods, which are again used in the production of a final output, then the theory to be outlined here may be valid for each process or stage of production, with the individual machines as micro units, without it being valid for the vertically integrated process leading from the basic inputs to the final output with the enterprise as the micro unit and the intermediate goods suppressed in the formulation of the model.

On the basis of the assumptions suggested above it is useful to distinguish between the following four concepts of production functions:

(1) The ex ante function at the micro level.
(2) The ex post function at the micro level.
(3) The short-run (or transient) function at the macro level.
(4) The long-run (or steady state) function at the macro level.

---

[1] Suggestions of elements for such a more general theory may be found in Svennilson (1964), Scheper (1968), Park (1966) and Hu (1970). Park introduces "ex post substitution" by letting a more or less restricted part of the ex ante isoquant map describe the available substitution possibilities also ex post. This seems to me to be somewhat artificial. Scheper and Hu introduce a CES-function as the ex post production function.

[2] A study which goes some way in the direction of allowing for such effects is Gort and Boddy (1967).

A preliminary survey of these concepts of production functions and their interrelations will be given in this chapter. They will all be taken up for more careful discussion in subsequent chapters.

Most of the time we shall, for ease of exposition, consider production processes with only two current inputs besides capital equipment. Generalizations to an arbitrary number of inputs should be straight-forward on almost all points.

2.2. *The ex ante function at the micro level*

The basic description of technology must start at the micro level.

The ex ante function at the micro level indicates the possibilities from which we have to choose when a new micro unit is to be established. It may be said to summarize the relevant technological knowledge at a certain point of time. In the words of Salter it is "the production function which includes all possible designs".[3]

In describing a new production unit we have to talk about capacity and inputs at full capacity operation rather than actual output and inputs as in a traditional production function. We introduce the following notation:

$\bar{x}$ = capacity (measured by maximum output) of the new production unit;

$\bar{v}_1$ = input of factor No. 1 when the unit is operated at full capacity;

$\bar{v}_2$ = defined correspondingly for factor No. 2;

$\bar{k}$ = amount of capital invested in the production unit.

We shall generally assume that there are substitution possibilities between all inputs at this stage so that the range of possible choices can be appropriately described by a function

$$\bar{x} = \phi(\bar{v}_1, \bar{v}_2, \bar{k}) \qquad (2.1)$$

with such properties as are usually attributed to traditional production functions.[4] In particular we shall assume that there exists, for each relative factor combination $\bar{v}_1 : \bar{v}_2 : \bar{k}$ an optimal scale, i.e. a level of capacity $\bar{x}$ at which

---

[3] See Salter (1960) p. 15.

[4] When I introduced an ex ante production function in my 1959 paper I suggested that the total capacity already established in a sector might be included as an additional argument in the ex ante function for further expansion as an expression of pressure on natural resources or of external economies or diseconomies, see Johansen (1959) pp. 160–161 and 166. I still think this would be realistic in many cases, but the idea will not be pursued here.

inputs per unit of output at full capacity operation are lower or at least not higher than for all other capacity levels.[5]

A few comments on the interpretation of the variables introduced in (2.1) may be called for.

First of all, output $\bar{x}$ and current inputs $\bar{v}_1$ and $\bar{v}_2$ must have the dimension amount (volume, weight, etc.) per unit of time.

Underlying the definition of concepts referring to *capacity* there must be some assumption about working hours per day (week, month, year). If the concepts are defined on the basis of normal working hours and one shift, and we then go over to considering two-shift work and both shifts are equivalent, then we might still use the function (2.1) as it is if we reckon inputs and output per hour of operation. If we, as will often be the case, measure inputs and output per day, we would have to redefine the function into

$$\bar{x} = \phi^0(\bar{v}_1, \bar{v}_2, \bar{k}) \equiv 2\phi\left(\frac{\bar{v}_1}{2}, \frac{\bar{v}_2}{2}, \bar{k}\right).$$

With twice as much of current inputs per day we obtain twice as much of output per day on the basis of the same invested amount $\bar{k}$. If the second shift is less efficient than the first shift, an appropriate way of indicating the situation may be to say that an amount of investment creates *two* micro units, one first shift unit and one second shift unit, with different characteristics. We will touch upon this point again later on.

The measurement of capital is usually considered to be a very dubious and controversial affair. In the present context it is not necessarily all that difficult. There will, at least for most of the analysis, be no need for aggregating capital equipment over different vintages. On the other hand, it may be necessary to face the fact that production units to be established at the same time may have different capital equipment – qualitatively different, or consisting of different combinations of basic elements – according to which factor proportions they are designed for. Formally there is no difficulty in conceiving of a function like (2.1) with all such aspects of capital specified as arguments of the function, and this would not change much of the following analysis. Mainly for expository reasons we shall, however, retain the

---

[5] This assumption is not absolutely indispensable for the analysis. The essential point is that there is something which restricts the size of each unit to be established so that we get a number of production units in the sector under consideration. Many parts of the analysis will be more relevant when there is a large number of micro units in the sector than when there is a small number.

simple formulation (2.1). If capital is heterogeneous as suggested above we may think of our sector as a price taker in the capital goods market and $\bar{k}$ as the value of the capital equipment acquired for a new production unit calculated on the basis of the given prices. Starting out from a more fundamental production function with several arguments pertaining to capital input, (2.1) may then be established by an efficiency requirement with regard to types and composition of capital stock for each given set of values for $\bar{v}_1$, $\bar{v}_2$ and $\bar{k}$.

One aspect which cannot so easily be accomodated by such an approach is the durability aspect of capital, because when different durabilities can be chosen efficiency considerations could only reduce capital measurement to one dimension on the basis of assumptions about the future. When this aspect is important we could therefore add the expected durability as a fourth argument in (2.1).[6]

The ex ante function was described above as "summarizing the relevant technological knowledge at a certain point of time". Consequently it is a rather relative concept. The question which has to be answered in order to give precise meaning to the concept is – technological knowledge *where* or in the possession of *whom*? Unless there is perfect knowledge everywhere, in the sense that know-how available somewhere or to somebody is freely available everywhere and to everybody interested in it, there will be a whole nest of ex ante functions, one for every group or quarter. We may then define the *efficient ex ante function* by associating with each $\bar{v}_1$, $\bar{v}_2$, $\bar{k}$-combination the largest $\bar{x}$-value which can be obtained from this input-combination on the basis of any individual ex ante function. The efficient ex ante function thus defined may coincide with one special ex ante function over its whole domain, but it will in general consist of segments from several individual functions. The individual ex ante functions are relevant for a theory aiming at explaining actual development, since actual investment decisions have to be taken on the basis of such ex ante functions. (There are of course interesting problems of trade in know-how etc. involved.) For normative studies the efficient ex ante function is of particular importance, but when costs of information, organization etc. are taken into account it does not follow that all investments taking place in a certain period should result in $\bar{x}$, $\bar{v}_1$, $\bar{v}_2$, $\bar{k}$-points obeying the efficient ex ante function.

Even apart from the relativity of the concept as explained above, the ex ante function is a somewhat vague concept. It may be reasonably well de-

---

[6] Cf. Salter (1960), pp. 18–19.

fined for factor combinations that have been tried out in practice before, but for virgin parts of the domain of the function there may be considerable uncertainty about it. One might say, of course, that although there is no empirically founded knowledge about it in such regions of the domain, it nevertheless "is there". For theoretical purposes at least I think this is an acceptable idea, but it does not remove all doubts about the concept. There will necessarily be some "Research and Development" work involved in designing equipment not of the traditional type. The more R & D-efforts are put into it, the better results as measured by the variables $\bar{v}_1$, $\bar{v}_2$, $\bar{k}$ and $\bar{x}$ will presumably be obtained. Should we then define the ex ante function on the basis of no R & D-input (in which case the scope for substitution in the ex ante function would be more or less confined to previously used factor proportions), on the basis of some sort of average amount of R & D-inputs, or on the basis of the maximum conceivable amount of R & D-inputs during a given period of time? Or could we escape by introducing the amount of R & D-efforts as an additional argument in the function? I think there are no easy answers to these questions. To some extent the answers will have to depend on the purpose of the study. For the mainly theoretical purposes of the present study we shall not need to come to a decision concerning all such issues; we shall rather proceed on the assumption that we are dealing with a sector of production where these ambiguities are not of paramount importance.[7] On the other hand, as soon as one attempts to study ex ante functions empirically, one will have to delve somewhat more deeply into these questions.

Although it will not be our concern in the present study, I think the considerations presented above suggest an opening for linking studies of the diffusion of technological knowledge to production function studies such as those outlined in this and the following chapters.

2.3. *The ex post function at the micro level*

We now consider a production unit which has already been established on the basis of an ex ante function like (2.1), i.e. special values have been chosen for $\bar{k}$, $\bar{v}_1$, $\bar{v}_2$, implying a certain value of $\bar{x}$ which is the output capacity of this production unit. Thus $\bar{x}$, $\bar{v}_1$, $\bar{v}_2$ and $\bar{k}$ are no longer variables. The

---

[7] As in previous instances this assumption is not crucial for the whole study. In particular, the study of the short-run production function at the macro level, which makes up a major part of the book, is unaffected by the problems mentioned above.

production possibilities embodied in this unit are then assumed to be as follows:

$$0 \leqq x \leqq \bar{x};$$

$$v_1 = \frac{\bar{v}_1}{\bar{x}} x, \text{ or } v_1 = \xi_1 x, \text{ where } \xi_1 = \frac{\bar{v}_1}{\bar{x}}; \qquad (2.2)$$

$$v_2 = \frac{\bar{v}_2}{\bar{x}} x, \text{ or } v_2 = \xi_2 x, \text{ where } \xi_2 = \frac{\bar{v}_2}{\bar{x}}.$$

The symbols without bars denote actual output and actual current inputs. The first line in (2.2) then reflects the output capacity of the unit, while the second and third line indicate that current inputs are required in the same proportions to output as they would be at full capacity utilization. For a given unit of time one may think of the variation in x and the accompanying variations in v_1 and v_2 e.g. in the form of using the equipment for a larger or smaller portion of total time, but other interpretations are also possible.

The symbols ξ_1 and ξ_2 have been introduced in (2.2) for notational convenience, indicating input per unit of output for the two current inputs. We shall talk about ξ_1 and ξ_2 as current input coefficients. They are variables ex ante, but fixed coefficients ex post, i.e. when the equipment is installed. From the ex ante point of view their range of variation is determined by the requirement that they have to fulfil (2.1), i.e. we must have

$$\bar{x} = \phi(\xi_1 \bar{x}, \xi_2 \bar{x}, \bar{k}). \qquad (2.3)$$

In (2.2) v_1 and v_2 are actually used amounts of inputs. If we instead let v_1 and v_2 denote *available* amounts we must have $v_1 \geqq \xi_1 x$ and $v_2 \geqq \xi_2 x$, and we could write instead of (2.2):

$$x = \text{Min} \left[\frac{\bar{x}}{\bar{v}_1} v_1, \frac{\bar{x}}{\bar{v}_2} v_2, \bar{x} \right] = \text{Min} \left[\frac{v_1}{\xi_1}, \frac{v_2}{\xi_2}, \bar{x} \right]. \qquad (2.4)$$

However, in the following it will in most cases be more appropriate to consider the amounts of inputs actually used in the production process, and then formulation (2.2) is the relevant one.

I am of course aware of the restrictiveness of the formulation given above. In practice there is obviously some scope for substitution also ex post. Let me speculate a little bit on a more general formulation.[8]

---

[8] The following paragraphs are not necessary for the reading of the rest of the book.

Previous suggestions[9] employ an ex post function in the same variables as the ex ante function, using only one current input – labour – in addition to capital. This holds also for Professor Solow's more special vintage model (Solow 1960), which assumes the same function ex post as ex ante. It seems to me that a better formulation is to specify the ex post function only in terms of current inputs, the capital stock once installed playing the part of a fixed factor. A rather general formulation would then be something like the following. Let in general

$$x = \lambda \ (v_1, v_2, t), \ (v_1, v_2) \in D_{\lambda t} \tag{2.5}$$

represent an ex post production function in terms of actually consumed inputs, where the input combination has to belong to a domain $D_{\lambda t}$ in the v_1, v_2-space. (If we instead specify the function in terms of *available* amounts of inputs, we would not have to specify the domain $D_{\lambda t}$; we could then let the ex post function be defined over the whole non-negative quadrant for v_1, v_2.) When in the sequel we speak about the function $\lambda()$ it is understood that we also include the specification of its domain $D_{\lambda t}$. The argument t is meant to measure time from the date investment is made and is intended to reflect changes in production possibilities due to detereoration of equipment etc. In general the domain will also change. In the special case of "sudden death" $\lambda()$ and D will remain unaltered up to a certain time, and then collapse to zero.

With such ex post functions it would be necessary to reconsider also the formulation of the ex ante function.

By means of investments of various types and amounts it will be possible to establish various ex post functions. We may accordingly define a set Λ, which is the set of all ex post production functions which can be established through an act of investment, i.e. Λ is the set of all possible $\lambda()$'s. The specification of Λ is one element of the specification of the ex ante function in the general case. It might be natural to consider it as the range of the ex ante function, but in what follows we shall reverse the viewpoint and consider it as its domain.

For a full specification of the ex ante possibilities we must also consider the capital requirement.

Let us first consider the case where capital input can be measured by one single variable k. It then seems plausible that each ex post function $\lambda()$ which

---

[9] See the footnote on p. 5.

can be established requires a certain amount of capital so that we could now write the ex ante function in the following form:

$$\bar{k} = \phi^*(\lambda), \lambda \in \Lambda, \tag{2.6}$$

i.e. ϕ^* is a function which to each possible ex post function $\lambda()$ in the set Λ assigns a real number which is to be interpreted as the amount of capital which must be invested in a new production unit in order to start the ex post function operating.

Since the same amount of capital can be "shaped" in different forms, the function (2.6) cannot necessarily be inverted. In other words, the same amount of capital can give rise to various different ex post functions.

If we more generally consider the investment not as one variable, but rather as a vector, a more complicated formulation than (2.6) would be necessary. One might e.g. find it useful to define "indifference classes" in the investment space, one such class containing all investment vectors which establish the same ex post function. With a sufficiently detailed description of the investment (a sufficiently large number of components in the vector) one might establish a one-to-one correspondence between non-overlapping indifference classes and ex post functions $\lambda()$ in Λ.

Let me briefly return to the question as to whether the capital stock invested in a production unit should be retained in the ex post function. Presumably the reason for retaining it – as is done by some authors mentioned above – is that the capital stock will decline or deteriorate as a result of wear and tear and accordingly production possibilities will shrink. This is taken care of in the formulation above by letting $\lambda()$ (and its domain D) depend on t. Now, if we are absolutely free to define any time function we might find appropriate for the changes in capital stock due to the passing of time, anything which can be described in one of the frameworks can also be covered by the other one. The choice between the two then appears to be mainly a matter of terminology. However, there are conceivable time profiles of $\lambda(v_1, v_2, t)$ which it would seem rather artificial to ascribe to changes in the amount of capital; e.g., it is not unknown that the capacity or efficiency of a production unit increases for some time after the equipment has been installed.

Within the framework suggested above the one extreme vintage model, the Solow model which assumes the same substitution possibilities ex ante and ex post could be specified in the following way (with two current inputs instead of only one). The class Λ is a parametric class consisting of functions $\lambda(v_1, v_2, he^{-\delta t})$, where $\lambda()$ is now a specified functional form, e.g. the Cobb-

Douglas function, δ is a constant, and h is a parameter, $h \geqq 0$. Each element of Λ is characterized by a value of the parameter h, and (2.6) could then be given the simple form of a function of h, and indeed the very simple form $\bar{k} = \phi^*(\lambda) = h$.

The other extreme case, defined by (2.2), which we have chosen to adopt here, can be viewed as a special case of the general formulation in the following way. The class of possible ex post functions Λ is the class of "Leontief functions" with limited capacity. Each function can be specified in terms of three parameters ξ_1, ξ_2 and $\bar{x}$, in such a way that $x = v_1/\xi_1$, where the domain of the function $D_{\lambda t}$ is restricted by $v_2 = (\xi_2/\xi_1)v_1$ and $v_1 \leqq \xi_1\bar{x}$. If the equipment retains its efficiency unchanged for a certain duration and then breaks down, we may express this (as suggested above) by saying that the domain collapses into the single point 0, 0 for v_1, v_2 after this duration. The full class Λ of possible ex post functions is defined by all production functions of the type described above for such values of the parameters $\xi_1, \xi_2, \bar{x}$ as satisfy (2.3) for some value of $\bar{k}$. The ex ante function, which is in general of the form (2.6), can in this special case be given as a function of $\xi_1, \xi_2, \bar{x}$ since these parameters identify uniquely the member of the class; in fact it is $\bar{k}$ as a function of ξ_1, ξ_2 and $\bar{x}$ as implicitly defined by (2.3).

Alternatively we could have based the formulation of Λ on the form (2.4) of the ex post function.

These formulations are of course rather cumbersome if we have in mind only such special cases as those mentioned above. However, a formulation like the one given here in terms of $\lambda()$, Λ and ϕ^* seems to me to be convenient if one wants to cover both such extreme cases as well as various intermediate cases like those referred to on p. 5.

In principle it would certainly be possible to work through the material in the following sections and chapters on the basis of such a more general model. It is a matter of judgement that I think the formulation (2.2) (in some contexts with some generalized interpretations to be mentioned later on) is a good approximation to realities in many cases. When (2.2) is a good approximation, then much more specific and interesting conclusions can be obtained on the basis of this formulation than by sticking to the general formulation in order to give some slight scope for ex post substitution.

2.4. The short-run production function at the macro level

The sector to which the production function at the macro level refers, will at any given moment of time comprise a certain number of production units.

On the basis of the assumptions made above each of these production units will have the simple structure given by (2.2), however in general with different production capacities and different input coefficients ξ_1 and ξ_2. Total production will be obtained as a result of a combination of activities of the type (2.2). If we now let superscript $i = 1, 2, \ldots, N$ refer to the production units, and furthermore let X, V_1 and V_2 denote output and available inputs for the sector as a whole, then we must have:

$$X = \sum_{i=1}^{N} x^i, \tag{2.7a}$$

$$V_1 \geqq \sum_{i=1}^{N} \xi_1^i x^i, \tag{2.7b}$$

$$V_2 \geqq \sum_{i=1}^{N} \xi_2^i x^i, \tag{2.7c}$$

$$0 \leqq x^i \leqq \bar{x}^i \quad (i = 1, 2, \ldots, N). \tag{2.7d}$$

The conditions in (2.7) indicate the production possibilities of the sector. Without further assumptions they do, however, not define a production function in the sense of a unique value of X for every given V_1, V_2.

We now introduce the assumption of efficiency for the sector as a whole. This means that for every given V_1, V_2 we assume that X defined by (2.7a) be maximized subject to the conditions given in (2.7b–d). This is a rather common approach to aggregation in economics. As usual two interpretations could be placed on this: we may assign a normative significance to it, or we may consider it as positive theory under certain assumptions about market behaviour under decentralized decision-making.

The optimization problem raised above is a simple linear programming problem. The nature of the solution can best be studied by considering the dual problem. For this purpose we first rewrite the conditions of the problem in the following form

$$
\begin{array}{rcl|l}
\xi_1^1 x^1 + \xi_1^2 x^2 + \ldots + \xi_1^N x^N & \leqq V_1 & & q_1 \\
\xi_2^1 x^1 + \xi_2^2 x^2 + \ldots + \xi_2^N x^N & \leqq V_2 & & q_2 \\
x^1 & \leqq \bar{x}^1 & & r^1 \\
x^2 & \leqq \bar{x}^2 & & r^2 \\
& \vdots & & \vdots \\
x^N & \leqq \bar{x}^N & & r^N.
\end{array}
\tag{2.8}
$$

The objective function is (2.7a).

To the right in (2.8) we have assigned (non-negative) dual variables to the various conditions: q_1 and q_2 correspond to the restrictions on factor uses and $r_1, r_2, \ldots, r_N$ correspond to capacity limitations.

The full dual problem is to minimize

$$q_1 V_1 + q_2 V_2 + r^1 \bar{x}^1 + r^2 \bar{x}^2 + \ldots + r^N \bar{x}^N \tag{2.9}$$

under the conditions

$$q_1 \xi_1^i + q_2 \xi_2^i + r^i \geqq 1 \qquad (i = 1, 2, \ldots, N), \tag{2.10}$$

which are obtained by transposing the coefficient matrix in (2.8) and using the coefficients 1 of the objective function (2.7a) as constants to the right in (2.10).

From the correspondences between the solutions of the direct and the dual problem it follows that equality in (2.10) is necessary (but not sufficient) for $x^i > 0$. Furthermore $r^i > 0$ implies that the capacity limit $\bar{x}_i$ is reached. The possible situations are represented in the following scheme:

	$r^i = 0$	$r^i > 0$
$q_1 \xi_1^i + q_2 \xi_2^i + r^i = 1$	$0 \leqq x^i \leqq \bar{x}^i$	$x^i = \bar{x}^i$
$q_1 \xi_1^i + q_2 \xi_2^i + r^i > 1$	$x^i = 0$	impossible

$$\tag{2.11}$$

The case marked "impossible" is impossible if $\bar{x}^i > 0$ since the row condition implies $x^i = 0$ and the column condition implies $x^i = \bar{x}^i$.

The cases in (2.11) can equally be put down in the following form, since $q_1 \xi_1^i + q_2 \xi_2^i + r^i > 1$ and $r^i = 0$ is equivalent to $q_1 \xi_1^i + q_2 \xi_2^i > 1$ etc.:

$$q_1 \xi_1^i + q_2 \xi_2^i > 1 \Rightarrow x^i = 0; \tag{2.12a}$$

$$q_1 \xi_1^i + q_2 \xi_2^i = 1 \Rightarrow 0 \leqq x^i \leqq \bar{x}^i; \tag{2.12b}$$

$$q_1 \xi_1^i + q_2 \xi_2^i < 1 \Rightarrow x^i = \bar{x}^i. \tag{2.12c}$$

The variables q_1 and q_2 can evidently be interpreted as shadow prices of the inputs in terms of units of output. Whether a production unit is to be operated or not is then, according to (2.12), decided by whether current operation costs calculated at these shadow prices would be lower than or exceed unity. When operation costs equal unity we have a marginal production unit in the sense that it may or may not be operated in the optimal solution.

For convenience we shall introduce the symbol s^i defined by

$$s^i = 1 - q_1\xi_1^i - q_2\xi_2^i.$$ (2.13)

This can clearly be interpreted as quasi rent measured in terms of and per unit of output which would be obtained by operating production unit No. i when current input prices in terms of units of output are q_1 and q_2. When $s^i \geq 0$ it is identical to the dual variable r^i introduced above, but whereas r^i is restricted by $r^i \geq 0$, s^i defined by (2.13) is not restricted in this way. In terms of the concept of quasi rent (calculated at the shadow prices for current inputs) the conditions in (2.12) can be rephrased by saying that optimization requires that production units which are only able to earn a negative quasi rent should not be operated, whereas production units which are able to earn a positive quasi rent should be operated at full capacity. Production units which would earn zero quasi rent are "marginal units", and may or may not be operated according to what is required by the given total amounts of current inputs V_1 and V_2.

On the basis of such an optimization as has been described above total output X will now be a function of total inputs V_1 and V_2 for the sector. This constitutes the short-run macro production function. How does this function look? The method of constructing isoquants in the case of a number of activities with different factor proportions is well known from activity analysis. However, the usual construction is not applicable in the present case since it disregards the capacity limitations for the various activities.

A simple construction for the case of limited capacities is given in Figure 2.1. Here there are three production units with input coefficients ξ_1^i, ξ_2^i for $i = 1, 2, 3$. These are indicated in the usual way by arrows from the origin in the figure. Furthermore the capacities of the three production units are indicated in the figure in the following way: The coordinates of E indicate the inputs of factors 1 and 2 when production unit No. 1 is used to full capacity, i.e. the coordinates are $\xi_1^1 \bar{x}^1$ and $\xi_2^1 \bar{x}^1$. In a corresponding way points F and A indicate full capacity utilization of production units Nos. 2 and 3. Now for total factor amounts corresponding to V_1, V_2-points within the parallelogram $OFDEO$ production is possible and efficient with utilization of production units Nos. 1 and 2.[10] The isoquants in this region are construct-

---

[10] The fact that all V_1, V_2-points in the region $OFDEO$ can be reached by combining operation of units Nos. 1 and 2 follows from the following consideration: For any point such as D' in Figure 2.1 the degrees to which the two processes 1 and 2 are required to be operated are indicated by the points E' and F' obtained by completing the parallelogram from D'. Then clearly no point within the region $OFDEO$ will require more than full capacity utilization for units Nos. 1 and 2 (whereas points outside this region cannot be reached by operating only units Nos. 1 and 2).

ed in the usual way, i.e. parallel to the line between (ξ_1^1, ξ_2^1) and (ξ_1^2, ξ_2^2). Correspondingly, for factor amounts corresponding to points within the parallelogram $OABFO$ production is possible and efficient with utilization of production units Nos. 2 and 3. Isoquants in this region are also constructed in the usual way. For total factor combinations corresponding to points in the region $FBCDF$ it is necessary to use all three production units. Since the production process of unit No. 2 is superior to combinations of the processes of units Nos. 1 and 3, this unit will always be used to full capacity in this region, whereas units Nos. 1 and 3 are combined to produce output in excess of the full capacity output of unit No. 2. The slope of the isoquants in this region is accordingly determined by the input coefficients of production units Nos. 1 and 3, i.e. it is equal to the slope of the line between (ξ_1^1, ξ_2^1) and (ξ_1^3, ξ_2^3), which is dotted in the figure.

At point C all production units are utilized to full capacity. This point then determines the capacity of the sector as a whole.

In Figure 2.1 we now have a well-defined production function with piece-wise linear isoquants within the region $OABCDEO$. If we consider only actually used inputs, the production function does not exist outside this

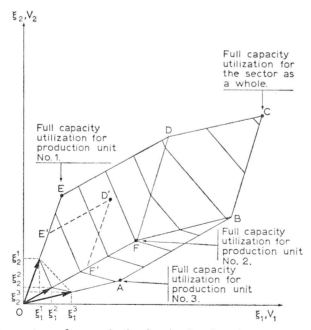

Fig. 2.1. Isoquant map for a production function based on three processes with limited capacities.

region. If we consider total production as a function of *available* amounts, whether these be used or not, then we could extend the isoquants by horizontal lines east of $OABC$ and by vertical lines north of $OEDC$. North-east of C total output would be constant, i.e. the surface representing the function would be flat.

Similar constructions to the one shown in Figure 2.1 could of course be made for cases with more production units than three. The number of regions which would have to be distinguished would then increase. A feature of such constructions is that production units which would appear to be inefficient in the usual constructions where there are no capacity limitations, will be called into use by certain total input combinations in such constructions as ours when capacity is fully utilized in more efficient units. Thus with capacity limitations no production units (processes) can be eliminated by efficiency considerations regardless of the available amounts of production factors, as is done in the traditional activity analysis construction of isoquants.

It is easy to compare the criterion (2.12) or the corresponding criterion in terms of quasi rent s^i with the construction in Figure 2.1 and see which of the cases in (2.12) hold for the various production units in the various regions of the figure. Considering e.g. the interior of the region $FBCDF$ we could say that production unit No. 2 earns a positive quasi rent, whereas the two other units earn zero quasi rent in this region (corresponding to $s^2 > 0$ and $s^1 = s^3 = 0$). In the other regions one of the units would earn a negative quasi rent and should not be operated.

The considerations given above indicate how the maximization of total output X in (2.7) subject to the constraints given there defines a production function. This is a short-run function since it is based on existing capacities and on the factor proportions which are given for each of the existing production units. In the following we shall write such a function as $F(V_1, V_2)$ where we specify only the arguments which are variable in the short run, namely V_1 and V_2.

It follows from the fact that q_1 and q_2 are dual variables associated with the constraints (2.7b–c) that these variables can be interpreted as marginal productivities in the function $F(V_1, V_2)$.

Although it is not of interest in the short-run context, it will prove useful for some of the following considerations also to put on record the fact, likewise following from the relations between the dual and the direct optimization problem, that the variable r^i entering (2.8–2.11) measures the increase in total output X which could be achieved by a slight increase in the capacity $\bar{x}^i$ of production unit No. i (retaining the input coefficients ξ_1^i, ξ_2^i unaltered), for $i = 1, 2, \ldots, N$. For a production unit which is to be operated in the optimal solution, this variable is equal to the quasi rent per unit of output of this production unit, as defined by (2.13). Formula (2.13) has a very natural interpretation: If the capacity $\bar{x}^i$ is increased by "one unit" of output, while total inputs V_1 and V_2 remain constant, then total output X can be increased by 1 minus the loss in production by other production units by withdrawal of the required amounts of inputs ξ_1^i and ξ_2^i from these other units. Since q_1 and q_2 express marginal productivities, this loss is $q_1\xi_1^i + q_2\xi_2^i$. Thus quasi rent also has a sort of marginal productivity interpretation, but it measures the marginal productivity of a factor which is fixed in the short run and is accordingly of a more hypothetical nature than the marginal productivities of V_1 and V_2.

The type of production function developed above has many interesting properties, which will be explored in some of the following chapters. However, it is not always convenient to explore these aspects on the basis of the linear programming formulation given above when the number of production units is very large. It is then, at least for theoretical purposes, convenient and illuminating to change over to a formulation which takes as the starting-point the distribution of production units with respect to their input coefficients instead of starting out from a collection of identifiable individual production units. This leads to, and provides an interpretation of, the type of production functions proposed by professor Houthakker in the 1955–56 paper referred to before. At the same time it will give a background for a discussion of whether or not the special case proposed by Houthakker – a Cobb-Douglas function derived on the basis of a generalized Pareto distribution of production units with respect to input coefficients – is a realistic and empirically interesting case.

2.5. The long-run production function at the macro level

The three types of production functions which have been introduced above are all in principle observable in the sense that technical choices and current production at any moment of time can be considered as empirical counterparts of the variables in these functions. The long-run production function which will now be defined in what I think is the customary way, is a more hypothetical construct.

Let us assume that there is available for the sector as a whole at a given moment of time quantities K, V_1 and V_2 of capital and current inputs. Let us furthermore assume (and this is the assumption that makes the long-run production function a hypothetical construct) that this amount of capital can be given any concrete form that we might desire. Under these conditions, maximize total output X. The value of X thus determined will be a function of K, V_1 and V_2. This function is the long-run production function.

This function must clearly be closely related to the ex ante function at the micro level which defines the technological possibilities from which the choice has to be made[11] (and is accordingly also afflicted with the same ambiguities that we discussed towards the end of Section 2.2.)

We now make two assumptions:

(1) For every factor proportion $\bar{v}_1 : \bar{v}_2 : \bar{k}$ in (2.1) there is an optimal scale of production, i.e. a scale at which output per unit of input is maximized.

(2) For the sector as a whole we consider factor amounts V_1, V_2 and K which are "large" as compared with factor inputs at a production unit of optimal size.

With these assumptions, and assuming "classical" curvature of the ex ante function, the maximization of X will be obtained by establishing a number of equal production units of optimal size.

Let the factor proportions for the sector as a whole be represented by V_1/K and V_2/K. Factor inputs at a production unit of optimal size will then be functions of these two ratios:

$$\bar{v}_1 = \bar{v}_1 \left(\frac{V_1}{K}, \frac{V_2}{K} \right), \quad \bar{v}_2 = \bar{v}_2 \left(\frac{V_1}{K}, \frac{V_2}{K} \right), \quad \bar{k} = \bar{k} \left(\frac{V_1}{K}, \frac{V_2}{K} \right), \quad (2.14)$$

i.e. $\bar{v}_1$, $\bar{v}_2$, $\bar{k}$ defined by (2.14) is the point along the factor ray corresponding to the proportions V_1/K, V_2/K which minimizes inputs per unit of output. It is the point along this ray where the scale elasticity of $\phi(\bar{v}_1, \bar{v}_2, \bar{k})$ is equal to one (passing through one from higher to lower values).[12] Output from a production unit of optimal size will then be determined by the ex ante function (2.1) with the amounts (2.14) inserted:

---

[11] Compare Salter's reflections (1960, p. 15) to the effect that "there seems to be a clear case for regarding the version of the production function which includes all possible designs as the most relevant concept, *at least for long-run analysis*" (my italics, L.J.). This suggests that we could identify a "long-run production function at the *micro* level" with what we have called the ex ante function. In the main text we shall, however, be concerned with the long run function at the *macro* level which is related to, but in general not identical with, the micro ex ante function.

[12] See Frisch (1965), pp. 70–71 and 120–25. (Frisch uses the term "passus coefficient" for the scale elasticity.)

$$\bar{x} = \phi \left\{ \bar{v}_1 \left(\frac{V_1}{K}, \frac{V_2}{K} \right), \ \bar{v}_2 \left(\frac{V_1}{K}, \frac{V_2}{K} \right), \ \bar{k} \left(\frac{V_1}{K}, \frac{V_2}{K} \right) \right\} \equiv \phi^* \left(\frac{V_1}{K}, \frac{V_2}{K} \right). \quad (2.15)$$

The function ϕ^* is defined by the latter identity.[13]

Inputs per unit of output for production units of optimal size will now be determined by

$$\xi_1 = \frac{\bar{v}_1(V_1/K, V_2/K)}{\phi^*(V_1/K, V_2/K)}, \quad \xi_2 = \frac{\bar{v}_2(V_1/K, V_2/K)}{\phi^*(V_1/K, V_2/K)}, \quad \xi_3 = \frac{\bar{k}(V_1/K, V_2/K)}{\phi^*(V_1/K, V_2/K)}.$$

$$(2.16)$$

If we eliminate V_1/K and V_2/K from (2.16) we will obtain a relationship between ξ_1, ξ_2 and ξ_3, which is a technical relationship between inputs per unit of output for production units of optimal size. It is convenient to let this relation be written as

$$\Psi(\xi_1, \xi_2, \xi_3) = 1. \quad (2.17)$$

This relation will be referred to as "the technique relation".

The connection between the technique relation (2.17) and the ex ante function (2.1) can be further elucidated by the following consideration. Take any set of values of inputs and outputs $\bar{v}_1$, $\bar{v}_2$, $\bar{k}$, $\bar{x}$ which satisfy the ex ante function (2.1). By forming the ratios $\xi_1 = \bar{v}_1/\bar{x}$, $\xi_2 = \bar{v}_2/\bar{x}$, $\xi_3 = \bar{k}/\bar{x}$ the point $(\bar{v}_1, \bar{v}_2, \bar{k}, \bar{x})$ can be transformed to a point in the ξ_1, ξ_2, ξ_3-space. By transforming all points $(\bar{v}_1, \bar{v}_2, \bar{k}, \bar{x})$ which satisfy the ex ante function in this way, we obtain a set of feasible points in the ξ_1, ξ_2, ξ_3-space, i.e. a set of feasible input coefficient constellations. Now for every ray through the origin in the ξ_1, ξ_2, ξ_3-space we pick out the point which is nearest to the origin among the feasible points along this ray. The set of points thus selected is the set of input coefficient combinations corresponding to optimal scales for all input proportions, i.e. it is the set of input coefficient combination which satisfy the technique relation (2.17). In other words, in the ξ_1, ξ_2, ξ_3-space the ex ante function defines the feasible set, whereas the technique relation defines the efficiency frontier towards the origin of this set.[14]

The technique relation is thus closely connected with the ex ante function at the micro level. The long-run macro production function is again directly connected with the technique relation.

We have stated above that we obtain maximal total output for given V_1,

---

[13] The use of the symbol ϕ^* here is not related to its use for the more general function ϕ^* in (2.6).

[14] This consideration has been elaborated in detail by Førsund (1969). See also Bentzel and Johansson (1959) and Førsund (1970).

V_2 and K by establishing a number of similar production units of optimal size. This holds true provided that we do not run into a non-integer number of such production units. Assumption No. 2 above is adopted in order to permit us to neglect this difficulty.[15] We will then have

$$V_1 = \xi_1 X, \quad V_2 = \xi_2 X, \quad K = \xi_3 X. \tag{2.18}$$

The long-run macro production function is then implicitly determined by insertion into the technique relation (2.17) since the production units are to have the best possible input coefficients corresponding to the given proportions:

$$\Psi \left(\frac{V_1}{X}, \frac{V_2}{X}, \frac{K}{X} \right) = 1. \tag{2.19}$$

It is clear from (2.19) that the long-run production function at the macro level is homogeneous of degree 1.

Alternatively to the derivation given above the macro production function could be formulated in the following way. For any given combination V_1, V_2, K the number N of production units of optimal size will be a function $N(V_1, V_2, K)$ of these variables. Total output when we have this number of equal production units will be

$$X = N(V_1, V_2, K) \, \phi \left(\frac{V_1}{N(V_1, V_2, K)}, \frac{V_2}{N(V_1, V_2, K)}, \frac{K}{N(V_1, V_2, K)} \right) \tag{2.20}$$

which also shows homogeneity of degree 1 since the function $N(V_1, V_2, K)$ will clearly be homogeneous of degree 1.[16]

This formulation summarizes more in one big jump by introducing the function $N(V_1, V_2, K)$. However, the formulation in terms of the technique relation (2.17–2.19) will, for most purposes, be more useful.

The relationship between the two formulations can be shown by writing $N(V_1, V_2, K)$ as $XN(V_1/X, V_2/X, K/X)$, which is permissible since $N()$ is homogeneous of degree 1. Then (2.20) appears as

---

[15] A careful treatment of this problem, showing that what we do in the text is permissible "asymptotically", is given by Samuelson (1967).

[16] This latter formulation corresponds to the one used by Bentzel and Johansson (1959) in a study of the question of homogeneity of production functions in relation to aggregation from micro to macro. The term "technique relation" for (2.17) corresponds to their "technique line" in the case of two production factors. Compare also footnote 7 in my paper (1959) and pp. 172–174 of my paper (1960).

$$N\left(\frac{V_1}{X}, \frac{V_2}{X}, \frac{K}{X}\right) \times$$

$$\phi\left(\frac{V_1/X}{N(V_1/X, V_2/X, K/X)}, \frac{V_2/X}{N(V_1/X, V_2/X, K/X)}, \frac{K/X}{N(V_1/X, V_2/X, K/X)}\right) = 1, \quad (2.21)$$

which is one possible way of expressing (2.19).

Using now the formulation based on (2.14–2.19) the following observations can be made.

The way of representing the technique relation as shown by (2.17) is not unique. It is clear that if we have another function $\Psi^*(\xi_1, \xi_2, \xi_3)$ which is equal to unity when and only when $\Psi(\xi_1, \xi_2, \xi_3) = 1$, then the technique relation (2.17) can be equivalently represented by

$$\Psi^*(\xi_1, \xi_2, \xi_3) = 1. \quad (2.22)$$

In particular it is possible to select a function Ψ^* which is homogeneous of degree 1 in the variables ξ_1, ξ_2, ξ_3, and there is only one way of doing this, namely as follows: For any given ξ_1, ξ_2, ξ_3, determine a number α such that

$$\Psi\left(\frac{\xi_1}{\alpha}, \frac{\xi_2}{\alpha}, \frac{\xi_3}{\alpha}\right) = 1. \quad (2.23)$$

This α will be uniquely determined. Then put $\Psi^*(\xi_1, \xi_2, \xi_3) = \alpha$ for all ξ_1, ξ_2, ξ_3-points. The function $\Psi^*()$ thus obtained is clearly homogeneous of degree 1, and it is equal to unity when and only when (2.17) is fulfilled. When this special representation of the technique relation is chosen we can write the long–run macro production function implicitly determined by (2.19) in the explicit form:

$$X = \Psi^*(V_1, V_2, K). \quad (2.24)$$

When we, in the following chapters, use the technique relation and the corresponding long-run production function we shall assume that we have chosen this special representation without indicating this by an asterisk.

The construction indicated by (2.22–2.24) shows that the technique relation represents one special isoquant surface of the long-run macro function, namely the isoquant surface corresponding to one unit of output. The other isoquants are generated by projecting this special isoquant along rays from the origin, i.e. the isoquant surfaces are radially related projections of one another.

If the ex ante function at the micro level is *homogeneous of degree 1*, then inputs per unit of output are constant along any factor ray, and no uniquely determined optimal size exists. In this case we may simply define the technique relation $\Psi(\xi_1, \xi_2, \xi_3) = 1$ so as to coincide with the isoquant corresponding to a capacity of one unit of output in the ex ante function, and the long-run macro function will have the same form as the ex ante micro function.

As another special case of some interest let us consider an ex ante function ϕ which can be written in the following way

$$\phi(\bar{v}_1, \bar{v}_2, \bar{k}) = g(\hat{\phi}(\bar{v}_1, \bar{v}_2, \bar{k})), \tag{2.25}$$

where $\hat{\phi}()$ is homogeneous of degree 1 and g is a strictly increasing function of one argument. Then ϕ is a *homothetic function*.[17] In this case the surface in the $\bar{v}_1, \bar{v}_2, \bar{k}$-space corresponding to optimal scale of production will coincide with an isoquant surface; it will correspond to a value of $\hat{\phi}()$ in (2.25), which makes the elasticity of $g()$ equal to unity, and all combinations of $\bar{v}_1, \bar{v}_2, \bar{k}$ which give this value of $\hat{\phi}()$, and only these, will yield the same value of $\bar{x} = \phi(\bar{v}_1, \bar{v}_2, \bar{k})$. Let this value $\bar{x}^0$. Using (2.15–2.16) we then have

$$\phi(\bar{x}^0 \xi_1, \bar{x}^0 \xi_2, \bar{x}^0 \xi_3) = g(\hat{\phi}(\bar{x}^0 \xi_1, \bar{x}^0 \xi_2, \bar{x}^0 \xi_3)) = \bar{x}^0.$$

Using the inverse function $g^{-1}()$ and using the fact that $\hat{\phi}$ is homogeneous of degree 1, the technique relation can then be written as

$$\frac{\bar{x}^0}{g^{-1}(\bar{x}^0)} \hat{\phi}(\xi_1, \xi_2, \xi_3) = 1, \tag{2.26}$$

where the left-hand side corresponds to $\Psi^*()$ in (2.22), and the long-run macro function can be written as

$$X = \frac{\bar{x}^0}{g^{-1}(\bar{x}^0)} \hat{\phi}(V_1, V_2, K) \tag{2.27}$$

corresponding to (2.24). Thus, apart from the constant factor $\bar{x}^0/[g^{-1}(\bar{x}^0)]$, which could by appropriate conventions regarding $g()$ and $\hat{\phi}()$ be set equal

---

[17] There are some different definitions of homotheticity in the literature, and the problem about equivalence of the various definitions seems not to be entirely clear, at least when there are more than two factors of production. (There is however an unpublished paper by Hanoch (1969), which goes a long way towards clarification.) Sometimes homotheticity is defined as in the text above, but with $\hat{\phi}()$ homogeneous of degree q, where q is any positive number, see e.g. Newman (1969), pp. 303–304. However, if $\hat{\phi}()$ is homogeneous of degree $q > 0$, but $q \neq 1$, then we could replace $\hat{\phi}()$ by $(\hat{\phi}())^{1/q}$, which is homogeneous of degree 1 and redefine $g()$ accordingly. We may therefore just as well assume $\hat{\phi}()$ to be homogeneous of degree 1 from the outset.

to unity, the homogeneous kernel of the homothetic ex ante micro function appears as the long-run macro function. The two functions have the same family of isoquants, but the output labels on the isoquants are the same only at output level $\bar{x}^0$.

In the case of non-homothetic ex ante functions the form of the isoquants of the long-run macro function will in general be different from the form of the isoquants of the ex ante function. But, as pointed out above, it still holds that the isoquants of the long-run macro function are radial projections of the surface corresponding to the technique relation, which is derived from the ex ante function, as explained above.

2.6. *Some preliminary comments on dynamics and the relationships between the various concepts of production functions*

We have seen above that there is a clear mathematical relationship between the ex ante production function at the micro level and what we have called the long-run production function at the macro level at any given moment of time. The actual production possibilities for the sector as a whole at a given moment of time are, however, not determined by this long-run production function, but rather by the short-run production function at the macro level, which is dependent upon the technical characteristics and capacities of existing production units. These characteristics and capacities are related to the ex ante function in the sense that each production unit has at some time been "extracted" from the ex ante function that existed at that time; but the relationship is not clear-cut. We may say that the short-run macro production function reflects both the history of ex ante functions over time and the actual choices made from these ex ante functions.

The actual observations of factor inputs and output at the macro level at any point of time will of course be observations from the short-run production function (provided that the underlying optimization hypothesis is valid, cf. the discussion in Sections 3.6 and 6.6). These will clearly be inferior to points which obey the long-run macro function. However, under very special circumstances such observations may approximate the long-run production function. These special circumstances are: An approximately constant ex ante function (or possibly such neutral shifts in the ex ante function as are matched by disembodied technological progress); approximately constant factor prices (including the interest rate) so that approximately the same factor proportions are chosen at all times; and no wear and tear which make production on old equipment more input-consuming than production on new equipment. In short we may say that these are circumstances characterizing a "steady state". The long-run production function would therefore be spanned out by observations if we had the opportunity to observe alternative steady states, and we might call it a "steady state production function" (although it has relevance under some more general circumstances, as will be shown in Chapter 7). The short-run production function corresponding to each of these steady states would be characterized by all production units having the same technical characteristics, which would in a figure like Figure 2.1 mean that all the arrows indicating the input coefficients of the various production units would coincide, and the whole area of possible input constellations $OABCDEO$ would collapse into a ray of a certain length. There would be alternative such rays for alternative steady states, the maximum point of each of them corresponding to a point on the long-run or steady state production function.

For such comparisons between the short-run and the long-run production functions it would perhaps be better to consider also the short-run function as a function of three variables, V_1, V_2 and K, where K is now capital stock actually used. There would be no difficulty in doing this by supplementing (2.7–2.12). However, unless there are some special costs attached to the use of capital equipment, not accounted for through the current inputs v_1 and v_2, then only the frontier of this function which corresponds to zero price for using existing equipment will be relevant. (Figure 2.1 may be considered as a projection down into the V_1, V_2-plane of such a frontier.) On this frontier the amount of capital actually used will follow the current inputs V_1, V_2 as a "shadow factor".

In the following chapters we will be much concerned with the short-run function. There are two reasons for this: In the first place, the short-run function as generated from the distribution of the production units with respect to technological characteristics has many properties which are of interest in themselves; in the second place, since the realized production at any point of time must (with the proviso mentioned above) be compatible with the short-run function, while in general not with the steady state function, a study of the *dynamics* of production of a sector requires a study of how the short-run production function changes through time.

Because of its role in such a dynamic context we might also use the expression "transient production function" for the short-run production function. We shall revert to some questions of how the short-run function changes through time after having considered some of its properties at a given moment of time.

The considerations presented above indicate a basic difficulty in the empirical analysis of production *at the macro level* (to the extent of course that our model is reasonably realistic). Time series observations at the macro level are realizations from the short-run function rather than the long-run function. It is therefore very doubtful whether long-run functions can be estimated from such data. On the other hand, the short-run function is itself shifting through time in such a way that time series observations do not provide a basis for estimating *one* such function.

If the ex ante function at the micro level changes through time as a result of increasing know-how, then the long-run function will of course also change through time. This change will represent technological change. The changes in the short-run function through time will be generated by many more factors than technological progress, as represented by changes in the ex ante function, and one might therefore expect the changes in the short–run function to be more complicated and less accessible to a representation in terms of a limited number of parameters than in the case of the long-run function.

CHAPTER 3

Establishing the short-run production function
at the macro level

3.1. *The capacity distribution*

In the preceding chapter we suggested the derivation of the short-run production function at the macro level on the basis of the distribution of micro production units with respect to input coefficients. It is in principle clear how this could be done on the basis of a linear programming approach, as illustrated in connection with Figure 2.1. However, many of the theoretical properties of this type of function can be more efficiently revealed by shifting over to considering a continuum of such production units at the micro level instead of keeping track of a finite number of individual units. In the sequel we shall assume that there exists such a distribution over a two-dimensional region in the ξ_1, ξ_2-plane.

This distribution, to be called *the capacity distribution*, will be denoted by $f(\xi_1, \xi_2)$. The meaning of this function is that

$$f(\xi_1^0, \xi_2^0)\Delta\xi_1\Delta\xi_2 \tag{3.1}$$

indicates approximately the total capacity of production with input coefficient No. 1 in the interval between ξ_1^0 and $\xi_1^0+\Delta\xi_1$ and input coefficient No. 2 in the interval between ξ_2^0 and $\xi_2^0+\Delta\xi_2$, $\Delta\xi_1$ and $\Delta\xi_2$ being "small"; or, more precisely, if we consider a region in the ξ_1, ξ_2-plane, then total capacity of production with input coefficients in this region is obtained by integrating $f(\xi_1, \xi_2)$ over this region. The function $f(\xi_1, \xi_2)$ is thus a continuous analogue to the discrete capacity distribution which could be indicated by the collection of numbers $\xi_1^i, \xi_2^i, \bar{x}^i$ ($i = 1, 2, \ldots, N$) in the case studied in Sections 2.3 and 2.4, and the integration of $f(\xi_1, \xi_2)$ corresponds to the summation of capacities $\bar{x}^i$ for production units with input coefficients in a certain region in the discrete case.

In special cases one might consider capacity distributions concentrated only along a one-dimensional curve in the ξ_1, ξ_2-diagram. In such cases (3.1) above would have to be replaced by

$$f(\xi_1^0, \xi_2^0)\Delta s, \tag{3.2}$$

where Δs is the length of a small arc of the curve from the point ξ_1^0, ξ_2^0, and $f(\xi_1, \xi_2)$ indicates capacity per unit of length along the curve, or similar expressions if the capacity distribution along the curve is indicated in other ways than per unit of length. Corresponding to the integration over a region as mentioned in connection with (3.1), we would now have line integrals.

By means of sufficiently general notation and concepts of integration the two cases mentioned above could be treated as one. We shall, however, most of the time assume that the capacity distribution extends in two dimensions in the ξ_1, ξ_2-plane, treating the case of capacity distribution along a curve more by supplementary remarks and by examples. Most of what will be derived for the two-dimensional case carries over to the one-dimensional case without difficulty.

It is perhaps wise to remind oneself that the case of a continuous distribution, be it one-dimensional or two-dimensional, is in our context an approximation adopted for the sake of convenience. We should therefore not indulge in mathematical subtilties created by the representation of the capacity distribution in a continuous form, and we shall allow ourselves to speak about the production units as identifiable entities, although this does not correspond to the formal representation of the capacity distribution.

Whether we choose a one-dimensional or a two-dimensional distribution is a matter of approximations. I think the two-dimensional case is the more relevant in practical cases. I will briefly review some reasons for this, partly repeating some suggestions from the preceding chapter.

In this discussion we shall use the term "*region of positive capacity*" for that part of the ξ_1, ξ_2-plane where $f(\xi_1, \xi_2) > 0$. Talking about the form of the region of positive capacity the "length" of the region refers to its extension in the direction from the south-west to the north-east, i.e. in the direction along rays from the origin, while the "breadth" or "width" of it refer to its extension in the direction from the north-west to the sourth-east, i.e. across rays from the origin.

(1) *Factor prices for current inputs* have been changing in the past. This has induced different choices from the ex ante function, exploiting the ex ante substitution possibilities. In the ξ_1, ξ_2-plane this substitution effect would tend to broaden the region of positive capacity. If the optimal amount of investment per unit of production capacity were the same in all production units, then the point mentioned here would produce a distribution along the curve in the ξ_1, ξ_2-plane corresponding to the technique relation (2.17) for fixed ξ_3, but in general this will not be so.

(2) With the type of technology assumed here, not only current prices, but

also *expected future prices* are relevant for technological choices. Individual investors may then have had different expectations about the future even at the same moment of time. The effect on the form of the region of positive capacity is the same as under point (1) above.

(3) Now existing production units have been established under *different proportions of capital goods prices to current input prices* (and different expectations as to the development of input prices). This fact has induced different choices of capital intensities. In general, if lower capital intensities have been chosen in the more distant past, this would (assuming a constant ex ante function) be reflected by lower ξ_3-values matched by higher ξ_1, ξ_2-values. A dispersion of ξ_3-values chosen in the past would accordingly tend to create a longer region of positive capacity. This holds at least if capital in the ex ante function is a substitute for both the current inputs while leaving the rate of substitution between the two current inputs unaffected. If the two current inputs are e.g. labour and raw materials, then one would expect capital to be a substitute mainly for labour, and the effect of the differences in ξ_3 chosen for the various vintages would be reflected by an extension of the region of positive capacity mainly in the labour input direction, i.e. in a direction intermediate between the length and the breadth dimension.

(4) *Changes in the rate of interest* in the past may have left their marks on the capacity distribution in a similar way to that mentioned under point (3). Besides there may have been an effect upon the *durability*, or more generally the time profile of the capacity of the production units as represented by the argument t in the ex post function (2.5). To the extent that there is a trade-off between this aspect and current input requirements there will also be effects of this upon the form of the capacity distribution and the region of positive capacity.

(5) The effects mentioned under points (1)–(4) above operate under the assumption of a common ex ante function known to all investors. However, investment decisions are taken on the basis of more or less *imperfect knowledge* about technological possibilities. We have suggested towards the end of Section 2.2 that we should in principle consider a whole nest of ex ante functions, one for every group or quarter where investment decisions are made. Alternatively we might consider an "efficient ex ante function" representing the best technological knowledge available somewhere, in which case most projects would fail to reach an efficiency in terms of input coefficients corresponding to this ex ante function. Whichever way we prefer to look at it, the result is a tendency to enlarge the region of positive capacity in the

ξ_1, ξ_2-plane. The effect may operate both in the length and in the breadth dimension.

(6) We may get similar effects if there are differences in production efficiency due to *geographical factors*, assuming that there are limited amounts available of each quality of "land". (This factor may call for a generalization of the concept of ex ante function.)

(7) By point (5) we relaxed the assumption of perfect knowledge about technology. If we also *relax the assumption of "perfect markets"* (in addition to recognising the existence of different price expectations as under points (2) and (3)), then we get additional effects creating spread in the capacity distribution. Particularly important is perhaps more or less severe lack of investible funds for some individual investors, which will tend to create production units of sub-optimal scale. These units will be represented by input coefficients which are more distant from the origin than those satisfying the technique relation (2.17), cf. the interpretation of the technique relation as representing a frontier of feasible points in Section 2.5. This will largely tend to create dispersion in the length dimension of the region of positive capacity, but there may be "biased" effects as mentioned under point (3). Some investment decisions may also have been taken under influence of a desire to safeguard against shortages of some input factors in the future (apart from what is reflected through price expectations). This will operate in the breadth dimension of the region of positive capacity.

(8) Other types of "imperfections" are *side effects* attached to different types of production equipment having to do with safety, welfare, prestige, etc. If these are appraised differently by different investors, it will tend to produce some variety in the technological decisions, conceivably in any direction.

(9) As suggested in Section 2.2 we may in certain cases interpret our model in such a way that the *same piece of production equipment gives rise to different processes* represented by different points in the ξ_1, ξ_2-diagram. A practical example is the operation of a production unit in overtime work. The same piece of equipment may then be represented firstly by a ξ_1, ξ_2-point corresponding to regular hours of work, and in addition by a point corresponding to overtime work, where the latter may in many cases be less efficient than the former one. This may work in different directions in the ξ_1, ξ_2-plane, but perhaps mainly to create dispersion in the labour input direction.

(10) Up to now we have not mentioned *technological progress*. In fact the various production units existing at a certain moment of time have usually

been picked from different ex ante functions, due to increasing technological know-how which changes the ex ante function through time. The strongest effect of this will perhaps be in the length dimension of the region of positive capacity, but biases in the progress may of course also have effects in the breadth dimension.

(11) In addition to point (10) we may have *technological progress affecting already existing production units* (disembodied technological progress). According to when and where a ξ_1, ξ_2-point entered the capacity distribution it may move through time along various paths in the ξ_1, ξ_2-diagram and contribute to creating dispersion.

(12) A production unit entering the capacity distribution at a certain point of time may clearly be affected by *wear and tear* in such a way that its capacity declines through time. It is, however, also possible that its ξ_1, ξ_2-point moves through time; e.g. increasing repair and maintenance requirements may increase the labour input coefficients, or, for a motor or engine, fuel requirements may increase with age. As suggested before the efficiency of a production unit will sometimes increase for a limited period of time before such factors as those mentioned above begin to make themselves felt. The effects mentioned here would probably tend to extend the region of positive capacity in various directions. (Such factors are not taken care of in the main case of the model outlined above, but it was suggested that they might be covered by the time argument in the more general formulation of the ex post function towards the end of Section 2.3).

(13) As in the case of prices not only the current situation with respect to technology is relevant for investment decisions. Also *expectations with respect to future technological development* are relevant. Partly this point will overlap with the effects of price expectations, but there will also be independent effects. E.g., expectations with respect to embodied technological progress, which can only be utilized by new investments, may influence the choice of durability of equipment which may again be somehow correlated with input requirements. If disembodied technological progress, affecting the efficiency of already installed equipment, is expected not to be neutral as between different types of equipment, then this will also influence investment decisions. Since expectations of different investors are not likely to be identical we have an additional factor tending to create dispersion in the capacity distribution in the ξ_1, ξ_2-plane.

(14) In addition to the more or less systematic factors listed above we may of course have *random elements* affecting the individual production units. We could perhaps distinguish between two types of random influences.

First there are "embodied random elements". These operate in the construction of the production units: a piece of equipment is "born" with certain random, but unalterable characteristics reflected in the values of the current input coefficient. Next there are "disembodied random elements" affecting the production unit after it has been put in operation. These could perhaps be further subdivided into temporary and lasting or irreversible factors. (If we recognize the existence of such random elements the ex ante function may perhaps be interpreted as a frontier in the sense that it represents the efficiency of the production units which can be constructed on the basis of the best technological knowledge and provided that the random elements take zero values. In this case the random elements in the input coefficients would be non-negative. Alternatively one could of course define the ex ante function in terms of expected values, in which case the random elements affecting the input coefficients could be positive, zero or negative.)

The above list of factors creating dispersion in the capacity distribution is probably almost exhaustive (and certainly so if all elements not mentioned under points (1)–(13) are considered as random and thereby included under point (14)). It is seen that some factors work mainly along the length dimension, others along the breadth dimension, while still others have a more ambiguous effect. Some of the points would need further analysis in order to achieve precision. However, I think enough has been said about them to justify an approach in which it is assumed in the main case that there is a capacity distribution over a region of positive capacity which has some extension in two dimensions in the ξ_1, ξ_2-plane.

We have formulated many of the remarks under the various points above as if we have an economy consisting of individual investors who operate in a market. Most of the effects pointed out would, however, though sometimes in other disguises and to different degrees, also operate under other institutional arrangements. On the whole one would perhaps expect a more narrowly concentrated capacity distribution under a system of central planning than under a market system since the same technological knowledge would underlie a higher proportion of investment decisions, prices would fluctuate to a lesser degree, decisions would be taken on the basis of more centralized or uniform expectations about future prices and technology, and weights attached to such side effects as are mentioned under point (8) would tend to be more uniform. On the other hand, under a market system production units with "abnormal" input coefficients would perhaps be squeezed out of business at a faster rate.

I think it would be a very interesting source of information on the working of various systems if data on the development of the capacity distribution for economies on comparable levels of technology, but with different systems of management, were available.

We have listed above a multitude of factors influencing the form of the capacity distribution. In analyses where we start out from a given capacity distribution it is not difficult to recognize the influence of all these factors in the history up to now. For dynamic studies in which one wants to consider the process of selections from the ex ante function, the various effects which change the distribution of production units with respect to input coefficients, and furthermore the corresponding changes in the short-run function through time – all this in an integrated fashion – it is of course much more difficult to include all these aspects explicitly in the study. Therefore, in some theoretical models, notably growth models, which assume basically a similar type of technological structure as the one we have adopted here, the implied short-run function at any moment of time would perhaps more often correspond to a distribution of the individual production units along a one-dimensional curve in the ξ_1, ξ_2-diagram. However, most growth models assume only one current input – labour – so that the problem is not faced explicitly.[1]

3.2. *The feasible production set*

We now assume the existence of a capacity distribution $f(\xi_1, \xi_2)$, which is to be interpreted as explained in connection with (3.1). Before we derive the short-run macro production function we shall make some observations concerning the feasible production set in the V_1, V_2, X-space.

A feasible point in the V_1, V_2, X-space is reached by exploiting to some extent the capacity in various parts of the region of positive capacity in the

---

[1] Solow illustrates the idea of a production function derived from a capacity distribution with only one current input and draws attention to the relation of this formulation to the construction of a so-called Lorenz-curve, see Solow (1967) pp. 46–48. Levhari (1968) exploits this idea in a study of the case of only one current input in which he, for special cases, solves the reversed problem, i.e. the problem of deriving the form of the capacity distribution from a known production function.

Growth and capital theory papers which contain ideas for the case of one current input which can on some points be compared with the present study are Solow (1962, 1963), Thănh (1966), Solow et al. (1966), Whitaker (1965) and Bliss (1968).

ξ_1, ξ_2-plane. We shall describe the pattern of exploitation of capacity by means of a function $u(\xi_1, \xi_2)$ with the interpretation

$u(\xi_1, \xi_2) =$
proportion employed of capacity with input coefficients ξ_1, ξ_2. (3.3)

In the discrete case represented by (2.7) the corresponding proportion would be $x^i/\bar{x}^i$ for $i = 1, 2, \ldots, N$.

The function $u(\xi_1, \xi_2)$ will be referred to as the *capacity utilization function*. The function (3.3) must clearly be restricted by

$$0 \leq u(\xi_1, \xi_2) \leq 1. \tag{3.4}$$

It would not be reasonable to require $u(\xi_1, \xi_2)$ to be continuous, since we might e.g. be interested in cases where $u = 1$ over a certain region and $u = 0$ outside this region, i.e. full utilization of capacity of certain types while leaving other capacity idle. On the other hand, it does not seem that we miss anything of interest by assuming $u(\xi_1, \xi_2)$ to be *continuous almost everywhere* (i.e., the set of points where $u(\xi_1, \xi_2)$ is discontinuous is of measure zero).

Having chosen a certain pattern of capacity utilization represented by $u(\xi_1, \xi_2)$, total output and inputs can be written as

$$X = \int \int u(\xi_1, \xi_2) f(\xi_1, \xi_2) d\xi_1 d\xi_2 \tag{3.5}$$

$$V_i = \int \int \xi_i u(\xi_1, \xi_2) f(\xi_1, \xi_2) d\xi_1 d\xi_2 \qquad (i = 1, 2) \tag{3.6}$$

since the capacity of a "cell" $\Delta\xi_1\Delta\xi_2$ is $f(\xi_1, \xi_2)\Delta\xi_1\Delta\xi_2$ and the proportion $u(\xi_1, \xi_2)$ of this is utilized, and furthermore ξ_i units of input No. i is required per unit of output for the type of equipment localized in this cell.

The integrations in (3.5–3.6) are performed over the whole region of positive capacity. Since we have $f(\xi_1, \xi_2) = 0$ outside this region we may also think of the integrals in (3.5–3.6) as being taken over the whole positive quadrant in the ξ_1, ξ_2-plane.

Equations (3.5–3.6) are the counterparts of (2.7a–c) in the discrete case.

As a special case we may, as suggested above, have a capacity utilization function which is equal to 1 everywhere in a region G and equal to 0 outside this region:

$$\begin{aligned} u(\xi_1, \xi_2) &= 1 \quad \text{for} \quad (\xi_1, \xi_2) \in G, \\ u(\xi_1, \xi_2) &= 0 \quad \text{for} \quad (\xi_1, \xi_2) \notin G. \end{aligned} \tag{3.7}$$

In this case (3.5–3.6) can be written as

$$X = \int\int_G f(\xi_1, \xi_2)d\xi_1 d\xi_2, \tag{3.8}$$

$$V_i = \int\int_G \xi_i f(\xi_1, \xi_2)d\xi_1 d\xi_2 \ (i = 1,2). \tag{3.9}$$

When $u(\xi_1, \xi_2)$ takes the form (3.7) we shall refer to G as the *utilization region*.

The feasible production set is now generated by varying the capacity utilization function over the whole class of functions (continuous almost everywhere) which satisfy (3.4) and taking V_1, V_2 and X as defined by (3.5–3.6) into the V_1, V_2, X-space.

It is easy to verify that this feasible production set is *convex*. Consider two arbitrary points

$$(V_1^1, V_2^1, X^1) \ and \ (V_1^2, V_2^2, X^2) \tag{3.10}$$

in the feasible set. We must verify that any point V_1^*, V_2^*, X^* constructed as a convex combination

$$V_i^* = \lambda V_i^1 + (1-\lambda)V_i^2$$
$$\qquad\qquad\qquad\qquad (0 \leq \lambda \leq 1) \tag{3.11}$$
$$X^* = \lambda X^1 + (1-\lambda)X^2$$

also belongs to the feasible set.

Since the points in (3.10) are feasible, they must be generated by some utilization functions $u^1(\xi_1, \xi_2)$ and $u^2(\xi_1, \xi_2)$. Now construct another function $u^*(\xi_1, \xi_2)$ by

$$u^*(\xi_1, \xi_2) = \lambda u^1(\xi_1, \xi_2) + (1-\lambda)u^2(\xi_1, \xi_2). \tag{3.12}$$

This is clearly a permissible utilization function: When $u^1()$ and $u^2()$ satisfy (3.4), $u^*()$ does so as well, and like $u^1()$ and $u^2()$ $u^*()$ will be continuous almost everywhere.

A new point V_1^*, V_2^*, X^* in the feasible region is thus generated when $u^*()$ is substituted for $u()$ in (3.5–3.6). It is seen immediately that this point satisfies (3.11).

Since this construction can be done for any two points (3.10) in the feasible set and any λ, $0 \leq \lambda \leq 1$, we can conclude that the feasible production set is convex.

The counterpart of this in the case of the discrete model of Section 2.4 follows of course from the basic theorem about the convexity of the feasible region in a linear programming problem.

It seems reasonable to assume that the region of positive capacity be bounded. With a capacity distribution $f(\xi_1, \xi_2)$ which is finite it is then clear that the feasible set in the V_1, V_2, X-space will be *bounded*.

The convexity and boundedness of the production set are properties of clear economic significance. For analytical tidiness it may also be of interest to mention the problem of *openness or closedness* of the production set, although there are hardly any observable or verifiable counterparts of this distinction in the underlying economic reality. A full discussion of this would require more mathematical sophistication than seems necessary for our purposes. While it seems somewhat doubtful whether the feasible set is closed when only $u(\xi_1, \xi_2)$-functions which are continuous almost everywhere are permitted, it is possible to conclude that the set is closed if we permit all measurable u-functions.[2] Although it is difficult to attach economic significance to u-functions which are measurable, but not continuous almost everywhere, there does not seem to be any danger involved in permitting them in order to allow us to think of the production set as being closed.

In some of the mathematical illustrations, which will be provided later on, the boundedness assumption will be temporarily given up. Otherwise we shall proceed on the basis of the conclusions that the feasible production set in the V_1, V_2, X-space is convex, bounded and closed.

3.3. *Establishing the macro function by analogy with the linear programming case*

The short-run macro production function is defined by considering the maximal value of total output X that can be obtained for every given combination of total inputs V_1, V_2. In Section 2.4 we gave a preliminary discussion of this function on the basis of a finite set of discrete production units.

---

[2] A sketch of the reasoning: We consider the integrals in (3.5–3.6) over a compact region which contains the region of positive capacity. The set of permissible u-functions (measurable functions which satisfy (3.4)) over this region is compact. The integrals (3.5–3.6) define a continuous function from the set of u-functions to R^3, i.e. it defines a continuous image in R^3 of the compact set of u-functions. This image, which is our feasible production set, is then itself compact, and hence closed since compactness in R^3 implies closedness.

We saw that the selection of production units to be utilized could be done on the basis of quasi rents as calculated by (2.13), where q_1 and q_2 are (non-negative) shadow prices of the two current inputs. Zero quasi rent signified the border between production units which should be operated and units which should not be operated.

In the continuous case with a capacity distribution $f(\xi_1, \xi_2)$ the decision about which units should be utilized, and to what degree, is represented by the choice of a utilization function as introduced by (3.3). The macro production function is accordingly defined by maximization of X given by (3.5) subject to the conditions that V_1 and V_2 as obtained from (3.6) assume given values, where the functional form $u()$ is our "free variable" in the maximization. In other words, the production function is defined as the frontier in the X-direction of the feasible production set discussed in Section 3.2, or, in order to limit consideration to the economically interesting part of it, the frontier in the direction of increasing X and decreasing V_1 and V_2. Since the set is convex, bounded and closed, there is no problem about the existence of such a frontier defining the production function.

In analogy with the discrete case we may expect that the maximal X for given V_1, V_2 can be obtained on the basis of a quasi rent consideration, utilizing all capacity which yields positive quasi rent and leaving idle all capacity that would yield negative quasi rent, since the macro function in the continuous case may be considered as a limiting case of the type of macro function discussed in Section 2.4 and illustrated in Figure 2.1 when the number of production units increases beyond all limits, rendering each of them negligible in size as proportion of the total. What to do with capacity which yields exactly zero quasi rent is irrelevant in the continuous case since this capacity is of measure zero.

This suggests that we should define a *zero quasi rent line* by

$$q_1\xi_1 + q_2\xi_2 = 1 \tag{3.13}$$

and let this be the border-line between capacity which should be fully utilized and capacity which should be left idle. We thus define a region $G(q_1, q_2)$ by

$$
\begin{aligned}
&q_1\xi_1 + q_2\xi_2 \leq 1, \\
&\xi_1 \geq 0, \quad \xi_2 \geq 0, \\
&[\text{i.e. } G(q_1, q_2) = \{(\xi_1, \xi_2) \mid \xi_1 \geq 0, \ \xi_2 \geq 0, \ q_1\xi_1 + q_2\xi_2 \leq 1\}]
\end{aligned}
\tag{3.14}
$$

and let this region be the utilization region. We then have, cf. (3.7–3.9):

$$X = \int \int_{G(q_1, q_2)} f(\xi_1, \xi_2) d\xi_1 d\xi_2,$$

$$V_i = \int \int_{G(q_1, q_2)} \xi_i f(\xi_1, \xi_2) d\xi_1 d\xi_2 \qquad (i = 1, 2).$$

(3.15)

The macro production function is now implicitly defined by (3.15). We have three equations between the five variables X, V_1, V_2, q_1, q_2. By eliminating q_1 and q_2 we would obtain one equation relating X, V_1 and V_2. This defines the production function at the macro level, which we shall denote by

$$X = F(V_1, V_2).$$

(3.16)

This production function is essentially the type of production function proposed by professor Houthakker in his paper (1955–56). Thus, within our framework his type of production function falls into place as representing the short-run production function at the macro level, while the distribution function $f(\xi_1, \xi_2)$ on which it is based represents the history of choices from ex ante functions at the micro level at various points of time in the past together with influences from other factors reviewed in Section 3.1. Houthakker establishes such a function by reasoning which is drawn from discrete activity analysis similar to what is done above. Other types of reasoning more directly appropriate for the continuous case will be presented in the following section.

Establishing the production function at the macro level in the way given above, is a purely technical matter. Thus, the parameters q_1 and q_2 may be considered simply as parameters which are helpful in the implicit determination of the production function. It is, however, clear that they can be given an interpretation in terms of prices, and we have already referred to them as "shadow prices". Let there be a price of output P and current input prices Q_1 and Q_2. Let us assume furthermore that production processes which yield a negative quasi rent are not employed. We would then utilize all processes which are characterized by input coefficients ξ_1, ξ_2 which satisfy

$$P - Q_1\xi_1 - Q_2\xi_2 \geqq 0.$$

(3.17)

This is clearly the same as the first line of (3.14) when q_1 and q_2 are defined by

$$q_1 = \frac{Q_1}{P}, q_2 = \frac{Q_2}{P}.$$

(3.18)

This simply demonstrates the classical proposition that efficiency for the sector as a whole is obtained when prices are given and decisions about utilization of production processes is taken on the basis of non-negativity of quasi rents. We may accordingly think of the production function at the macro level as being generated by varying the prices and observing the corresponding variations in inputs and output. Since the absolute level of the prices is unimportant in this connection, only the two relative prices q_1 and q_2 are necessary.

Various properties of this type of production function will be discussed in Chapter 4.

3.4. *Direct reasoning for the continuous case*

This section will establish no new conclusions, but only prove the conclusion of the preceding section by direct reasoning for the case of a capacity distribution over a continuum of production units. Besides, this section will perhaps provide a more direct and lucid argument in so far as it does not invoke the duality theory of linear programming. Readers who feel that the reasoning of Section 3.3, relying on the analogy with discrete activity analysis, is sufficient, may however skip this section.

We know from before that efficient points exist in the sense that there is for every feasible V_1, V_2 a maximum for X, or, for every feasible V_1, X (V_2, X) a minimum for V_2 (V_1). This follows from the boundedness and closedness of the feasible set in the V_1, V_2, X-space. Furthermore, because of the convexity of the set there is no problem about local optima which are not global optima.

We shall now show that any utilization function $u(\xi_1, \xi_2)$ which is not of the form that $u(\xi_1, \xi_2) = 1$ for ξ_1, ξ_2 in a set $G(q_1, q_2)$ and $u(\xi_1, \xi_2) = 0$ outside $G(q_1, q_2)$ where $G(q_1, q_2)$ is defined by (3.14), cannot give an efficient point in the V_1, V_2, X-space. In other words, for any such $u(\xi_1, \xi_2)$-function it is possible to construct another $u(\xi_1, \xi_2)$-function such that either X is increased without V_1 and/or V_2 being increased, or V_1 (V_2) is decreased without X being decreased and/or V_2 (V_1) being increased.

As a first step, let us consider a utilization function $u(\xi_1, \xi_2)$ which is such that $u(\xi_1, \xi_2) > 0$ in a region ε_A containing a point A given by ξ_1^A, ξ_2^A, while we have $u(\xi_1, \xi_2) < 1$ in a region ε_B containing a point B given by ξ_1^B, ξ_2^B, where either $\xi_1^B < \xi_1^A, \xi_2^B \leq \xi_2^A$, or $\xi_1^B \leq \xi_1^A, \xi_2^B < \xi_2^A$, or both (and where $f(\xi_1, \xi_2) > 0$ in both regions). Since A and B are distinct points we can choose the regions so small that these relations are fulfilled by comparisons of every point in ε_B with every point in ε_A. Then it is clearly possible to decrease the utilization function in the region ε_A by a term $u_A^-(\xi_1, \xi_2)$ and increase it by a term $u_B^+(\xi_1, \xi_2)$ in the region ε_B in such a way that total output is left unaffected. The condition is, by requiring the modifications of the expression for X in (3.5) to cancel out:

$$\int\int_{\varepsilon_B} u_B^+(\xi_1, \xi_2)f(\xi_1, \xi_2)d\xi_1 d\xi_2 = \int\int_{\varepsilon_A} u_A^-(\xi_1, \xi_2)f(\xi_1, \xi_2)d\xi_1 d\xi_2.$$

(3.19)

From (3.6) we have the change in input V_i:

$$\Delta V_i = \int\int_{\varepsilon_B} \xi_i u_B^+(\xi_1, \xi_2)f(\xi_1, \xi_2)d\xi_1 d\xi_2 -$$

(3.20)

$$\int\int_{\varepsilon_A} \xi_i u_A^-(\xi_1, \xi_2)f(\xi_1, \xi_2)d\xi_1 d\xi_2.$$

If $\bar{\xi}_i^B$ is the upper bound for ξ_i in ε_B and $\bar{\xi}_i^A$ is the lower bound for ξ_i in ε_A we have from (3.19–3.20):

$$\Delta V_i \leqq (\bar{\xi}_i^B - \bar{\xi}_i^A) \int\int_{\varepsilon_A} u_A^-(\xi_1, \xi_2)f(\xi_1, \xi_2)d\xi_1 d\xi_2 \quad (i = 1, 2). \quad (3.21)$$

The integral is positive. Furthermore the difference $\bar{\xi}_i^B - \bar{\xi}_i^A$ is non-positive, and can be made negative for at least one of the inputs under the conditions stated above. Thus the modification of the utilization function decreases one or both inputs while leaving output unaffected.

From this it follows that we can restrict further attention to utilization functions which are equal to unity south-west of and equal to zero north-east of a non-increasing boundary curve in the ξ_1, ξ_2-plane since all other types of utilization functions are non-efficient by the above argument (in the region of positive capacity; it is of course immaterial how we think of the utilization function outside this region).

Now consider a case where this curve is not a straight line through the region of positive capacity. Then we will have at least one part of the curve as indicated in Figure 3.1, either case (a) or (b), with points A, B and C belonging to the region of positive capacity. Consider case (a). Here we have two points $A = (\xi_1^A, \xi_2^A)$ and $B = (\xi_1^B, \xi_2^B)$ with neighbourhoods ε_A and ε_B, where $u(\xi_1, \xi_2) = 0$, while there is a third point $C = (\xi_1^C, \xi_2^C)$ with a neighbourhood ε_C, where $u(\xi_1, \xi_2) = 1$, the points being located such that C is outside the straight line through A and B. If $f(\xi_1, \xi_2)$ is continuous only *almost* everywhere, we select A, B and C and the corresponding neighbourhoods such that $f(\xi_1, \xi_2)$ is continuous over these neighbourhoods.

Let us now modify the utilization function by introducing fractions u_A^+ and u_B^+ in the neighbourhoods ε_A and ε_B, while reducing the utilization function in ε_C by u_C^-. We may let u_A^+, u_B^+ and u_C^- be constant.

The increase in output X by this modification will be

$$\Delta X = u_A^+ \iint_{\varepsilon_A} f\,\mathrm{d}\xi + u_B^+ \iint_{\varepsilon_B} f\,\mathrm{d}\xi - u_C^- \iint_{\varepsilon_C} f\,\mathrm{d}\xi, \qquad (3.22)$$

where we have for brevity written $f\,\mathrm{d}\xi$ for $f(\xi_1, \xi_2)\,\mathrm{d}\xi_1\,\mathrm{d}\xi_2$. The corresponding changes in inputs will be

$$\Delta V_i = u_A^+ \iint_{\varepsilon_A} \xi_i f\,\mathrm{d}\xi + u_B^+ \iint_{\varepsilon_B} \xi_i f\,\mathrm{d}\xi - u_C^- \iint_{\varepsilon_C} \xi_i f\,\mathrm{d}\xi \quad (i = 1, 2). \qquad (3.23)$$

To economize on notation, let now ε_A, ε_B and ε_C denote the *size* of the neighbourhoods. By choosing the neighbourhoods sufficiently small we may to any desired degree of approximation write (3.22) as

$$\Delta X = u_A^+ f(A)\varepsilon_A + u_B^+ f(B)\varepsilon_B - u_C^- f(C)\varepsilon_C \qquad (3.24)$$

and (3.23) as

$$\Delta V_i = u_A^+ \xi_i^A f(A)\varepsilon_A + u_B^+ \xi_i^B f(B)\varepsilon_B - u_C^- \xi_i^C f(C)\varepsilon_C \quad (i = 1, 2), \qquad (3.25)$$

where we have written $f(A)$ for $f(\xi_1^A, \xi_2^A)$, etc.

We now select u_A^+, u_B^+ and u_C^- (we might also use the sizes of the neighbourhoods) in such a way that inputs are unaffected by the modifications, i.e. $\Delta V_1 = 0$ and $\Delta V_2 = 0$. This requires

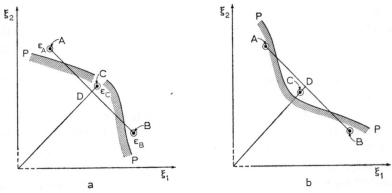

Fig. 3.1. Curve PP is the boundary curve for the utilization region.

$$f(A)\xi_1^A \frac{u_A^+ \varepsilon_A}{u_C^- \varepsilon_C} + f(B)\xi_1^B \frac{u_B^+ \varepsilon_B}{u_C^- \varepsilon_C} = f(C)\xi_1^C,$$

$$f(A)\xi_2^A \frac{u_A^+ \varepsilon_A}{u_C^- \varepsilon_C} + f(B)\xi_2^B \frac{u_B^+ \varepsilon_B}{u_C^- \varepsilon_C} = f(C)\xi_2^C. \tag{3.26}$$

For such a choice to be possible (with positive u_A^+, u_B^+, u_C^-) it is necessary and sufficient that the following determinants are not zero and have the same sign:

$$\begin{vmatrix} f(A)\xi_1^A & f(B)\xi_1^B \\ f(A)\xi_2^A & f(B)\xi_2^B \end{vmatrix} = f(A)f(B)\,(\xi_1^A\xi_2^B - \xi_2^A\xi_1^B), \tag{3.27}$$

$$\begin{vmatrix} f(A)\xi_1^A & f(C)\xi_1^C \\ f(A)\xi_2^A & f(C)\xi_2^C \end{vmatrix} = f(A)f(C)\,(\xi_1^A\xi_2^C - \xi_2^A\xi_1^C), \tag{3.28}$$

$$\begin{vmatrix} f(C)\xi_1^C & f(B)\xi_1^B \\ f(C)\xi_2^C & f(B)\xi_2^B \end{vmatrix} = f(B)f(C)\,(\xi_1^C\xi_2^B - \xi_2^C\xi_1^B). \tag{3.29}$$

Since all points A, B and C belong to the region of positive capacity we have $f(A), f(B), f(C) > 0$. By inspecting Figure 3.1a and interpreting $\xi_1^A\xi_2^B$ etc. as sizes of various rectangles it is furthermore easy to see that the expressions in parentheses on the right in (3.27–3.29) are all negative.

Since Equations (3.26) only determine the proportions u_A^+/u_C^- and u_B^+/u_C^-, it is clearly possible to select all u_A^+, u_B^+ and u_C^- in the permissible interval between 0 and 1.

Now divide through (3.26) by $f(C)$ and introduce the following (positive) "weights":

$$P_A = \frac{f(A)u_A^+\varepsilon_A}{f(C)u_C^-\varepsilon_C}, \qquad P_B = \frac{f(B)u_B^+\varepsilon_B}{f(C)u_C^-\varepsilon_C}, \tag{3.30}$$

Then (3.26) can be written as:

$$\frac{P_A}{P_A+P_B}\,\xi_1^A + \frac{P_B}{P_A+P_B}\,\xi_1^B = \frac{\xi_1^C}{P_A+P_B} = \xi_1^D,$$

$$\frac{P_A}{P_A+P_B}\,\xi_2^A + \frac{P_B}{P_A+P_B}\,\xi_2^B = \frac{\xi_2^C}{P_A+P_B} = \xi_2^D. \tag{3.31}$$

The first and second line in (3.31) can now be interpreted as the coordinates of a new point in the ξ_1, ξ_2-plane; we call this $D = (\xi_1^D, \xi_2^D)$. Since we have $\xi_2^D/\xi_1^D = \xi_2^C/\xi_1^C$ from the expressions to the right in (3.31), this new point is located on the ray from the origin through point C. Furthermore, from the expressions to the left in (3.31) we see that point D is formed as a convex combination (positive weights adding up to unity) of points A and B, i.e. it is located on the straight line connecting A and B. The situation is summarized in Figure 3.1a, where point D is marked off.

Now by assumption point C is located outside the straight line connecting A and B. From the equalities to the right in (3.31) it then follows that

$$P_A + P_B = \frac{f(A)u_A^+ \varepsilon_A + f(B)u_B^+ \varepsilon_B}{f(C)u_C^- \varepsilon_C} > 1. \tag{3.32}$$

Comparing with (3.24) we see that this is the same as $\Delta X > 0$, i.e. output has increased by the modification of the utilization function (while inputs have remained constant).

By exactly parallel reasoning for the case illustrated by Figure 3.1b, we can show that output can be increased while inputs are kept constant by reducing the utilization function in the regions ε_A and ε_B and increasing it in ε_C.

Since now any non-linear borderline for the utilization region through the region of positive capacity must for some part of the curve allow either case (a) or case (b) of Figure 3.1 and thus permit modifications of the utilization function which increase output while leaving inputs constant, no non-linear borderline can represent an efficient utilization function.

On the other hand, it is clear that when the borderline is linear, no increase in output is possible with constant total inputs.

By this we have established the conclusion of Section 3.3 without appealing to the duality theory of linear programming and discrete activity analysis.

The advantage of the proof given above is that it shows in a rather transparent way why a utilization region $G(q_1, q_2)$ as given by (3.14) is optimal.

When the conclusion is known, a much shorter proof can be given.[3]

For any utilization function $u(\xi_1, \xi_2)$, write the functions defined by (3.5–3.6) as $X(u)$, $V_1(u)$ and $V_2(u)$. Let there be given available amounts $\overline{V}_1$ and $\overline{V}_2$ of V_1 and V_2. Consider an arbitrary utilization function which is permissible under these given values $\overline{V}_1$ and $\overline{V}_2$, i.e. we have

$$V_1(u) \leqq \overline{V}_1, \qquad V_2(u) \leqq \overline{V}_2,$$

---

[3] The following proof was constructed by Mr. A. Seierstad.

or

$$\bar{V}_1 - V_1(u) \geqq 0, \qquad \bar{V}_2 - V_2(u) \geqq 0. \qquad (3.33)$$

Then we have for output $X(u)$, with $q_1, q_2 \geqq 0$:

$$X(u) \leqq X(u) + q_1\bar{V}_1 + q_2\bar{V}_2 - q_1V_1(u) - q_2V_2(u)$$

or

$$X(u) \leqq \int\int (1 - q_1\xi_1 - q_2\xi_2)u(\xi_1, \xi_2)f(\xi_1, \xi_2)d\xi_1d\xi_2 + q_1\bar{V}_1 + q_2\bar{V}_2. \qquad (3.34)$$

Now, since $G(q_1, q_2)$ defined by (3.14) is the region where $1 - q_1\xi_1 - q_2\xi_2 \geqq 0$, the right-hand side of (3.34) will not decrease if we restrict integration to $G(q_1, q_2)$, i.e. we have

$$X(u) \leqq \int\int_{G(q_1, q_2)} (1 - q_1\xi_1 - q_2\xi_2)u(\xi_1, \xi_2)f(\xi_1, \xi_2)d\xi_1d\xi_2 \\ + q_1\bar{V}_1 + q_2\bar{V}_2. \qquad (3.35)$$

Furthermore, since $u(\xi_1, \xi_2) \leqq 1$, we have from (3.35):

$$X(u) \leqq \int\int_{G(q_1, q_2)} (1 - q_1\xi_1 - q_2\xi_2)f(\xi_1, \xi_2)d\xi_1d\xi_2 + q_1\bar{V}_1 + q_2\bar{V}_2. \qquad (3.36)$$

We now use the assumption that q_1 and q_2 are appropriate to the given amounts $\bar{V}_1$ and $\bar{V}_2$, i.e. we have

$$\int\int_{G(q_1, q_2)} \xi_i f(\xi_1, \xi_2)d\xi_1d\xi_2 = \bar{V}_i \qquad (i = 1, 2). \qquad (3.37)$$

Then (3.36) is the same as

$$X(u) \leqq \int\int_{G(q_1, q_2)} f(\xi_1, \xi_2)d\xi_1d\xi_2. \qquad (3.38)$$

Thus, under the condition of given upper limits on the use of production factors, no other utilization function can yield larger output than the characteristic function of $G(q_1, q_2)$, i.e. the function which is 1 on $G(q_1, q_2)$ and 0 outside this region.

Finally it is worth mentioning that the most economic way of establishing our conclusion is simply to refer to the generalized fundamental lemma of Neyman and Pearson in the theory of testing statistical hypotheses.[4] Our result is an immediate consequence of this theorem, in fact so immediate that

---

[4] See e.g. Lehmann (1959), pp. 83–84, Theorem 5.

it is just a question of translating the symbols.[5] But this does of course not give much insight into the economics of the problem.

3.5. *Reflections on possible generalizations, I*

We have assumed above that the ex post function at the micro level is of the form described in Section 2.3, i.e. we have assumed fixed input coefficients by production in the range between zero output and full capacity utilization. This assumption can be somewhat relaxed without rendering the conclusions in the preceding sections of this chapter invalid.

We have already suggested before that e.g. the possibility that a production unit can be utilized for overtime work in addition to normal hours of work can be accommodated in our framework by thinking of this production unit as represented formally by two ξ_1, ξ_2-points; the point corresponding to overtime work would have ξ_1 and/or ξ_2 higher than the point corresponding to normal hours of work, and would not be called into operation by such optimization as we have studied unless normal hours of work are already utilized. (Alternatively we might extend our considerations to three dimensions, letting normal hours and overtime work be considered as different inputs.)

This suggestion can be generalized to ex post functions where input coefficients vary with the degree of capacity utilization in such a way that marginal input requirements are non-decreasing, and at least one of them increasing with output. Now assume that we have, instead of (2.2),

$$0 \leqq x \leqq \bar{x};$$

$$v_1 = g_1(x), \ g_1' = \frac{dg_1}{dx} > 0, \ \frac{d^2g_1}{dx^2} \geqq 0;$$

$$v_2 = g_2(x), \ g_2' = \frac{dg_2}{dx} > 0, \ \frac{d^2g_2}{dx^2} \geqq 0, \tag{3.39}$$

where g_1 and g_2 are input requirement functions and dg_1/dx and dg_2/dx are marginal input requirements (and at least one of the second derivatives is positive). In a ξ_1, ξ_2-diagram we may represent this case by a capacity distribution along a certain curve. Approximately we may think of a ξ_1, ξ_2-point with a capacity $\overline{\Delta x}$ and input coefficients $\xi_1 = g_1'(x)$ and $\xi_2 = g_2'(x)$.

---

[5] This was pointed out to me by Mr. T. Schweder.

We would then have, approximately, for this "production unit", input functions like $\Delta v_1 = g_1'(x)\Delta x$, $\Delta v_2 = g_2'(x)\Delta x$ $(0 \leq \Delta x \leq \overline{\Delta x})$. We may then clearly, in the limit when we let these artificial units become small, think of a capacity distribution along a curve in the ξ_1, ξ_2-plane determined by

$$\xi_1 = g_1'(x), \quad \xi_2 = g_2'(x) \tag{3.40}$$

or

$$\xi_2 = g_2' \left(g_1'^{-1}(\xi_1) \right), \tag{3.41}$$

where $g_1'^{-1}$ is the inverse function of $g_1'(x)$ (assuming $d^2 g_1/dx^2 > 0$). (3.41) might be called the expansion curve in the ξ_1, ξ_2-diagram. If we now let x indicate the point on this curve as we move outwards from the origin, we have a capacity density of 1 along the curve. Output and inputs when we utilize capacity along the curve from zero up to a certain point will be

$$x = \int_{y=0}^x dy, \quad v_1 = \int_{y=0}^x \xi_1 dy, \quad v_2 = \int_{y=0}^x \xi_2 dy, \tag{3.42}$$

which, when (3.40) is inserted, are of course equivalent to $v_1 = g_1(x)$ and $v_2 = g_2(x)$ (assuming $g_1(0) = 0$ and $g_2(0) = 0$).

If we prefer instead to measure capacity along the curve in other ways, the integrals in (3.42) should be transformed in the appropriate way.

As an example, assume that the input functions are of the form

$$v_1 = g_1(x) = ax + Ax^\alpha, \quad v_2 = g_2(x) = bx + Bx^\beta \quad (\alpha > 1, \beta > 1).$$

Then (3.40) takes the form

$$\xi_1 = a + A\alpha x^{\alpha-1}, \quad \xi_2 = b + B\beta x^{\beta-1}$$

and the curve along which the capacity should be considered as distributed is, corresponding to (3.41):

$$\xi_2 = b + B\beta \left(\frac{\xi_1 - a}{A\alpha} \right)^{\frac{\beta-1}{\alpha-1}},$$

which is an increasing curve in the ξ_1, ξ_2-plane from the point a, b.

If we have several production units of this type, each of them will have its capacity distributed along such a curve. According to the previous sections we should for efficiency exploit capacity lying south-west of a zero quasi rent line $q_1\xi_1 + q_2\xi_2 = 1$. The marginal capacity is that for which this equality is fulfilled. In such cases as those studied here this would amount to

$$q_1 g_1'(x) + q_2 g_2'(x) = 1. \tag{3.43}$$

This means that production units with ex post input functions which imply increasing marginal input requirements are utilized up to a point where marginal costs at shadow prices (in terms of output) q_1, q_2 are equal as between themselves and equal to unity (provided that their expansion curves intersect at all with the zero quasi rent line). This is of course the same result as we would obtain by formulating the optimization problem directly on the basis of the input functions instead of the distribution along the expansion curves in the ξ_1, ξ_2-diagram.

With a number of production units of this type the situation may be as suggested in Figure 3.2. In a ξ_1, ξ_2-diagram we have here placed a number of expansions paths along which we have distributed the capacity as explained above. If there are sufficiently many such curves we may approximate the whole structure by introducing a capacity distribution function in two dimensions, $f(\xi_1, \xi_2)$ which is such that $f(\xi_1, \xi_2)\Delta\xi_1\Delta\xi_2$ for a small cell $\Delta\xi_1, \Delta\xi_2$ approximates the total capacity of the parts of all expansion paths that fall inside this cell as suggested in the figure. On the basis of the assumptions made above we may thus operate with a distribution function as we did in Sections 3.1–3.4 and derive the macro function in exactly the same way. The only difference is that each physically identifiable production unit is now no longer represented by one point in the ξ_1, ξ_2-diagram, but rather has its share in various parts of the capacity distribution. For empirical analysis this of course complicates matters considerably, but it does not affect the theoretical analysis in the following chapters.

The generalization explained above covers decreasing marginal returns to inputs. It is also possible to generalize in other directions.

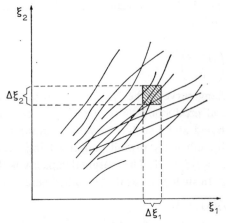

Fig. 3.2. Capacity distribution along curves in the ξ_1, ξ_2-plane.

In our main case we started out by assuming ex post functions, as represented by fixed input coefficients ξ_1, ξ_2 for each production unit, to be valid for any output level between zero and full capacity. The utilization function $u(\xi_1, \xi_2)$ was accordingly permitted to take any value in the interval $0 \leqq u(\xi_1, \xi_2) \leqq 1$. However, in the optimal solution only $u(\xi_1, \xi_2) = 0$ and $u(\xi_1, \xi_2) = 1$ were used. Then our solution would clearly be optimal also if $u(\xi_1, \xi_2)$ were from the outset restricted to taking only the values 0 or 1. The interpretation of this is that our way of establishing the macro function is valid even if the individual production units are such that they can only be operated at zero level or at full capacity.

If we combine this idea with the preceding one, we can cover quite a wide class of ex post functions. Again let the input requirement functions for a production unit be $g_1(x)$ and $g_2(x)$. Now assume first that marginal input requirements are decreasing over the whole range up to full capacity, in contrast with the assumptions in (3.39). Then again the solution previously derived is still valid if we represent a production unit by its average input coefficients at full capacity utilization. By proceeding as if the ex post function were as in (2.2) we obtain a solution where each unit is either fully utilized or not utilized at all. No unit is utilized at intermediate levels. The fact that the production units are less productive at intermediate levels than they are formally assumed to be clearly does not disturb the optimality of the calculated solution: when intermediate levels do not come into the optimal solution under assumptions of constant input requirements per unit of output, they will clearly not come into the optimal solution when they are less favourable compared to the end-points zero and full capacity output.

Next assume that the input requirement functions are of the form that marginal input requirements are decreasing up to a certain output level, and next increasing up to full capacity utilization $\bar{x}$. Let the output level where *average* input requirements start increasing be x^* (the same for both inputs). Then we may first represent the capacity x^* by a point in the ξ_1, ξ_2-plane, relying on the argument just presented. The rest of the capacity, $\bar{x} - x^*$, may be spread out along a curve, as explained in connection with (3.39–3.42). This curve will start at the point corresponding to average input requirements at output level x^*. By the optimization a unit of production of this type would be utilized at a level of output between x^* and $\bar{x}$ where marginal cost calculated as by (3.43) equals 1 if its expansion line between x^* and $\bar{x}$ intersects with the zero quasi rent line.[6]

---

[6] It seems not to be possible to cover in this way cases where minimum average input requirements occur at different levels of output for the different inputs.

In general we may now within an industry have a mixture of cases like those described above in addition to the ordinary case. Within a cell $\Delta\xi_1\Delta\xi_2$ as marked off in Figure 3.2 we would then have a total capacity consisting of capacity concentrated in discrete points and capacity distributed along parts of curves passing through this cell. If there are sufficiently many and sufficiently varied cases represented it may still be possible to approximate this by a distribution function $f(\xi_1, \xi_2)$ as introduced before.

By these generalizations we cover cases of indivisibilities and increasing returns to scale which usually cause difficulties in price and allocation theory. The reason why they do not create difficulties for the theoretical analysis in our context is of course that the "marginal production units" are in any case of a negligible order of magnitude.[7] As soon as we return to reality, where production units are of finite size and of a finite number, it is a matter of empirical facts, purpose of analysis and judgement to decide to what extent such an idealized theory is a useful approximation.

3.6. Reflections on possible generalizations, II

While the generalizations suggested in Section 3.5 were concerned with the technology at the micro level underlying the short-run macro function, this section will take up the assumption about efficiency. A macro function where the aggregation problem is solved by an assumption about efficiency, as is done in the previous sections, is of interest from many points of view. For positive theory and for forecasts without normative significance, one may however feel that a macro function based on less than full efficiency might be more realistic.

In an actual case, when the individual units are faced with given factor prices Q_1 and Q_2 and a given output price P, there may be several reasons – readjustment costs, market imperfections, incomplete information etc. – why the selection of production units to be operated will not be perfect. On

---

[7] At this point our reflections on generalizations touch some modern developments in allocation theory which build on assumptions about a "continuum" or "measure space" of economic agents and which can dispense with the traditional concavity or convexity assumptions of theoretical economics. See e.g. Hildenbrand (1968) and works by Auman, Debreu, Vind and others referred to there. For an earlier discussion of relevance to this point, see Farrell (1959), Rothenberg (1960) and contributions to the discussion by Koopmans, et al. in *The Journal of Political Economy* 1961. A recent and rigorous re-statement of some of the conlusions from this discussion is given in Hildenbrand (1969).

the other hand, comparing production units which are able to earn a clearly positive quasi rent with units which are able to earn only a negative quasi rent, one would expect a larger proportion of the capacity in the former group to be operated. This suggests the introduction of the following non-decreasing function:

$u(s)$ = the proportion operated of capacity which is able to
earn a quasi rent s per unit of output value.   (3.44)

Quasi rent per unit of output value for a production unit with input coefficients ξ_1 and ξ_2 will be

$$s = \frac{P - Q_1\xi_1 - Q_2\xi_2}{P} = 1 - q_1\xi_1 - q_2\xi_2.$$ (3.45)

Compare (2.13) and (3.18).

Total output and total factor use can now be expressed as

$$X = \int\int u(1 - q_1\xi_1 - q_2\xi_2)f(\xi_1, \xi_2)d\xi_1 d\xi_2,$$

$$V_i = \int\int \xi_i u(1 - q_1\xi_1 - q_2\xi_2)f(\xi_1, \xi_2)d\xi_1 d\xi_2 \qquad (i = 1, 2),$$ (3.46)

where the integrals are taken over the whole positive quadrant (with effectively positive contributions to the integrals only from the region of positive capacity).

The function $u(s)$ must satisfy $0 \leq u(s) \leq 1$ and is likely to be non-decreasing. Otherwise it is not easy to specify the form of $u(s)$. In Figure 3.3 possible forms are suggested.

In the case of curve I full capacity utilization would not obtain even at very profitable prices. With curve II full capacity utilization for the sector as a whole would obtain if prices are such that even the most inefficient units earn a quasi rent of s_1 or greater. The case of perfect optimization,

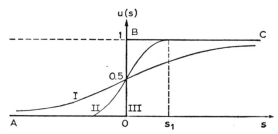

Fig. 3.3. Possible forms of the function $u(s)$ defined by (3.44).

which we have discussed in the previous sections, corresponds to a $u(s)$-function following the step curve $AOBC$ in the figure, i.e. to $u(s)$ being defined by

$$u(s) = \begin{cases} 0 \text{ when } s < 0 \\ 1 \text{ when } s \geq 0. \end{cases} \qquad (3.47)$$

In the previous sections the macro function $F(V_1, V_2)$ was defined by the elimination of q_1 and q_2 from the system (3.15). In a corresponding way the macro function in the present case, say $F(V_1, V_2; u)$, where u represents the functional form $u(s)$, can be obtained from (3.46) by elimination of q_1 and q_2.

Obviously we will have $F(V_1, V_2; u) < F(V_1, V_2)$ when $u(s)$ is different from (3.47). Otherwise the effects of the introduction of a $u(s)$-function different from (3.47) have not been fully explored.

A further generalization would be to introduce total output in proportion to full capacity output as another argument in u, i.e. to write

$$u\left(s, \frac{X}{\overline{X}}\right), \qquad (3.48)$$

where $\overline{X}$ is total capacity for the sector as a whole and X is actual output. The reason for introducing this argument in the function could be that buyers adhere more or less to their customary suppliers, while these on their side more or less let the wish to retain the customers override the short-run profitability considerations. Another reason might be cartel agreements. An extreme case would be if u depends *only* on $X/\overline{X}$. It then follows from insertion in the first equation in (3.46) that $u = X/\overline{X}$ since we have

$$X = \int \int u\left(\frac{X}{\overline{X}}\right) f(\xi_1, \xi_2) d\xi_1 d\xi_2 =$$

$$u\left(\frac{X}{\overline{X}}\right) \int \int f(\xi_1, \xi_2) d\xi_1 d\xi_2 = u\left(\frac{X}{\overline{X}}\right) \overline{X}. \qquad (3.49)$$

From the last equations of (3.46) one has

$$V_i = \int \int \xi_i \frac{X}{\overline{X}} f(\xi_1, \xi_2) d\xi_1 d\xi_2 = \frac{\overline{V}_i}{\overline{X}} X = \bar{\xi}_i X \quad (i = 1, 2), \qquad (3.50)$$

where $\overline{V}_1$ and $\overline{V}_2$ are total factor inputs at full capacity utilization, and $\bar{\xi}_1$ and $\bar{\xi}_2$ are average input coefficients for all production units. Thus, in this extreme case the short-run production function at the macro level is of the Leontief type for $X \leq \overline{X}$ regardless of the distribution $f(\xi_1, \xi_2)$.

The generalization suggested in this section is of a purely positive significance, whereas the case on which we concentrate through most of this
study may be said to be similar to other theories of perfect competition in
that it allows both a normative and positive interpretation (cf. Section 2.4
after Equation (2.7)).

Whereas the discussion in the following chapters about the various properties of the short-run macro function, the demand and supply functions
derived from it and some distributional aspects remains valid under the
generalizations suggested in Section 3.5, the generalization suggested in this
section would require modifications on some points in the following chapters.
Some hints will be given here and there, but, as already mentioned, the full
implications have not been worked out.

CHAPTER 4

On the form of the short-run macro function

4.1. Introduction

The short-run macro function is determined implicitly by (3.15), where the region $G(q_1, q_2)$ is determined by (3.14). Rewriting the zero quasi rent condition $q_1\xi_1 + q_2\xi_2 = 1$ in the form

$$\xi_2 = \frac{1}{q_2} - \frac{q_1}{q_2}\xi_1 \tag{4.1}$$

we can cover the region $G(q_1, q_2)$ by integration over ξ_1 from 0 to $1/q_1$ and over ξ_2 from 0 to the value given by (4.1). For convenience we then rewrite (3.15) in the form

$$X = \int_0^{\frac{1}{q_1}} \int_0^{\frac{1}{q_2} - \frac{q_1}{q_2}\xi_1} f(\xi_1, \xi_2)d\xi_2 d\xi_1 = g(q_1, q_2),$$

$$V_1 = \int_0^{\frac{1}{q_1}} \int_0^{\frac{1}{q_2} - \frac{q_1}{q_2}\xi_1} \xi_1 f(\xi_1, \xi_2)d\xi_2 d\xi_1 = h_1(q_1, q_2),$$

$$V_2 = \int_0^{\frac{1}{q_1}} \int_0^{\frac{1}{q_2} - \frac{q_1}{q_2}\xi_1} \xi_2 f(\xi_1, \xi_2)d\xi_2 d\xi_1 = h_2(q_1, q_2). \tag{4.2}$$

We have here introduced the functions $g(q_1, q_2)$, $h_1(q_1, q_2)$ and $h_2(q_1, q_2)$, which represent output and inputs corresponding to any given set of values of q_1 and q_2. These functions are convenient for notational brevity, but they also have a direct economic interpretation as supply and factor demand functions in terms of relative prices, i.e. factor prices deflated by output price. We shall revert to this interpretation in Chapter 6.

Equations (4.1–4.2) are not strictly valid when $q_1 = 0$ or $q_2 = 0$, but we may consider these cases as limiting cases of (4.2).

We now consider the two last equations of (4.2) as a transformation from q_1, q_2 to V_1, V_2. Inverting this transformation[1] we obtain

---

[1] It will be seen below that the Jacobian of this transformation is positive.

$$q_1 = h_1^{-1}(V_1, V_2), \quad q_2 = h_2^{-1}(V_1, V_2). \tag{4.3}$$

Inserting this into the first equation of (4.2) we have an expression for the short-run macro function

$$X = F(V_1, V_2) \equiv g\left(h_1^{-1}(V_1, V_2), h_2^{-1}(V_1, V_2)\right). \tag{4.4}$$

In the remainder of this chapter we shall explore various questions concerning the form of such production functions. It is clear that a wide variety of forms are possible; on the other hand, not all increasing functions of two arguments with "correct" curvature of the isoquants can be established in this way on the basis of a capacity distribution function $f(\xi_1, \xi_2)$ even if we are free to choose the form of this distribution. We therefore have a narrower class of functions than those traditionally considered as eligible production functions. This should not be considered as a weakness of the model; it is rather a strong point since it means that the model has empirically meaningful implications.

4.2. Marginal productivities, isoquants, and expansion lines

An isoquant of the macro function (4.4) is generated by varying V_1 and V_2 in (4.2) in such a way that X remains constant. Under this variation q_1 and q_2 will of course vary. From the price interpretation of q_1 and q_2 it is intuitively clear that the slope of an isoquant (the marginal rate of substitution) will be related to the ratio between q_1 and q_2. In the case of (2.7–2.12) this follows from the shadow price interpretation of q_1 and q_2. We shall however derive this relationship more directly and explicitly for the present case, particularly since some of the formulas which we shall then come across will be useful also for other purposes.

From (4.2) we have by differentiation:

$$\mathrm{d}X = \frac{\partial g}{\partial q_1}\,\mathrm{d}q_1 + \frac{\partial g}{\partial q_2}\,\mathrm{d}q_2,$$

$$\mathrm{d}V_1 = \frac{\partial h_1}{\partial q_1}\,\mathrm{d}q_1 + \frac{\partial h_1}{\partial q_2}\,\mathrm{d}q_2,$$

$$\mathrm{d}V_2 = \frac{\partial h_2}{\partial q_1}\,\mathrm{d}q_1 + \frac{\partial h_2}{\partial q_2}\,\mathrm{d}q_2. \tag{4.5}$$

For further exploration we need the partial derivatives involved in (4.5). Consider first the derivative $\partial g/\partial q_1$. For this differentiation we may think of $g(q_1, q_2)$ written in the form

$$X = g(q_1, q_2) = \int_0^{\frac{1}{q_1}} f^*(q_1, q_2, \xi_1) d\xi_1, \tag{4.6}$$

where

$$f^*(q_1, q_2, \xi_1) = \int_0^{\frac{1}{q_2} - \frac{q_1}{q_2}\xi_1} f(\xi_1, \xi_2) \, d\xi_2. \tag{4.7}$$

From (4.6) we have by differentiation with respect to q_1 which enters both in the upper limit of the integral and in the integrand

$$\frac{\partial g}{\partial q_1} = -\frac{1}{q_1^2} f^*\left(q_1, q_2, \frac{1}{q_1}\right) + \int_0^{\frac{1}{q_1}} \frac{\partial f^*(q_1, q_2, \xi_1)}{\partial q_1} \, d\xi_1. \tag{4.8}$$

From (4.7) we have

$$\frac{\partial f^*}{\partial q_1} = -\frac{\xi_1}{q_2} f\left(\xi_1, \frac{1}{q_2} - \frac{q_1}{q_2}\xi_1\right). \tag{4.9}$$

We now collect the full expression for $\partial g/\partial q_1$. The first term in (4.8) is obtained from (4.7) by inserting $1/q_1$ for ξ_1 in $f^*(q_1, q_2, \xi_1)$. It is then seen that the upper limit of the integral reduces to zero, i.e. we have $f^*(q_1, q_2, 1/q_1) = 0$. Then from (4.8–4.9) we obtain the simple expression

$$\frac{\partial g}{\partial q_1} = -\frac{1}{q_2} \int_0^{\frac{1}{q_1}} \xi_1 f\left(\xi_1, \frac{1}{q_2} - \frac{q_1}{q_2}\xi_1\right) d\xi_1. \tag{4.10}$$

In order to obtain $\partial g/\partial q_2$ we proceed in a similar manner. From (4.6) we have

$$\frac{\partial g}{\partial q_2} = \int_0^{\frac{1}{q_1}} \frac{\partial f^*(q_1, q_2, \xi_1)}{\partial q_2} d\xi_1. \tag{4.11}$$

The derivative under the integral is obtained from (4.7)

$$\frac{\partial f^*}{\partial q_2} = -\frac{1}{q_2}\left(\frac{1}{q_2} - \frac{q_1}{q_2}\xi_1\right) f\left(\xi_1, \frac{1}{q_2} - \frac{q_1}{q_2}\xi_1\right), \tag{4.12}$$

which by insertion in (4.11) yields

$$\frac{\partial g}{\partial q_2} = -\frac{1}{q_2} \int_0^{\frac{1}{q_1}} \left(\frac{1}{q_2} - \frac{q_1}{q_2} \xi_1 \right) f\left(\xi_1, \frac{1}{q_2} - \frac{q_1}{q_2} \xi_1 \right) d\xi_1. \tag{4.13}$$

It is easy to carry out the differentiations of $h_1(q_1, q_2)$ and $h_2(q_1, q_2)$ in the same way. Collecting the results we have:

$$\frac{\partial g}{\partial q_1} = -\frac{1}{q_2} \int_0^{\frac{1}{q_1}} \xi_1 f\left(\xi_1, \frac{1}{q_2} - \frac{q_1}{q_2} \xi_1 \right) d\xi_1,$$

$$\frac{\partial g}{\partial q_2} = -\frac{1}{q_2} \int_0^{\frac{1}{q_1}} \left(\frac{1}{q_2} - \frac{q_1}{q_2} \xi_1 \right) f\left(\xi_1, \frac{1}{q_2} - \frac{q_1}{q_2} \xi_1 \right) d\xi_1,$$

$$\frac{\partial h_1}{\partial q_1} = -\frac{1}{q_2} \int_0^{\frac{1}{q_1}} \xi_1^2 f\left(\xi_1, \frac{1}{q_2} - \frac{q_1}{q_2} \xi_1 \right) d\xi_1,$$

$$\frac{\partial h_1}{\partial q_2} = -\frac{1}{q_2} \int_0^{\frac{1}{q_1}} \xi_1 \left(\frac{1}{q_2} - \frac{q_1}{q_2} \xi_1 \right) f\left(\xi_1, \frac{1}{q_2} - \frac{q_1}{q_2} \xi_1 \right) d\xi_1,$$

$$\frac{\partial h_2}{\partial q_1} = -\frac{1}{q_2} \int_0^{\frac{1}{q_1}} \xi_1 \left(\frac{1}{q_2} - \frac{q_1}{q_2} \xi_1 \right) f\left(\xi_1, \frac{1}{q_2} - \frac{q_1}{q_2} \xi_1 \right) d\xi_1,$$

$$\frac{\partial h_2}{\partial q_2} = -\frac{1}{q_2} \int_0^{\frac{1}{q_1}} \left(\frac{1}{q_2} - \frac{q_1}{q_2} \xi_1 \right)^2 f\left(\xi_1, \frac{1}{q_2} - \frac{q_1}{q_2} \xi_1 \right) d\xi_1. \tag{4.14}$$

These formulas can be interpreted in terms of averages. For this purpose it is convenient to introduce the following integral:

$$J = \frac{1}{q_2} \int_0^{\frac{1}{q_1}} f\left(\xi_1, \frac{1}{q_2} - \frac{q_1}{q_2} \xi_1 \right) d\xi_1. \tag{4.15}$$

For any variable y which is a function of ξ_1, or of ξ_1 and ξ_2 where ξ_2 is again related to ξ_1 by (4.1), we introduce the following notation:

$$M(y) = \frac{\dfrac{1}{q_2} \displaystyle\int_0^{\frac{1}{q_1}} y f\left(\xi_1, \frac{1}{q_2} - \frac{q_1}{q_2} \xi_1 \right) d\xi_1}{J}. \tag{4.16}$$

The interpretation of $M(y)$ is evidently the average value of y along the line $q_1 \xi_1 + q_2 \xi_2 = 1$ from the point $0, 1/q_2$ to the point $1/q_1, 0$. Intuitively we may speak of $M(y)$ as the average of y for marginal production units, since the line $q_1\xi_1 + q_2\xi_2 = 1$ signifies the border-line of production units to be employed. When necessary we shall write $M(y; q_1, q_2)$ to indicate that this average will of course depend upon q_1 and q_2. For convenience we shall however retain the shorter notation most of the time.

With the notation introduced by (4.16) and writing ξ_2 for $(1/q_2) - (q_1/q_2)\xi_1$ we can write (4.14) in the following way:

$$\frac{\partial g}{\partial q_1} = -J\,M(\xi_1), \qquad \frac{\partial g}{\partial q_2} = -J\,M(\xi_2),$$

$$\frac{\partial h_1}{\partial q_1} = -J\,M(\xi_1^2), \qquad \frac{\partial h_1}{\partial q_2} = -J\,M(\xi_1\xi_2),$$

$$\frac{\partial h_2}{\partial q_1} = -J\,M(\xi_1\xi_2), \qquad \frac{\partial h_2}{\partial q_2} = -J\,M(\xi_2^2). \tag{4.17}$$

Inserting these expressions in (4.5) we obtain

$$-\frac{1}{J}dX = M(\xi_1)dq_1 + M(\xi_2)\,dq_2$$

$$-\frac{1}{J}dV_1 = M(\xi_1^2)dq_1 + M(\xi_1\xi_2)dq_2$$

$$-\frac{1}{J}dV_2 = M(\xi_1\xi_2)dq_1 + M(\xi_2^2)dq_2. \tag{4.18}$$

We now introduce the variances and the covariance of ξ_1 and ξ_2 along the line $q_1\xi_1 + q_2\xi_2 = 1$ given by

$$\sigma_i^2 = M\{[\xi_i - M(\xi_i)]^2\} = M(\xi_i^2) - [M(\xi_i)]^2 \qquad (i = 1, 2),$$

$$\sigma_{12} = M\{[\xi_1 - M(\xi_1)][\xi_2 - M(\xi_2)]\} = M(\xi_1\xi_2) - M(\xi_1)M(\xi_2). \tag{4.19}$$

Since ξ_1 and ξ_2 are linearly related by $q_1\xi_1 + q_2\xi_2 = 1$, or $\xi_2 = (1/q_2) - (q_1/q_2)\xi_1$, in the "population" of marginal production units, we have the following relationships:

$$q_1M(\xi_1) + q_2M(\xi_2) = 1, \text{ or } M(\xi_2) = \frac{1}{q_2} - \frac{q_1}{q_2}M(\xi_1),$$

$$\sigma_2^2 = \left(\frac{q_1}{q_2}\right)^2\sigma_1^2, \qquad \sigma_{12} = -\frac{q_1}{q_2}\sigma_1^2 = -\sigma_1\sigma_2. \tag{4.20}$$

Using these relationships we can derive a simple expression for the determinant of the second order moments entering the two last equations of (4.18):

$$\begin{vmatrix} M(\xi_1^2) & M(\xi_1\xi_2) \\ M(\xi_1\xi_2) & M(\xi_2^2) \end{vmatrix} = \begin{vmatrix} \sigma_1^2 + [M(\xi_1)]^2 & \sigma_{12} + M(\xi_1)M(\xi_2) \\ \sigma_{12} + M(\xi_1)M(\xi_2) & \sigma_2^2 + [M(\xi_2)]^2 \end{vmatrix}$$

$$= \{\sigma_1^2 + [M(\xi_1)]^2\} \{\sigma_2^2 + [M(\xi_2)]^2\} - \{\sigma_{12} + M(\xi_1)M(\xi_2)\}^2$$

$$= \sigma_1^2\sigma_2^2 + \sigma_2^2[M(\xi_1)]^2 + \sigma_1^2[M(\xi_2)]^2 + [M(\xi_1)]^2[M(\xi_2)]^2 - \sigma_{12}^2$$

$$- 2\sigma_{12}M(\xi_1)M(\xi_2) - [M(\xi_1)]^2[M(\xi_2)]^2.$$

Here σ_{12}^2 cancels against $\sigma_1^2\sigma_2^2$ according to the second line of (4.20). Furthermore, expressing σ_2^2 and σ_{12} in terms of σ_1^2 we can write the last formula as

$$\sigma_1^2\{[M(\xi_2)]^2 + \left(\frac{q_1}{q_2}\right)^2 [M(\xi_1)]^2 + 2\frac{q_1}{q_2} M(\xi_1)M(\xi_2)\}$$

$$= \frac{1}{q_2^2} \sigma_1^2\{q_1^2[M(\xi_1)]^2 + q_2^2[M(\xi_2)]^2 + 2q_1q_2M(\xi_1)M(\xi_2)\}.$$

By squaring the first equation in (4.20) it is seen that the term in brackets in this expression reduces to 1. Accordingly we have the following simple result:

$$\begin{vmatrix} M(\xi_1^2) & M(\xi_1\xi_2) \\ \\ M(\xi_1\xi_2) & M(\xi_2^2) \end{vmatrix} = \frac{1}{q_2^2} \sigma_1^2 = \frac{1}{q_1^2} \sigma_2^2. \tag{4.21}$$

If there is any spread at all among the marginal production units, and we assume there is, the determinant in (4.21) is positive.[2]

We can now solve the two last equations in (4.18) with respect to dq_1 and dq_2 so as to obtain:

$$dq_1 = \frac{q_2^2}{J\sigma_1^2} [-M(\xi_2^2)\,dV_1 + M(\xi_1\xi_2)dV_2],$$

$$dq_2 = \frac{q_2^2}{J\sigma_1^2} [M(\xi_1\xi_2)\,dV_1 - M(\xi_1^2)dV_2]. \tag{4.22}$$

---

[2] From (4.17) and (4.21) it is now seen that the Jacobian mentioned in footnote 1 on p. 54 is

$$\begin{vmatrix} \dfrac{\partial h_1}{\partial q_1} & \dfrac{\partial h_1}{\partial q_2} \\ \\ \dfrac{\partial h_2}{\partial q_1} & \dfrac{\partial h_2}{\partial q_2} \end{vmatrix} = \begin{vmatrix} -JM(\xi_1^2) & -JM(\xi_1\xi_2) \\ \\ -JM(\xi_1\xi_2) & -JM(\xi_2^2) \end{vmatrix} = \frac{J^2}{q_2^2} \sigma_1^2 > 0,$$

provided that q_1 and q_2 are such that the line $q_1\xi_1 + q_2\xi_2 = 1$ passes through the region of positive capacity so that $J > 0$.

Let us pause for a moment to consider these equations. While the last two equations in (4.18) indicate the changes in factor inputs V_1 and V_2 for given changes in the parameters q_1 and q_2, the equations in (4.22) indicate the changes in the parameters q_1 and q_2 for given changes in total factor inputs V_1 and V_2. In (4.22) the ratios before the brackets are positive numbers. Furthermore all moments M are positive. It is clear then that a "shadow price" q_i is negatively influenced by an increase in the corresponding input V_i and positively influenced by an increase in the other input. In Figure 4.1

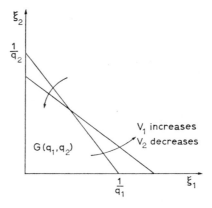

Fig. 4.1. Rotation of the border-line $q_1\xi_1+q_2\xi_2 = 1$ when V_1 increases and V_2 decreases (q_1 decreases, q_2 increases).

we have illustrated how the border-line $q_1\xi_1+q_2\xi_2 = 1$ of the region $G(q_1, q_2)$ defined by (3.14) rotates when input V_1 increases while at the same time input V_2 decreases. As is intuitively obvious the rotation is such that some additional production capacity which is relatively intensive in factor No. 1 will be included while some capacity which is relatively intensive in factor No. 2 will be excluded from utilization.

Let us now consider the change in total output X. Inserting from (4.22) in the equation on the first line of (4.18) we obtain

$$dX = -\frac{q_2^2}{\sigma_1^2}\{[-M(\xi_1)M(\xi_2^2)+M(\xi_2)M(\xi_1\xi_2)]dV_1+$$

$$+[-M(\xi_2)M(\xi_1^2)+M(\xi_1)M(\xi_1\xi_2)]dV_2\}. \qquad (4.23)$$

Now consider the coefficient before dV_1 in this expression. This can be considerably simplified by the following steps, using (4.19–4.20):

$$- \frac{q_2^2}{\sigma_1^2} \{ -M(\xi_1)M(\xi_2^2) + M(\xi_2)M(\xi_1\xi_2) \}$$

$$= - \frac{q_2^2}{\sigma_1^2} \left\{ -M(\xi_1)M(\xi_2^2) + \frac{1-q_1M(\xi_1)}{q_2} M(\xi_1\xi_2) \right\}$$

$$= - \frac{q_2}{\sigma_1^2} \{ -M(\xi_1) [q_1M(\xi_1\xi_2) + q_2M(\xi_2^2)] + M(\xi_1\xi_2) \}.$$

Along the line $q_1\xi_1 + q_2\xi_2 = 1$, where the moments involved are calculated, we have $q_1\xi_1\xi_2 + q_2\xi_2^2 = \xi_2$ and hence $q_1M(\xi_1\xi_2) + q_2M(\xi_2^2) = M(\xi_2)$. Using this the last expression can be further developed in the following way:

$$- \frac{q_2}{\sigma_1^2} \{ M(\xi_1\xi_2) - M(\xi_1)M(\xi_2) \} = - \frac{q_2}{\sigma_1^2} \sigma_{12} = q_1.$$

The coefficient before dV_2 in (4.23) can be developed in the same way. Thus we end up with the simple formula

$$dX = q_1dV_1 + q_2dV_2. \tag{4.24}$$

It follows that the marginal productivities of the short-run macro function (4.4) are given by

$$\frac{\partial X}{\partial V_1} = q_1, \quad \frac{\partial X}{\partial V_2} = q_2 \tag{4.25}$$

and that the slope of an isoquant, i.e. the negative of the marginal rate of substitution, is given by

$$\left. \frac{dV_2}{dV_1} \right|_{dX = 0} = - \frac{q_1}{q_2}. \tag{4.26}$$

The results given in (4.24–4.26) are intuitively plausible on the basis of the interpretation of q_1 and q_2 as shadow prices in the corresponding discrete case. By the preceding analysis we have however shown these results by direct calculations without falling back upon the analogy with duality theory of linear programming.

To every position of the zero quasi rent line $q_1\xi_1 + q_2\xi_2 = 1$ corresponds a certain point in the V_1, V_2-plane, and vice versa. Through each such V_1, V_2-point passes an isoquant. The results given above may be restated in the following form: The slope of an isoquant through a V_1, V_2-point is the same as the slope of the zero quasi rent line which corresponds to the given V_1, V_2-point.

From the fact (shown in Section 3.2) that the feasible region in the

V_1, V_2, X-space is convex it follows that the isoquant curves in the V_1, V_2-plane are convex to the origin. The same result can now be seen by applying (4.26) in conjunction with the reasoning which was illustrated by Figure 4.1. First, since the marginal productivities q_1, $q_2 \geqq 0$, an isoquant goes from north-west towards south-east in the V_1, V_2-plane. Next, consider what happens to q_1 and q_2 when we move along an isoquant in this direction. Both the fact that V_1 increases and that V_2 decreases tend to decrease q_1; at the same time they tend to increase q_2 – see (4.22). Accordingly the zero quasi rent line rotates as shown in Figure 4.1 when we move along the isoquant in the direction mentioned, and since the slope of the isoquant is in every point the same as the slope of the corresponding zero quasi rent line it must be convex to the origin.

An expansion line in the factor diagram is a curve which connects points with the same slope on different isoquants. (In the terminology of Frisch this is an isocline curve, see Frisch (1965), pp. 56–57). In the traditional theory of production it cannot be shown that both inputs are non-decreasing along such an expansion line (in the direction of increasing output). The conditions under which an input is decreasing with increasing output along an expansion curve – referred to as an input being "regressive" – has been much debated in the literature in recent years.[3] Our short-run macro function cannot exhibit such regressivity. This follows easily from the correspondence between the slope of the zero quasi rent line and the slope of the isoquant. Because of this correspondence an expansion curve in the V_1, V_2-plane is clearly generated by a parallel shifting of the zero quasi rent line outwards in the ξ_1, ξ_2-plane (proportional reduction in q_1 and q_2). This parallel shifting of the zero quasi rent line enlarges the region $G(q_1, q_2)$ over which one integrates in the formulas (3.15) or (4.2) defining the short-run macro function; a region in the ξ_1, ξ_2-plane which has been included in $G(q_1, q_2)$ will never get out of it again. Hence, while output increases, inputs V_1 and V_2 cannot decrease under such a shifting of the zero quasi rent which generates an expansion line.[4]

4.3. *Compatibility of micro and macro calculation*

Our short-run macro function is an aggregate relationship. As such it sum-

---

[3] See Puu (1966, 1968) and literature referred to there. See also the comments by Frisch (1965), p. 164.
[4] Regressivity may well occur in the ex ante function at the micro level.

marizes a large amount of data at the micro level. An important question concerning such relationships is whether or not it can be used for further analysis without all the time having recourse to the underlying information at the micro level. Only if the answer is affirmative is the aggregate relationship a useful construct.

Now our macro function does of course correctly answer the question: Given total inputs V_1, V_2, what is the maximal output obtainable? This follows directly from the definition.

More interesting is the question about the compatibility of traditional marginal calculations applied to the short-run macro function, and decision-taking at the micro level, which with the fixed coefficients in the ex post micro functions is not of the marginalistic type.

Consider a situation in which the industry is faced with an output price P and input prices Q_1 and Q_2. These prices are considered as given data. The output and factor input response to these prices could now be calculated in two different ways:

(1) *Calculations from the micro level.* Let each individual decision-taker at the micro level decide whether or not to operate "his" production unit according as quasi rents $P - Q_1\xi_1 - Q_2\xi_2$ are positive or negative. Sum outputs and input requirements over all units with positive quasi rent so as to obtain X and V_1, V_2.

(2) *Calculation at the macro level.* Assume that the short-run macro function $X = F(V_1, V_2)$ is known. Under the given prices P, Q_1, Q_2, maximize total profits given by

$$PF(V_1, V_2) - Q_1 V_1 - Q_2 V_2 \qquad (4.27)$$

with respect to V_1 and V_2. This determines V_1, V_2 and X.

The calculations from the micro level correspond to calculations based on (4.2) for $q_1 = Q_1/P$ and $q_2 = Q_2/P$.

The calculation at the macro level yields the conditions

$$P \frac{\partial F}{\partial V_1} = Q_1, \quad P \frac{\partial F}{\partial V_2} = Q_2$$

or

$$\frac{\partial F}{\partial V_1} = \frac{Q_1}{P} = q_1, \quad \frac{\partial F}{\partial V_2} = \frac{Q_2}{P} = q_2. \qquad (4.28)$$

We have seen before that, for corresponding positions of the zero quasi rent line and points in the V_1, V_2-plane, the marginal productivities of

$F(V_1, V_2)$ are equal to the parameters q_1 and q_2 in the quasi rent condition. Then (4.28) clearly means that we have, by marginal calculations applied to the profit expression based on the macro production function, reached the same V_1, V_2-combination as by summation of results of calculations at the micro level.

We have in this case a type of aggregation in which the aggregate relationship is not simply a magnified reflection of processes at the micro level: There are substitution possibilities in the macro function without this being true for the micro processes. Correspondingly marginalistic calculations are justified at the macro level while simple unit price – unit cost comparisons are relevant at the micro level, and these two different types of calculations at the different levels are mutually compatible. In my opinion this is a very attractive feature. It fits in perfectly well with the observation that while economists, who are after all mainly concerned with macroeconomics, insist on the relevance of marginalistic calculations, they have not always succeeded in convincing people who are concerned with decision-making at the micro level. In view of the present model both parties may be right in their spheres, without this giving rise to any logical contradictions.[5]

4.4. Returns to scale

The degree of returns to scale in the short-run macro function, i.e. in $X = F(V_1, V_2)$ can be expressed by the elasticity

$$\varepsilon = \frac{\mathrm{d}X}{\mathrm{d}V_1} \frac{V_1}{X} = \frac{\mathrm{d}X}{\mathrm{d}V_2} \frac{V_2}{X} \tag{4.29}$$

defined for proportional factor variation, i.e. $\mathrm{d}V_1/V_1 = \mathrm{d}V_2/V_2$. This elasticity is known under various names in the literature. We shall use the term "scale elasticity".

From classical theory of production[6] it is well known that we have the following relationship:

---

[5] Another matter is the question about substitution possibilities in connection with investment decision. When production of machinery and equipment is separated from the use of machinery and equipment the usual market mechanisms may perhaps not be able to convey to the investor all the relevant information about the substitution possibilities in the micro ex ante function.

[6] See Frisch (1965), p. 73 or Danö (1966), p. 51.

$$\varepsilon X = V_1 \frac{\partial X}{\partial V_1} + V_2 \frac{\partial X}{\partial V_2}, \tag{4.30}$$

or using (4.25)

$$\varepsilon = q_1 \frac{V_1}{X} + q_2 \frac{V_2}{X}. \tag{4.31}$$

A simple geometrical illustration will provide an interpretation of (4.31) and at the same time show that $\varepsilon < 1$ for our function $F(V_1, V_2)$.

Consider first the factor inputs per unit of output for the sector as a whole, i.e. V_1/X and V_2/X. From (3.15) we see that we can interpret V_1/X, V_2/X as the centre of gravity of the "capacity mass" given by $f(\xi_1, \xi_2)$ over the utilization region $G(q_1, q_2)$, i.e.

$$\frac{V_i}{X} = \text{the average value of } \xi_i \text{ over the region } G(q_1, q_2)(i=1, 2). \tag{4.32}$$

In Figure 4.2 point A represents (4.32). This point will of course be located in the interior of the utilization region $G(q_1, q_2)$.

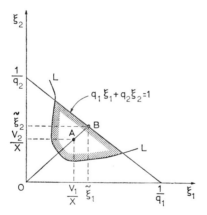

Fig. 4.2. Illustration of the expression for the scale elasticity of output, $\varepsilon = OA/OB$.

In the figure we have also marked off another point B, which is determined by the intersection of the ray from the origin through A with the boundary line $q_1\xi_1 + q_2\xi_2 = 1$. The coordinates of this point are $\tilde{\xi}_1$ and $\tilde{\xi}_2$, where

$$\frac{V_1}{X} = \alpha\tilde{\xi}_1, \quad \frac{V_2}{X} = \alpha\tilde{\xi}_2, \quad \alpha = \frac{OA}{OB}, \tag{4.33}$$

α being a factor of proportionality. It is clear from the figure that α is equal to the ratio between OA and OB as indicated to the right in (4.33).

Inserting from (4.33) in the expression (4.31) for the scale elasticity of output ε we obtain

$$\varepsilon = q_1 \frac{V_1}{X} + q_2 \frac{V_2}{X} = (q_1 \tilde{\xi}_1 + q_2 \tilde{\xi}_2)\alpha = \alpha \qquad (4.34)$$

since the values $\tilde{\xi}_1$ and $\tilde{\xi}_2$ satisfy the equation of the border-line in the figure.

Since α is equal to the ratio of OA to OB this provides a simple geometrical illustration of the magnitude of the scale elasticity. It is simply the proportion between the distance from the origin to the centre of gravity of utilized capacity in the ξ_1, ξ_2-plane and the distance along the same ray from the origin to the boundary of the utilization region; or, in other words, the proportion between the input coefficients of the average production unit and the input coefficients of the marginal production unit with the same factor proportion.

The following observation may further clarify the interpretation of point B in the figure. The total differential of the macro production function is given by (4.24). In terms of marginal input coefficients dV_1/dX and dV_2/dX this can be written as

$$q_1 \frac{dV_1}{dX} + q_2 \frac{dV_2}{dX} = 1. \qquad (4.35)$$

This shows that when we are in a production point V_1, V_2, X corresponding to the border-line $q_1 \xi_1 + q_2 \xi_2 = 1$ in the figure, then the marginal input coefficients for changes in production from this initial point have to satisfy the equation of this border-line. On the other hand any point on the border-line represents a possible pair of values dV_1/dX, dV_2/dX. This is natural since a further expansion of production will take place by including "more of the marginal production units" (or possibly including some new units and excluding others) which all have input coefficients satisfying this equation.

From this consideration it is clear that the coordinates of B are the marginal input coefficients by an expansion of production through increases in inputs which are proportional to their values in point A, i.e.

$$\xi_1 = \frac{V_1}{\alpha X} = \frac{dV_1}{dX}, \quad \xi_2 = \frac{V_2}{\alpha X} = \frac{dV_2}{dX}, \qquad (4.36)$$

and we have

$$\frac{\mathrm{d}X}{\mathrm{d}V_1}\frac{V_1}{X} = \frac{\mathrm{d}X}{\mathrm{d}V_2}\frac{V_2}{X} = \alpha, \tag{4.37}$$

which links up directly with the definition (4.29) so as to prove $\varepsilon = \alpha$.

It follows from the expressions given above that the scale elasticity ε will in general be less than unity, i.e. there will be decreasing returns to scale in the short-run macro function.

Furthermore it is possible to draw the conclusion that ε approaches the value $\varepsilon = 1$ when total output X tends to zero, provided that we are willing to make the very realistic assumption that all available production units have a finite efficiency. To see this, let us distinguish the region in the ξ_1, ξ_2-diagram where $f(\xi_1, \xi_2) > 0$ from the region where $f(\xi_1, \xi_2) = 0$. The former region has been called "the region of positive capacity". The assumption mentioned above then means that the region of positive capacity is bounded away from the origin in the diagram. Let e.g. the region of positive capacity be the region north-east of the curve L–L in Figure 4.2. A reduction in production will now mean that the border-line $q_1\xi_1 + q_2\xi_2 = 1$ will shift towards the south-west. Point A in the figure will have to remain within the region between the straight border-line and the curve L–L, i.e. the shaded area in the figure.[7] As $X \to 0$ this region will tend to vanish, and point B will of necessity approach point A, thus making the scale elasticity $\varepsilon = OA/OB$ tend to unity, i.e.

$$\varepsilon = \frac{OA}{OB} \to 1 \text{ as } X \to 0^+. \tag{4.38}$$

The assumption that the region of positive capacity is bounded away from the origin ensures that the distance OB does not tend to zero in this limiting process.

Apart from (4.38) and the fact that $\varepsilon < 1$ for $X > 0$ not much can be said in general about the variation in ε. In particular ε does not necessarily decrease monotonically with increasing output. It is easy to conceive of distributions $f(\xi_1, \xi_2)$ which are such that ε first decreases but later on passes through both increasing and decreasing phases as output X increases, although this may perhaps not be very realistic in practice.

4.5. *The elasticity of substitution*

The elasticity of substitution indicates the relative change in the factor

---

[7] Or in the convex hull of this region if it is not itself convex.

proportion V_2/V_1 per unit of change in the marginal rate of substitution $(-dV_2/dV_1)$ by movement along an isoquant.[8] As is well known this is an important characteristic of a production function, e.g. with regard to distributional aspects. Since it is characterizing the form of an isoquant it might have been natural to treat it in Section 4.2. However, as we shall see, it is convenient first to have discussed the scale elasticity treated in Section 4.4.

Since the marginal rate of substitution is in our case given by $-dV_2/dV_1 = q_1/q_2$ we may write the elasticity of substitution as

$$s_{12} = \frac{d(V_2/V_1)}{d(q_1/q_2)} \cdot \frac{q_1/q_2}{V_2/V_1} \qquad \text{for constant } X. \tag{4.39}$$

Underlying the definition of s_{12} are variations in V_1 and V_2, and corresponding variations in q_1 and q_2, such that $dX = 0$. In order to derive a simple expression for s_{12} we have to exploit the connections between the variations in q_1 and q_2 on the one hand and V_1 and V_2 on the other hand, which are given in (4.18), as well as the condition $dX = 0$.

Now we first have

$$d\left(\frac{V_2}{V_1}\right) = \frac{V_1 dV_2 - V_2 dV_1}{V_1^2}, \tag{4.40}$$

$$d\left(\frac{q_1}{q_2}\right) = \frac{q_2 dq_1 - q_1 dq_2}{q_2^2}. \tag{4.41}$$

Along the isoquant we have $dV_2 = -(q_1/q_2)\,dV_1$. Inserting this in (4.40) we have

$$d\left(\frac{V_2}{V_1}\right) = -\frac{q_1 V_1 + q_2 V_2}{q_2 V_1^2}\,dV_1. \tag{4.42}$$

In a similar way we have from the first line of (4.18), for $dX = 0$, $dq_2 = -[M(\xi_1)/M(\xi_2)]\,dq_1$, which inserted in (4.41) yields

$$d\left(\frac{q_1}{q_2}\right) = \frac{q_1 M(\xi_1) + q_2 M(\xi_2)}{q_2^2 M(\xi_2)}\,dq_1 = \frac{1}{q_2^2 M(\xi_2)}\,dq_1, \tag{4.43}$$

where the last simplification obtains because of the first line of (4.20).

In order to obtain s_{12} from (4.42–4.43) we have to relate dV_1 and dq_1. From (4.18), using $dq_2 = -[M(\xi_1)/M(\xi_2)]\,dq_1$, we have

$$dV_1 = -J\left[M(\xi_1^2) - \frac{M(\xi_1)}{M(\xi_2)}M(\xi_1\xi_2)\right]dq_1. \tag{4.44}$$

---

[8] See e.g. Danö (1966), pp. 57–59.

Then (4.42–4.43) can be combined to give

$$\frac{d(V_2/V_1)}{d(q_1/q_2)} = \frac{Jq_2}{V_1^2}(q_1V_1 + q_2V_2)[M(\xi_2)M(\xi_1^2) - M(\xi_1)M(\xi_1\xi_2)]. \quad (4.45)$$

Now the term in brackets here is of the same type as we encountered in (4.23). In a similar way as between (4.23) and (4.24) we can reduce it to $(1/q_2)\sigma_1^2$. Thus we have

$$\frac{d(V_2/V_1)}{d(q_1/q_2)} = \frac{J}{V_1^2}(q_1V_1 + q_2V_2)\sigma_1^2$$

and accordingly

$$s_{12} = J\frac{q_1}{q_2V_1V_2}(q_1V_1 + q_2V_2)\sigma_1^2. \quad (4.46)$$

Introducing the scale elasticity from the previous section and utilizing (4.30–4.31) this can furthermore be simplified to

$$s_{12} = J\frac{q_1}{q_2}\frac{X}{V_1V_2}\varepsilon\sigma_1^2 = J\frac{X}{V_1V_2}\varepsilon\sigma_1\sigma_2. \quad (4.47)$$

Here J, as before, is defined by (4.15), ε is the scale elasticity, and σ_1 and σ_2 are the standard deviations of input coefficients among marginal production units as defined by (4.19).

Let us make some remarks on the interpretation of (4.47).

First, it seems intuitively plausible that the variance σ_1^2 should enter as a multiplicative factor in the expression for the elasticity of substitution. For a vanishing σ_1^2 a rotation of the border-line of the utilization region which leaves X unaffected would evidently not induce any change in the ratio V_2/V_1, while it would do so when there is some variance in the distribution – compare the considerations in connection with Figure 4.1. In more concrete terms the question is whether the marginal production units are rather similar or quite different with regard to factor proportions.

The reason why the scale elasticity enters is perhaps also intuitively understandable, though not quite so clear as in case of the variance σ_1^2. Somewhat tentatively I submit the following consideration. Since the elasticity of substitution is a concept free of units of measurements it may be advantageous to rewrite the expression for s_{12} in such a form that it appears clearly as a combination of relative concepts:

$$s_{12} = 2\frac{J}{(2X)}\varepsilon\frac{\sigma_1}{V_1/X}\frac{\sigma_2}{V_2/X} = 2\frac{J}{(2X)}\varepsilon\frac{\sigma_1}{\bar{\xi}_1}\frac{\sigma_2}{\bar{\xi}_2}, \quad (4.48)$$

or, perhaps better, as

$$s_{12} = 2 \frac{J}{(2X)} \frac{1}{\varepsilon} \frac{\sigma_1}{\tilde{\xi}_1} \frac{\sigma_2}{\tilde{\xi}_2}. \qquad (4.48')$$

(The factorizing out of 2 will be explained later on.) We have here, to the right in (4.48), introduced the average input coefficients $\bar{\xi}_1$ and $\bar{\xi}_2$ for all capacity which is utilized. In (4.48') we have replaced these by $\tilde{\xi}_1$ and $\tilde{\xi}_2$ by means of (4.33), see also Figure 4.2. By this we have in the most natural way put the standard deviations in the distribution of marginal production units, σ_1 and σ_2, on a relative basis. The arguments given above can be interpreted as concerning the effects of the terms $\sigma_1/\tilde{\xi}_1$ and $\sigma_2/\tilde{\xi}_2$ in (4.48').

Now consider the effects of the scale elasticity ε in (4.48') under constant $\sigma_1/\tilde{\xi}_1$, $\sigma_2/\tilde{\xi}_2$ and J/X. If we have a low value of ε this means that point A in Figure 4.2 is located relatively near the origin, which again means that we have relatively small inputs V_1 and V_2. Then the rotation of the zero quasi rent line will induce changes in V_1 and V_2 which count relatively heavily compared with the initial values of V_1 and V_2 with the result that the elasticity of substitution, as defined by (4.39), will be relatively high.[9]

Thus the terms $\sigma_1/\tilde{\xi}_1$, $\sigma_2/\tilde{\xi}_2$ in (4.48') have to do with the width of the distribution of marginal production units, appropriately normalized, and ε has to do with the weighting of the increments in proportion to initial values of V_1 and V_2.

The term $J/2X$ expresses another effect. In order to understand this effect it is necessary to interpret the expression for J given by (4.15). For this purpose, consider a narrow strip of the ξ_1, ξ_2-plane along the zero quasi rent line $q_1\xi_1 + q_2\xi_2 = 1$. Let the strip be between this line and a line determined by $(q_1 + \Delta q_1)\xi_1 + (q_2 + \Delta q_2)\xi_2 = 1$, where $\Delta q_1/q_1 = \Delta q_2/q_2$ so that the second line is parallel with the first line. Let $\Delta q_1 > 0$. When Δq_1 and Δq_2 are small, we have from the first line of (4.5) that the capacity located in this strip is

$$\Delta X \approx \left| \frac{\partial g}{\partial q_1} \Delta q_1 + \frac{\partial g}{\partial q_2} \Delta q_2 \right|.$$

---

[9] It is well known that the elasticity of substitution can in general be written in such a form that the scale elasticity appears as a multiplicative factor, see e.g. Allen (1967), pp. 342–343, where the term $(af_a + bf_b)$ would correspond to our εX. However, in this form also the second order derivatives of the production function occur. Our formula for s_{12} could probably be developed from Allen's formula by first deriving $\partial^2 F/\partial V_1^2$, $\partial^2 F/\partial V_1 \partial V_2$ and $\partial^2 F/\partial V_2^2$ for our special production function, but this seems to be a more laborious route to follow than the one taken in the text above.

Utilizing the first line of (4.17) we further have

$$\Delta X \approx | J[M(\xi_1)\Delta q_1 + M(\xi_2)\Delta q_2] |$$

$$= \left| J[M(\xi_1)q_1 + M(\xi_2)q_2] \frac{\Delta q_1}{q_1} \right| = J \frac{\Delta q_1}{q_1},$$

where the last simplification obtains because of the first line of (4.20).

Next consider the size of the strip. It can evidently be considered as a parallelogram with base $(1/q_1) - 1/(q_1 + \Delta q_1) \approx \Delta q_1/q_1^2$ and height $1/q_2$ plus a triangle which is negligible when Δq_1 and Δq_2 are small. Hence we may say that the size of the strip is $\Delta q_1/q_1^2 q_2$. Now considering capacity per square unit in the strip we have as an approximation, which is exact in the limit when $\Delta q_1 \to 0$:

$$\frac{\text{capacity located in the strip}}{\text{size of the strip}} = J q_1 q_2. \tag{4.49}$$

The term which we want to interpret is $J/2X$. We can write this as

$$\frac{J}{2X} = \frac{J q_1 q_2}{X / \dfrac{1}{2 q_1 q_2}}. \tag{4.50}$$

In the denominator the expression $X/(1/2q_1 q_2)$ is capacity in proportion to the size of the whole utilization region $G(q_1, q_2)$ (see (3.14)), since this is a triangle with base $1/q_1$ and height $1/q_2$. Thus $J/2X$ expresses the capacity per square unit in a strip of marginal production units in the capacity distribution in proportion to the average density of capacity over the whole utilization region $G(q_1, q_2)$. Again it is intuitively plausible that this proportion should enter as it does in the expression for the elasticity of substitution since a rotation of the zero quasi rent line will evidently cause a larger shift in the factor proportion V_2/V_1 the more capacity mass we have, relatively, in the neighbourhood along the zero quasi rent line.

In the expression (4.48) we have factorized out the term 2 because $J/2X$ has a more convenient interpretation than J/X. The underlying reason is apparently that one of the regions involved in forming the proportion is (approximately) a parallelogram while the other is a triangle.

Thus, on the whole the expression we have found for the elasticity of substitution appears intuitively interpretable.

An expression like (4.48) or (4.48') might perhaps be useful if one were trying to solve the problem of finding the class of capacity distributions which would produce a Constant Elasticity of Substitution (CES) function as the short-run macro function.[10] According to Section 4.4 it would have to be a CES-function with decreasing returns to scale.

4.6. *The region of substitution*

The macro production function $F(V_1, V_2)$ defined by (3.14–3.16) or by (4.2) will be defined over a certain region in the factor diagram which we will call the region of substitution in accordance with classical theory of production. (The terms "efficient region" and "economic region" are also used.) In the interior of this region both marginal productivities will be effectively positive, while one of the marginal productivities will be zero on each of the boundaries of this region (and both of them zero if the two boundaries meet towards the north-east in the factor diagram).

In this section we are interested in the form of this region. In the special case which was studied by Houthakker (1955–56) it was assumed that the capacity distribution function $f(\xi_1, \xi_2)$ was of the (generalized) Pareto type over the whole positive quadrant, i.e. that what we have called the "region of positive capacity" covered the whole positive quadrant in the ξ_1, ξ_2-diagram. Then the region of substitution corresponding to the macro function $F(V_1, V_2)$ also covers the whole positive quadrant in the factor diagram. In the Houthakker case the function was proved to be of the Cobb-Douglas form.

This is a mathematically very elegant result, but it does not seem very realistic within our framework and interpretation. Assuming, as we do, that the capacity distribution function f represents existing and rigid capital equipment, it seems that the following properties are realistic:

(1) The region of positive capacity in the ξ_1, ξ_2-diagram is bounded away from the origin. This is, I think, an obligatory requirement. It means that all production units have a finite efficiency.

(2) All production units require only a finite amount of each input per unit of output, i.e. the region of positive capacity is bounded both in the ξ_1 and the ξ_2 direction. As an approximation one may perhaps neglect this restriction if one works with a form of the distribution function f which

---

[10] The corresponding problem in the case of only one variable input is solved by Levhari (1968). We shall give some elements of an answer in the two-factor case in Sections 5.3 and 5.4.

obtains very low values and in the limit tends to zero when ξ_1 or ξ_2 or both increase beyond all limits.

(3) Total capacity will be limited, i.e. the integral in (3.8) will obtain a finite value even when the region G includes the whole region of positive capacity.

(4) All production units require something of both current inputs. This means that the region of positive capacity in the ξ_1, ξ_2-diagram is bounded away from the axes of the diagram. This requirement is not obligatory, although it is likely to be fulfilled in most practical cases. One may of course conceive of cases in which the region of positive capacity is bounded away from one of the axes while including points on the other axis. But it is hard to think of cases where there is no labour input.

In the following discussion of the form of the region of substitution we shall observe these four conditions.

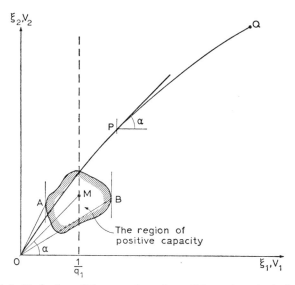

Fig. 4.3. Derivation of the upper boundary of the region of substitution.

In Figure 4.3 we illustrate the derivation of the upper boundary of the region of substitution. Along the horizontal axis we measure both ξ_1 and V_1, and along the vertical axis we measure ξ_2 and V_2.

The upper boundary is obtained by putting q_2 in (4.2) equal to zero since q_2 is the marginal productivity of V_2, and this should be equal to zero on the boundary in the V_2-direction. We then have

$$X = g(q_1, 0)$$
$$V_1 = h_1(q_1, 0) \tag{4.51}$$
$$V_2 = h_2(q_1, 0).$$

This means that the upper limit of integration over ξ_2 in (4.2) goes to infinity. This is however not problematic when condition No. 2 above is fulfilled since $f(\xi_1, \xi_2)$ will then be zero for sufficiently large values of ξ_2.

In Figure 4.3 the case represented by (4.51) means that all integrations are carried out over the region to the left of a vertical line such as the vertical indicated at $\xi_1 = 1/q_1$.

By eliminating q_1 from the two last formulas in (4.51) we would obtain the formula for the curve signifying the upper boundary of the region of substitution. By differentiation of these two formulas with respect to q_1 and use of (4.17) we obtain

$$\frac{\mathrm{d}V_2}{\mathrm{d}V_1} = \frac{M(\xi_1\xi_2;\, q_1, 0)}{M(\xi_1^2;\, q_1, 0)}, \tag{4.52}$$

where M as before denotes an average taken along the line $q_1\xi_1 + q_2\xi_2 = 1$; we have indicated that the averages are now taken for the case $q_2 = 0$, cf. the remarks between (4.16) and (4.17).

Since the averages in (4.52) are taken along a line where ξ_1 is constant and equal to $1/q_1$, we clearly have $M(\xi_1\xi_2;\, q_1, 0) = (1/q_1)M(\xi_2;\, q_1, 0)$ and $M(\xi_1^2;\, q_1, 0) = 1/q_1^2$.[11] Then (4.52) can be written as

$$\frac{\mathrm{d}V_2}{\mathrm{d}V_1} = \frac{M(\xi_2;\, q_1, 0)}{1/q_1} = q_1 M(\xi_2;\, q_1, 0). \tag{4.53}$$

For all given values of q_1 we obtain V_1, V_2 and X from (4.51). Let the point V_1, V_2 be point P in the figure. This is on the upper boundary of the region of substitution. The slope of the boundary line at this point is equal to the tangent of the angle α in the figure, which is the angle between OM and the horizontal axis, where M is the point $1/q_1$, $M(\xi_2;\, q_1, 0)$. The tangent of this angle is evidently equal to the expression in (4.53).

We could now trace the whole upper boundary from the origin by moving a vertical like the one in the figure from the left to the right. Positive amounts of inputs and output would first appear when this vertical reaches the region

---

[11] In order to ascertain the permissibility of these operations one should reconsider the formulation of the averages as given by (4.15–4.16). The integrals in these formulas are not defined for a constant value of ξ_1. For the case studied in the text above we should first substitute $\xi_2 = (1/q_2) - (q_1/q_2)\xi_1$ in the integrals in (4.15–4.16). Then there is no difficulty involved in setting $q_2 = 0$ so that ξ_1 becomes a constant equal to $1/q_1$.

of positive capacity at point A in the figure, and the slope of the upper boundary of the region of substitution corresponding to this point – i.e. its slope at the origin – would be equal to the slope of OA. Moving towards the right we finally end up at point B, where all capacity is exhausted. The corresponding V_1, V_2-point would be Q, where the slope of the boundary line is equal to the slope of OB.

In the figure we have drawn the curve OPQ with decreasing slope. This is not necessary; it is easy to conceive of cases in which the angle α increases at least for some parts as the vertical line moves towards the right (and in fact this occurred in the empirical study of Norwegian tankers which will be reported in Chapter 9).

A similar construction can be done for the boundary of the region of substitution in the V_1-direction. Now $q_1 = 0$ while the boundary is generated by letting q_2 change. In this case one obtains

$$\frac{\mathrm{d}V_2}{\mathrm{d}V_1} = \frac{M(\xi_2^2;\, 0, q_2)}{M(\xi_1\xi_2;\, 0, q_2)} = \frac{1}{q_2 M(\xi_1;\, 0, q_2)}. \tag{4.54}$$

The interpretation corresponds to the interpretation of (4.53).

In Figure 4.4 we have entered both the region of positive capacity in the ξ_1, ξ_2-plane and the region of substitution in the V_1, V_2-plane. In the region of substitution we have indicated some isoquants. These are vertical on the upper boundary of the region of substitution and horizontal on the boundary in the V_1-direction. In the figure the points P_A, P_B and P_C are on the same isoquant; point P_A corresponds to the position AA' of the line $q_1\xi_1 + q_2\xi_2 = 1$, point P_B corresponds to the position BB', and point P_C corresponds to the position CC'. In every case the capacity mass in $f(\xi_1, \xi_2)$ south-west of the border-line $q_1\xi_1 + q_2\xi_2 = 1$ is the same, and in every case the slope of the isoquant is the same as the slope of the zero quasi rent line $q_1\xi_1 + q_2\xi_2 = 1$. The upper and the right boundary of the region of substitution meets in point Q, which signifies the utilization of all existing capacity.

The illustration in Figure 4.4 satisfies all the four requirements stated in the introductory remarks of this section.

The figure gives some indication as to how the macro function $F(V_1, V_2)$ depends on the distribution of capacity $f(\xi_1, \xi_2)$. The scope for substitution in the short-run macro function depends essentially on the spread in the capacity distribution. In the limiting case when the region of positive capacity shrinks into one single point the short-run macro function degenerates into a Leontief function with no substitution possibilities (retaining however the property of having a limited capacity). If the region of positive capacity

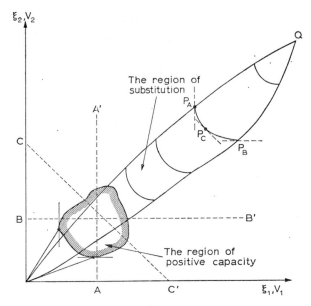

Fig. 4.4. The relationship between the isoquant map of $X = F(V_1, V_2)$ and the distribution $f(\xi_1, \xi_2)$ over the region of positive capacity.

shrinks into a narrow band (in the limit collapsing into a curve) which is monotonically increasing in the figure, then the short-run macro function collapses into a function with no substitution possibilities, but with decreasing returns to scale and not necessarily a constant ratio between V_2 and V_1. If the region of positive capacity shrinks into a narrow band of some other form, then the short-run macro function retains in the main the same properties as we have discussed above.

It is clear from the construction above that the scope for substitution in the macro function is in general not similar for different levels of total output. Depending on the form of the capacity distribution, many different cases are conceivable. But since both the upper and the right boundary of the region of substitution are necessarilily increasing curves in the figure, substitution possibilities must vanish gradually when we approach full capacity utilization for the sector as a whole.

The substitution possibilities in the short-run function will reflect the substitution possibilities in the ex ante function in the following sense: if there is little scope for substitution in the ex ante function (and the range of possible factor proportions in this function has not changed very much in the past due to technological change), then there must necessarily be little scope for substitution in the short-run macro function. On the other hand, if there is wide scope for substitution in the ex ante function, then there may or may not be wide scope for substitution in the short-run macro function depending on the actual choices made from the ex ante function in the past.

The case where the region of positive capacity shrinks into a very small region reflects a history of little change in this sector of the economy. The region collapses into one point in the case of a stationary economy, in which case the point Q in the figure and the corresponding amount of output and capital input represent one point on what we have called the long-run (or steady state) function at the macro level. On the other hand the case when the region of positive capacity is wide and big represents a less tranquil history in which at least some of the factors surveyed in Section 3.1 have had a strong impact.

4.7. Curves of constant marginal productivity

Contour lines for marginal productivities, i.e. curves along which one of the marginal productivities is constant, are not much used in expositions of production theory. However, their usefulness has recently been suggested by professor Palander and further analysed and illustrated (under the name iso-marginal productivity curves) by Puu and Skogh (1968). Particularly in connection with studies of input responses to changes in input prices such curves are a convenient tool.

For a production function generated from a capacity distribution in the way we are doing it is easy to construct such curves. Consider the problem of finding the curve representing a constant value of the marginal productivity of factor No. 1, i.e. $\partial F/\partial V_1$. Since this marginal productivity is equal to q_1, the contour line can be constructed by letting the zero quasi rent line $q_1\xi_1 + q_2\xi_2 = 1$ rotate around the point $\xi_1 = 1/q_1$, $\xi_2 = 0$ on the ξ_1-axis. For a sufficiently big value of q_2 the zero quasi rent line will not touch the region of positive capacity. Decreasing q_2 the line will first touch and later cut off a bigger and bigger share of the capacity distribution. It is clear that V_1, V_2 and X will all increase. At the same time it is clear that the contour curve will first be relatively near to the right boundary of the region of substitution since the slope $|q_1/q_2|$ of the isoquants which it intersects will first be small. Gradually the curve will get nearer to the upper boundary since the slope $|q_1/q_2|$ of the isoquants which it intersects will increase.

Comparing contour lines for different values of $q_1 = \partial F/\partial V_1$ it is clear that the line will be nearer to the right boundary of the region of substitution the lower is the value of $q_1 = \partial F/\partial V_1$.

A symmetric reasoning applies to contour curves for constant marginal productivity of factor No. 2.

Figure 4.5 suggests the form of the contour lines for the marginal productivities.

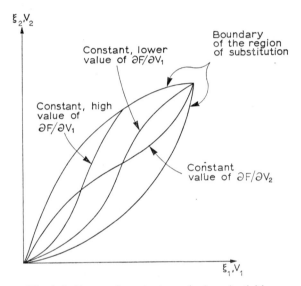

Fig. 4.5. Curves of constant marginal productivities.

Some functional forms which are used in production studies imply forms of the curves of constant marginal productivities which are not permissible within our framework. This applies e.g. to the transformed Cobb-Douglas function

$$X = A \exp\left(-\alpha V_1^{-\beta_1} V_2^{-\beta_2}\right), \tag{4.55}$$

which has been proposed for empirical work.[12]

Of course this fact does not mean that (4.55) cannot be a good functional form in other contexts in production studies, e.g. as an ex ante function, or in contexts not encompassed by our framework.

---

[12] See e.g. Ringstad (1967). The curves of constant marginal productivities for this function are depicted in Puu and Skogh (1968), and the forms shown are not compatible with the reasoning underlying our Figure 4.5.

In classical theory of production a pair of production factors are classified as technically complementary, independent or alternative according as the marginal productivity of one of the factors is increased, unaffected or reduced by a partial increase in the input of the other factor, i.e. according as $\partial^2 F / \partial V_i \partial V_j \gtreqless 0$.[13] From the reasoning in connection with Figure 4.5 it follows that production factors in our short-run function $F(V_1, V_2)$ are always complementary, or, as a limiting case, independent.[14]

---

[13] See Frisch (1965), p. 60.
[14] For a closer examination of this limiting case, see Section 5.4.

CHAPTER 5

Some mathematical illustrations of short-run macro production functions derived from capacity distributions

5.1. Introductory remarks

This chapter will illustrate the derivation of short-run macro production functions from given capacity distributions by means of simple mathematical examples. I shall also illustrate some of the general formulas pertaining to various characteristics of the form of the production function. This will perhaps appear somewhat unsystematic since it would be too much to illustrate all aspects in connection with every case. I shall let convenience dictate what to illustrate in each case.

The "classical" example in this field is of course Houthakker's derivation of the Cobb-Douglas production function on the basis of a generalized (two-dimensional) Pareto distribution of micro units with respect to input coefficients. This result, which will be briefly stated and discussed in Section 5.2 below, is of course very appealing since both the Cobb-Douglas function and the Pareto distribution are familiar to economists. However, this case does not satisfy the simple conditions suggested in Section 4.6, which seem realistic within our framework. First of all, it seems realistic to restrict the distribution of micro units to cover only a bounded region in the positive quadrant whose axes measure the input coefficients; in particular this region should be bounded away from the origin in order to conform with the fact that there are no infinitely efficient production processes available. One of the purposes of the sections following Section 5.2 is to present some examples which may be somewhat more satisfactory than the Pareto/Cobb-Douglas case in these respects.[1] On the other hand, attempts at handling cases which are realistic in all respects indicate that one easily runs into very messy formulas and calculations. The elements of realism gained in some of the examples to be presented below are therefore bought at the

---

[1] The case of a "generalized Pareto distribution" has been criticized on empirical grounds by Sanyal (1967). However, Sanyal seems to be wrong in his assertion that the Cobb-Douglas function obtains for a much wider class of capacity distributions than the Pareto class.

price of simplifying to the utmost degree on other accounts. In empirical work one would probably have to apply numerical methods which are not confined to cases which can be represented by nice mathematical formulas.

Most of the discussion in previous chapters has assumed that $f(\xi_1, \xi_2)$ is positive over a two-dimensional region in the ξ_1, ξ_2-diagram. However, as was suggested above, all the formulas easily carry over to the case where there is positive capacity distributed only along a curve in the ξ_1, ξ_2-diagram. One only has to adapt the integration to integration along the part (or in general those parts) of the curve which is located south-west of the zero quasi rent constraint $q_1\xi_1 + q_2\xi_2 = 1$. Some of the examples to be presented below are of this type.

Much of the material presented in Sections 5.3–5.7 below is taken from a previous joint report by Mr. Tor Hersoug and the present author.[2]

5.2. Professor Houthakker's derivation of the Cobb-Douglas function

Houthakker (1955–56) assumes the following form, which he calls a generalised Pareto distribution, for the capacity distribution ("input-output distribution" in his terminology):

$$f(\xi_1, \xi_2) = A\xi_1^{\alpha_1-1}\,\xi_2^{\alpha_2-1}, \qquad (5.1)$$

where A, α_1 and α_2 are constants.

On the basis of (5.1) he shows that we get a macro function of the Cobb-Douglas form

$$F(V_1, V_2) = C\,V_1^{\frac{\alpha_1}{\alpha_1+\alpha_2+1}}\,V_2^{\frac{\alpha_2}{\alpha_1+\alpha_2+1}}, \qquad (5.2)$$

where C is a constant depending on A, α_1 and α_2.

Houthakker assumes that $\alpha_1 \geqq 1$ and $\alpha_2 \geqq 1$. In this case the capacity density tends to zero when we approach the origin in the ξ_1, ξ_2-plane and increases as we move away from the origin, or is constant over the whole positive quadrant when we have $\alpha_1 = \alpha_2 = 1$. As far as I can see the derivation of (5.2) is still legitimate if we have α's less than 1, provided only that $\alpha_1 > 0$ and $\alpha_2 > 0$. If we have $0 < \alpha_1 < 1$ and $0 < \alpha_2 < 1$ the capacity density is higher the nearer we are to the origin, but still such that only a finite output is obtainable from a bounded region of utilization. The case assumed by Houthakker is, however, the less unacceptable.

---

[2] See Johansen and Hersoug (1969).

The scale elasticity of the macro function (5.2) is

$$\varepsilon = \frac{\alpha_1 + \alpha_2}{\alpha_1 + \alpha_2 + 1}, \tag{5.3}$$

which is constant and less than 1. The constancy of ε contradicts our conclusion (4.38). The reason is that the capacity distribution (5.1) fails to satisfy the condition of being bounded away from the origin, as we assumed in the arguments leading up to (4.38).

Let us, however, check the general expression for the scale elasticity given in connection with Figure 4.2 for the special case (5.1–5.3). According to the general result we should have $\varepsilon = OA/OB$, where OA and OB are as indicated in the figure.

From formulas given in Houthakker's paper it follows easily that we have

$$\frac{V_1}{X} = \frac{\alpha_1}{(\alpha_1 + \alpha_2 + 1)q_1}, \quad \frac{V_2}{X} = \frac{\alpha_2}{(\alpha_1 + \alpha_2 + 1)q_2}. \tag{5.4}$$

(These formulas also follow easily from (5.2) by using the fact that q_1 and q_2 represent marginal productivities.) The expressions in (5.4) give the coordinates of point A in Figure 4.2 for the special case under consideration.

The coordinates of point B, $\tilde{\xi}_1$ and $\tilde{\xi}_2$, are determined by the intersection between the zero quasi rent line $q_1\xi_1 + q_2\xi_2 = 1$ and the ray from the origin through A; i.e. we must have

$$q_1\tilde{\xi}_1 + q_2\tilde{\xi}_2 = 1; \quad \tilde{\xi}_2/\tilde{\xi}_1 = \frac{V_2}{X} \bigg/ \frac{V_1}{X}. \tag{5.5}$$

Using (5.4) we obtain

$$\tilde{\xi}_1 = \frac{\alpha_1}{q_1(\alpha_1 + \alpha_2)}, \quad \tilde{\xi}_2 = \frac{\alpha_2}{q_2(\alpha_1 + \alpha_2)}. \tag{5.6}$$

For the scale elasticity we then have

$$\varepsilon = \frac{OA}{OB} = \frac{V_1/X}{\tilde{\xi}_1} = \frac{\dfrac{\alpha_1}{(\alpha_1 + \alpha_2 + 1)q_1}}{\dfrac{\alpha_1}{(\alpha_1 + \alpha_2)q_1}} = \frac{\alpha_1 + \alpha_2}{\alpha_1 + \alpha_2 + 1} \tag{5.7}$$

in conformity with what is obtained directly from the production function.

Let us also see how formula (4.48) for the elasticity of substitution s_{12} works out in this special case. The various terms in (4.48) should offset each other in such a way that we arrive at $s_{12} = 1$.

First we need an expression for J which is defined by (4.15). This integral now takes the form

$$J = \frac{1}{q_2} \int_0^{\frac{1}{q_1}} A\xi_1^{\alpha_1-1} \left(\frac{1-q_1\xi_1}{q_2}\right)^{\alpha_2-1} d\xi_1. \tag{5.8}$$

In this integral we change the integration variable to $\eta = q_1\xi_1$ so as to obtain

$$J = \frac{A}{q_1^{\alpha_1}q_2^{\alpha_2}} \int_0^1 \eta^{\alpha_1-1}(1-\eta)^{\alpha_2-1} d\eta = \frac{A}{q_1^{\alpha_1}q_2^{\alpha_2}} B(\alpha_1, \alpha_2), \tag{5.9}$$

where $B(\alpha_1, \alpha_2)$ is the well-known Beta function[3] which is also involved in Houthakker's calculations in order to derive the Cobb-Douglas function.

From Houthakker we have the following expression for X in terms of q_1 and q_2 (p_1 and p_2 in his symbols):

$$X = \frac{(\alpha_1+\alpha_2+1)A}{\alpha_1\alpha_2 q_1^{\alpha_1}q_2^{\alpha_2}} B(\alpha_1+1, \alpha_2+1). \tag{5.10}$$

For the ratio J/X we get

$$\frac{J}{X} = \frac{\alpha_1\alpha_2 B(\alpha_1, \alpha_2)}{(\alpha_1+\alpha_2+1)B(\alpha_1+1, \alpha_2+1)}. \tag{5.11}$$

Now the Beta function is related to the Gamma function by

$$B(\alpha_1, \alpha_2) = \frac{\Gamma(\alpha_1)\Gamma(\alpha_2)}{\Gamma(\alpha_1+\alpha_2)}. \tag{5.12}$$

Furthermore we have

$$\Gamma(\alpha+1) = \alpha\Gamma(\alpha). \tag{5.13}$$

Using these formulas in connection with (5.11) we get

$$\frac{J}{X} = \frac{\alpha_1\alpha_2 \dfrac{\Gamma(\alpha_1)\Gamma(\alpha_2)}{\Gamma(\alpha_1+\alpha_2)}}{(\alpha_1+\alpha_2+1)\dfrac{\alpha_1\Gamma(\alpha_1)\alpha_2\Gamma(\alpha_2)}{(\alpha_1+\alpha_2+1)(\alpha_1+\alpha_2)\Gamma(\alpha_1+\alpha_2)}} = \alpha_1+\alpha_2. \tag{5.14}$$

The scale elasticity is already given by (5.3). Furthermore the average input coefficients $\bar{\xi}_1 = V_1/X$ and $\bar{\xi}_2 = V_2/X$ are given by (5.4).

---

[3] See e.g. Cramér (1946), pp. 126–128. The formulas used below are also given in Cramér's book.

What remain are then the formulas for the standard deviations σ_1 and σ_2 in the distribution of marginal production units. These are moments in a distribution as given by (4.16). The (normalized) density in this distribution is given by

$$
\phi(\xi_1) = \frac{\dfrac{1}{q_2} f\left(\xi_1, \dfrac{1-q_1\xi_1}{q_2}\right)}{J} = \frac{\dfrac{1}{q_2} A \xi_1^{\alpha_1-1} \left(\dfrac{1-q_1\xi_1}{q_2}\right)^{\alpha_2-1}}{\dfrac{A}{q_1^{\alpha_1}q_2^{\alpha_2}} B(\alpha_1, \alpha_2)}, \tag{5.15}
$$

which can be written as

$$
\phi(\xi_1) = q_1 \frac{(q_1\xi_1)^{\alpha_1-1}(1-q_1\xi_1)^{\alpha_2-1}}{B(\alpha_1, \alpha_2)}. \tag{5.16}
$$

Transforming to $\eta = q_1\xi_1$, where the range of variation for η is from 0 to 1 corresponding to the range from 0 to $1/q_1$ for ξ_1, we get the density in the distribution of η as

$$
\beta(\eta; \alpha_1, \alpha_2) = \frac{\eta^{\alpha_1-1}(1-\eta)^{\alpha_2-1}}{B(\alpha_1, \alpha_2)}, \tag{5.17}
$$

which is the density function of the Beta distribution.[4] Thus the generalized Pareto-distribution gives rise to a Beta distribution for the input coefficients (for $q_1\xi_1$, to be exact, and of course correspondingly for $q_2\xi_2$) among marginal production units, i.e. units located along the zero quasi rent line. This distribution is bell-shaped with a unique mode when $\alpha_1 > 1$ and $\alpha_2 > 1$. When $\alpha_1 = \alpha_2 = 1$ the distribution is rectangular (uniform between 0 and 1). When $\alpha_1 < 1$ and $\alpha_2 < 1$ it is U-shaped. In other cases $\beta(\eta; \alpha_1, \alpha_2)$ will increase as η approaches one of the boundaries 0 and 1 and tend to zero when η approaches the other boundary.

We now seek the variance σ_1^2 defined by (4.19). This is the variance of ξ_1 in the distribution of marginal production units, i.e. the variances of $\xi_1 = \eta/q_1$, where η follows the Beta distribution. Now the variance of η is given by[5] $(\alpha_1\alpha_2)/[(\alpha_1+\alpha_2)^2(\alpha_1+\alpha_2+1)]$ so that

$$
\sigma_1^2 = \frac{1}{q_1^2} \frac{\alpha_1\alpha_2}{(\alpha_1+\alpha_2)^2(\alpha_1+\alpha_2+1)}. \tag{5.18}
$$

A corresponding expression, only with q_2 replacing q_1, holds for the variance

---

[4] See Cramér (1946), pp. 243–244.
[5] See Cramér (1946), p. 244.

σ_2^2 of ξ_2. We then have for the last terms in the expression for the elasticity of substitution

$$\frac{\sigma_1}{\xi_1}\frac{\sigma_2}{\xi_2} = \frac{\dfrac{1}{q_1 q_2}\dfrac{\alpha_1\alpha_2}{(\alpha_1+\alpha_2)^2(\alpha_1+\alpha_2+1)}}{\dfrac{\alpha_1}{(\alpha_1+\alpha_2+1)q_1}\dfrac{\alpha_2}{(\alpha_1+\alpha_2+1)q_2}} = \frac{\alpha_1+\alpha_2+1}{(\alpha_1+\alpha_2)^2}. \tag{5.19}$$

Now collecting the terms from (5.14), (5.7) and (5.19) according to the general formula (4.48) for the elasticity of substitution we obtain

$$s_{12} = (\alpha_1+\alpha_2)\frac{\alpha_1+\alpha_2}{\alpha_1+\alpha_2+1}\frac{\alpha_1+\alpha_2+1}{(\alpha_1+\alpha_2)^2} = 1. \tag{5.20}$$

As is seen from the derivation above all the contributing factors to the elasticity of substitution discussed in connection with the general formula (4.48) are constant (depending on α_1 and α_2) when the capacity distribution is of the generalized Pareto type.

5.3. Distribution along a right-angled curve

In the first new example to be considered we assume all capacity to be distributed along a right-angled curve through the point P, corresponding to $\xi_1 = s_1$, $\xi_2 = s_2$, i.e. along the curve MPN in Figure 5.1. Furthermore we assume the distribution to be uniform along this curve. This is a rather peculiar case; it had perhaps better be considered as an approximation to a smooth curve, and the infinitely distant parts of PM and PN are not to be taken seriously. (We shall later on confine the distribution to the stretches k_1 and k_2 along PM and PN.) But the example is of interest in that it is about the simplest case one can imagine if one is to avoid assuming that infinitely efficient processes are available.

Integration should now be performed over those parts of MPN which are located south-west of the zero quasi rent line $q_1\xi_1 + q_2\xi_2 = 1$. In the figure this corresponds to integrating over the distances a and b along APB. Instead of expressing X, V_1 and V_2 in terms of the parameters q_1 and q_2 as is done in (4.2), it is simpler in this case to use a and b as parameters. There is of course a simple correspondence between a and b on the one hand and q_1 and q_2 on the other hand. Assuming for simplicity that the capacity per unit of length along the curve is 1, we clearly have

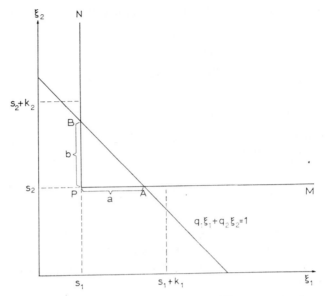

Fig. 5.1. Capacity distribution along the curve MPN. (The parameters k_1 and k_2 refer to a case, to be studied further on, where there is positive capacity only along the stretches k_1 and k_2 of PM and PN).

$$X = a+b,$$
$$V_1 = \int_{s_1}^{s_1+a} \xi_1 \, d\xi_1 + bs_1,$$
$$V_2 = as_2 + \int_{s_2}^{s_2+b} \xi_2 \, d\xi_2. \tag{5.21}$$

Carrying out the integrations we obtain

$$X = a+b,$$
$$V_1 = \tfrac{1}{2}a^2 + s_1 a + s_1 b,$$
$$V_2 = \tfrac{1}{2}b^2 + s_2 b + s_2 a. \tag{5.22}$$

The production function $X = F(V_1, V_2)$ is defined by (5.22) when a and b are eliminated. Inserting X for $a+b$ in the two last equations in (5.22) we have

$$V_1 = \tfrac{1}{2}a^2 + s_1 X, \text{ i.e. } a = \sqrt{2(V_1 - s_1 X)} \,;$$
$$V_2 = \tfrac{1}{2}b^2 + s_2 X, \text{ i.e. } b = \sqrt{2(V_2 - s_2 X)}. \tag{5.23}$$

Since only real and non-negative a and b are permissible, the square roots in (5.23) are taken to be positive, and we must require

$$V_1 \geqq s_1 X,$$
$$V_2 \geqq s_2 X. \tag{5.24}$$

Inserting back into $X = a+b$ from (5.23) we obtain the production function in implicit form:

$$X = \sqrt{2}\,(\sqrt{V_1 - s_1 X} + \sqrt{V_2 - s_2 X}). \tag{5.25}$$

Let us consider the region of substitution for this production function. The upper boundary of the region of substitution is generated by using as little as possible of input No. 1 and producing the required X by using the necessary amount of input No. 2. This clearly means that we should let A tend to P in the figure and adjust B so that the required X is achieved.[6] This is obtained by putting $a = 0$ in (5.22), i.e.

$$X = b, \quad V_1 = bs_1, \quad V_2 = \tfrac{1}{2}b^2 + s_2 b. \tag{5.26}$$

Eliminating b from the last two of these equations, and carrying out the corresponding operations for $b = 0$, we obtain the upper and the right boundaries for the region of substitution:

Upper boundary: $V_2 = \tfrac{1}{2}\left(\dfrac{V_1}{s_1}\right)^2 + s_2\left(\dfrac{V_1}{s_1}\right);$

Right boundary: $V_1 = \tfrac{1}{2}\left(\dfrac{V_2}{s_2}\right)^2 + s_1\left(\dfrac{V_2}{s_2}\right). \tag{5.27}$

(Equations (5.27) assume $s_1 > 0$, $s_2 > 0$.)

This region of substitution is indicated in Figure 5.2. Both the upper and the right boundary start out from the origin with the slope $dV_2/dV_1 = s_2/s_1$, i.e. they are tangential at the origin. Near the origin the region of substitution is accordingly very narrow, but it widens out more the farther we are away from the origin.

Let us verify the validity of the general formulas (4.53–4.54) for the slopes of the boundaries of the region of substitution for this special case. We then first need expressions for q_1 and q_2. These are obtained from the fact that points A and B of Figure 5.1 lie on the line $q_1\xi_1 + q_2\xi_2 = 1$, i.e.:

$$q_1(s_1 + a) + q_2 s_2 = 1,$$
$$q_1 s_1 + q_2(s_2 + b) = 1. \tag{5.28}$$

---

[6] This limiting case cannot be appropriately indicated by q_1 and q_2 since, if the line $q_1\xi_1 + q_2\xi_2 = 1$ is made vertical through P, it does not discriminate between points on PN. This is a special problem which only occurs when we have capacity concentrated along straight horizontal or vertical lines.

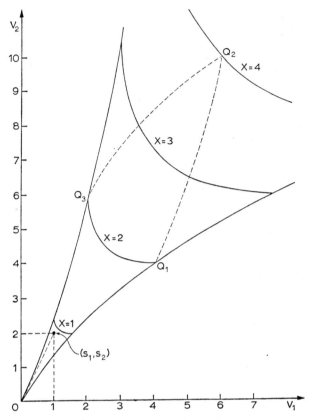

Fig. 5.2. The region of substitution and isoquants corresponding to a uniform distribution of capacity along the right-angled curve in Figure 5.1.

This yields

$$q_1 = \frac{b}{(s_1+a)\,(s_2+b)-s_1 s_2}, \quad q_2 = \frac{a}{(s_1+a)\,(s_2+b)-s_1 s_2}. \qquad (5.29)$$

Now consider formula (4.53) which gives the slope of the upper boundary of the region of substitution. Beside q_1 we need $M(\xi_2; q_1, 0)$, which is the average ξ_2 among the marginal production units corresponding to q_1 when $q_2 = 0$. In the present case this average is clearly the highest value of ξ_2 included, which is s_2+b. Since we have $q_2 = 0$, and also $a = 0$ when we are on the upper boundary, we then get from the general formula (4.53), when (5.29) is used:

$$\frac{dV_2}{dV_1} = \frac{1}{s_1}(s_2+b),\tag{5.30}$$

which is seen to conform with what is obtained by direct differentiation of the first formula in (5.27) when $V_1 = bs_1$ as it is on the upper boundary, see (5.26). In the same way (4.54) can be seen to hold. (The region of substitution is limited to $OQ_1Q_2Q_3O$ when the distribution in Figure 5.1 is restricted by k_1 and k_2.)

Since we now have expressions for q_1 and q_2, let us check by direct calculations that the marginal productivities really are equal to q_1 and q_2 as they should be according to Section 4.2. We consider $\partial F/\partial V_1$. By implicit differentiation in (5.25) we obtain

$$\frac{\partial X}{\partial V_1} = \sqrt{2}\left\{\frac{1}{2\sqrt{V_1-s_1X}}\left(1-s_1\frac{\partial X}{\partial V_1}\right) + \frac{1}{2\sqrt{V_2-s_2X}}\left(-s_2\frac{\partial X}{\partial V_1}\right)\right\}.\tag{5.31}$$

By using the expressions to the right in (5.23) this can be written as

$$\frac{\partial X}{\partial V_1} = \sqrt{2}\left\{\frac{1}{a\sqrt{2}}\left(1-s_1\frac{\partial X}{\partial V_1}\right) - \frac{1}{b\sqrt{2}}s_2\frac{\partial X}{\partial V_1}\right\},\tag{5.32}$$

which gives

$$\frac{\partial X}{\partial V_1} = \frac{b}{s_1b+s_2a+ab},\tag{5.33}$$

which is seen to be the same as the expression for q_1 given by (5.29).

The form of an isoquant within the region of substitution is obtained by keeping X fixed in (5.25). Solving for V_2 we obtain

$$V_2 = V_1 - X\sqrt{2(V_1-s_1X)} + \tfrac{1}{2}X^2 + (s_2-s_1)X.\tag{5.34}$$

It is easy to check that these isoquants are vertical at the upper and horizontal at the right boundary of the region of substitution. Isoquants for $X = 1, 2, 3$ are shown in Figure 5.2 (for $s_1 = 1, s_2 = 2$).

In order to illustrate the scale properties of the function we let for simplicity $s_1 = s_2 = s$ and consider variation along the factor ray $V_1 = V_2$. We then get from (5.25)

$$X = 2\sqrt{2}\sqrt{V_1-sX},\tag{5.35}$$

which can be solved for X (keeping only the meaningful root):

$$X = 2\sqrt{4s^2+2V_1-4s}.\tag{5.36}$$

From this follows the scale elasticity

$$\varepsilon = \frac{dX}{dV_1} \frac{V_1}{X} = \frac{V_1}{4s^2 + 2V_1 - 2s\sqrt{4s^2 + 2V_1}} \quad (s_1 = s_2 = s, \ V_2 = V_1). \quad (5.37)$$

It is easily seen that this approaches unity when $V_1 \to 0$, confirming (4.38), and declines towards $\frac{1}{2}$ when $V_1 \to \infty$.

This special case easily confirms that (5.37) is in accordance with the geometric construction in Figure 4.2, where ε is given by the proportion OA/OB. In the case under consideration this proportion is easily seen to be $(s+(a/4))/(s+(a/2))$. Using (5.22) and (5.36) this can be shown to be equivalent to (5.37).

It is worth noticing that in the limiting case where $s_1 = s_2 = 0$ the production function given implicitly by (5.25) simplifies to

$$X = \sqrt{2}(\sqrt{V_1} + \sqrt{V_2}), \quad (5.38)$$

which corresponds to a common text-book illustration of a production function. In this special case the region of positive capacity comprises the origin. Then (4.38) does no longer necessarily hold. Instead of decreasing from 1 towards $\frac{1}{2}$, the scale elasticity is for (5.38) constant at the level of $\frac{1}{2}$.

Equation (5.38) is a special member of the CES-family of production functions; its elasticity of substitution is constant at the value $\sigma_{12} = 2$.[7] It is tempting to check whether our formula (4.48) produces this simple result. The formalities are slightly different from what they were in Section 4.5, because we now have capacity distributed only along the axes. But let us try the interpretation which we placed upon (4.48).

Let us first work out the terms $\sigma_1/\bar{\xi}_1$ and $\sigma_2/\bar{\xi}_2$. In the present case, with $s_1 = s_2 = 0$, we have $a = 1/q_1$ and $b = 1/q_2$, see (5.28–5.29). The zero quasi rent line then goes from $(0, b)$ to $(a, 0)$ in the ξ_1, ξ_2-plane. Let us draw a parallel line through $(0, b+\Delta b)$ and $(a+\Delta a, 0)$, where $\Delta a/a = \Delta b/b$. Now marginal production units will be located in the interval Δa on the ξ_1-axis and in Δb on the ξ_2-axis. The input coefficient ξ_1 is a and 0 respectively; furthermore the capacities in these intervals are Δa and Δb. Hence we have the average input coefficient for marginal production units

$$M(\xi_1) = \frac{a \cdot \Delta a + 0 \cdot \Delta b}{\Delta a + \Delta b} = \frac{a\Delta a/\Delta b}{(\Delta a/\Delta b)+1} = \frac{a^2}{a+b}. \quad (5.39)$$

For the variance in the distribution of marginal units we get (cf. (4.19)):

---

[7] More general CES-functions will be produced in the following section.

$$\sigma_1^2 = \frac{\left(a - \dfrac{a^2}{a+b}\right)^2 \Delta a + \left(0 - \dfrac{a^2}{a+b}\right)^2 \Delta b}{\Delta a + \Delta b},$$

which, when we use $\Delta a/a = \Delta b/b$, simplifies to

$$\sigma_1^2 = \frac{a^3 b}{(a+b)^2}. \tag{5.40}$$

Correspondingly we have

$$\sigma_2^2 = \frac{ab^3}{(a+b)^2}. \tag{5.41}$$

The average input coefficients for the whole utilization region for the function under consideration are obtained from (5.22):

$$\bar{\xi}_1 = \frac{V_1}{X} = \frac{a^2}{2(a+b)}, \quad \bar{\xi}_2 = \frac{V_2}{X} = \frac{b^2}{2(a+b)}. \tag{5.42}$$

The scale elasticity is $\varepsilon = \frac{1}{2}$.

Now consider the term $J/2X$, which is capacity per square unit in the marginal strip in proportion to the same for the whole utilization region (see the discussion of (4.50)). In the present case the capacity in the marginal strip is $\Delta a + \Delta b$, while the size of the strip is (approximately) $\Delta a \cdot b$. The average density in the strip is accordingly

$$\frac{\Delta a + \Delta b}{\Delta a \cdot b} = \frac{a+b}{ab}.$$

For the whole utilization region the average density is

$$\frac{a+b}{\frac{1}{2}ab} = \frac{2(a+b)}{ab}.$$

Now collecting all the terms according to (4.48) we have

$$s_{12} = 2 \frac{\dfrac{a+b}{ab}}{\dfrac{2(a+b)}{ab}} \cdot \frac{1}{2} \cdot \frac{\dfrac{\sqrt{a^3 b}}{(a+b)}}{\dfrac{a^2}{2(a+b)}} \frac{\dfrac{\sqrt{ab^3}}{(a+b)}}{\dfrac{b^2}{2(a+b)}} = 2. \tag{5.43}$$

Hence the general interpretation of formula (4.48) is confirmed in the special case under consideration.

Let us finally consider the effect of confining the distribution of capacity to finite parts of the right-angled curve MPN in Figure 5.1. Along PM we restrict the capacity distribution to the distance k_1 from s_1, and along PN we restrict it to the distance k_2.

The upper boundary of the region of substitution given by (5.26–5.27) will now be valid only up to the point where $b = k_2$, i.e.:

$$V_1 = k_2 s_1, \quad V_2 = \tfrac{1}{2}k_2^2 + s_2 k_2. \tag{5.44}$$

From there on the boundary is determined by the two last equations of (5.22) for $b = k_2$. The formula for the boundary is obtained by eliminating a from these equations. Similarly, we obtain the formula for the right boundary, valid from the point

$$V_1 = k_1 s_2, \quad V_2 = \tfrac{1}{2}k_1^2 + s_1 k_1. \tag{5.45}$$

The formulas are:

$$\text{Upper boundary: } V_1 = \frac{1}{2s_2^2}(V_2 - \tfrac{1}{2}k_2^2 - k_2 s_2)^2 +$$

$$+ \frac{s_1}{s_2}(V_2 - \tfrac{1}{2}k_2^2 - k_2 s_2) + k_2 s_1 \, ;$$

$$\text{Right boundary: } V_2 = \frac{1}{2s_1^2}(V_1 - \tfrac{1}{2}k_1^2 - k_1 s_1)^2 +$$

$$+ \frac{s_2}{s_1}(V_1 - \tfrac{1}{2}k_1^2 - k_1 s_1) + k_1 s_2. \tag{5.46}$$

These curves are valid until they intersect at

$$V_1 = \tfrac{1}{2}k_1^2 + s_1 k_1 + s_1 k_2, \quad V_2 = \tfrac{1}{2}k_2^2 + s_2 k_2 + s_2 k_1. \tag{5.47}$$

At this point we have full capacity utilization, obtaining an output $X = k_1 + k_2$, as is easily checked by inserting from (5.47) into the production function (5.25).

Within the region of substitution now restricted by (5.46) in addition to (5.27) the isoquant curves remain as before.

In Figure 5.2 we have illustrated the effect of k_1 and k_2 on the region of substitution by drawing (in dotted lines) the boundaries (5.46) for the case $k_1 = 2, k_2 = 2$, i.e. the full region of substitution is in that case $OQ_1 Q_2 Q_3 O$.

From the figure as well as from a comparison between (5.27) and (5.46) it will be seen that the second part of the upper boundary is of the same form as the first part of the right boundary, and vice versa.

For the simple case treated in this section up to formula (5.43) we illustrated and checked almost all of the general propositions from Chapter 4. This will not be done to the same extent in the following examples.

5.4. Alternative one-factor processes

In the special case $s_1 = 0$, $s_2 = 0$ treated in the previous section, see (5.38–5.43), the production units are distributed along the ξ_1-axis and the ξ_2-axis. This means that each production unit uses only one of the inputs; we may say that we have a case of alternative one-factor processes. The two-factor macro production function is generated by an appropriate mixing of such alternative one-factor processes. Let us make some more general observations on such cases.

Let the capacity distributions along the two axes be given by $f_1(\xi_1)$ and $f_2(\xi_2)$. The macro production function is then generated by

$$X = \int_0^a f_1(\xi_1)\,d\xi_1 + \int_0^b f_2(\xi_2)\,d\xi_2,$$

$$V_1 = \int_0^a \xi_1 f_1(\xi_1)\,d\xi_1, \quad V_2 = \int_0^b \xi_2 f_2(\xi_2)\,d\xi_2, \tag{5.48}$$

where $a = 1/q_1$ and $b = 1/q_2$. This can evidently be written as

$$X = F_1(a) - F_1(0) + F_2(b) - F_2(0),$$

$$V_1 = G_1(a) - G_1(0), \quad V_2 = G_2(b) - G_2(0), \tag{5.49}$$

where F_1, F_2, G_1, G_2 are the integrals of $f_1(\xi_1)$, $f_2(\xi_2)$, $\xi_1 f_1(\xi_1)$, $\xi_2 f_2(\xi_2)$ respectively. By inverting G_1 and G_2 we thus obtain

$$X = F_1(G_1^{-1}(V_1 + G_1(0))) - F_1(0) + F_2(G_2^{-1}(V_2 + G_2(0))) - F_2(0). \tag{5.50}$$

This states the rather obvious fact that, on the basis of alternative one-factor processes, we obtain macro functions which are additive, i.e. the sum of two functions which contain only one input each. In other words, the two factors in the macro function are independent in the sense that the marginal productivity of one factor is independent of the input of the other factor.

It is also easy to see that this is the *only* case in which additive macro functions are generated. Consider Figure 4.1, where we now assume that there is some capacity in the interior of the positive quadrant, i.e. not only along the axes. We consider a location of the zero quasi rent line which goes through this interior capacity distribution. The rotation of the zero quasi rent line in Figure 4.1 orginally meant a movement such that output X remained constant. Let us now rotate the line such that V_1 increases while V_2 remains constant, i.e. we generate a partial increase in V_1. The rotation must be in the direction indicated in the figure. The centre of rotation must be somewhat displaced in comparison with the case of a constant output X. But, on the other hand, the centre of rotation must be in the interior of the quadrant, otherwise V_2 would also increase since we now assume some capacity in the interior. Then $1/q_2$ must decrease, and accordingly $q_2 = \partial F/\partial V_2$ increase. Thus a partial increase in one input affects the marginal productivity of the other input, and the macro function $F(V_1, V_2)$ cannot be additive.

The same result would follow from reasoning in connection with Figure 4.5, which shows curves of constant marginal productivities. In this connection we observed that V_1 and V_2 are in general complementary factors in $F(V_1, V_2)$. Only in the case of alternative one-factor processes at the micro level would the family of curves of constant marginal productivities degenerate into straight lines parallel with the axes over their whole range.[8]

As a somewhat more general case than (5.38) let us consider the case of Pareto distributions along the axes, i.e.

$$f_1(\xi_1) = A_1 \xi_1^{\alpha_1 - 1}, \quad f_2(\xi_2) = A_2 \xi_2^{\alpha_2 - 1}, \tag{5.51}$$

where A_1, A_2, α_1 and α_2 are constants, A_1 and $A_2 > 0$ and also α_1 and $\alpha_2 > 0$. If the last condition is not fulfilled the integrals below will not be meaningful. Assumption (5.51) bears some resemblance to the Houthakker case (5.1).

From (5.51) we get

$$X = \frac{A_1}{\alpha_1} a^{\alpha_1} + \frac{A_2}{\alpha_2} b^{\alpha_2}$$

$$V_1 = \frac{A_1}{\alpha_1 + 1} a^{\alpha_1 + 1}, \quad V_2 = \frac{A_2}{\alpha_2 + 1} b^{\alpha_2 + 1} \tag{5.52}$$

corresponding to (5.49). This yields, corresponding to (5.50), the production function

$$X = \frac{A_1}{\alpha_1} \left(\frac{\alpha_1 + 1}{A_1} V_1 \right)^{\frac{\alpha_1}{\alpha_1 + 1}} + \frac{A_2}{\alpha_2} \left(\frac{\alpha_2 + 1}{A_2} V_2 \right)^{\frac{\alpha_2}{\alpha_2 + 1}}. \tag{5.53}$$

---

[8] One might ask if separable macro functions, i.e. functions of the form
$$F(V_1, V_2) = \phi(\Psi_1(V_1) + \Psi_2(V_2))$$
can be generated by capacity distributions where there are processes at the micro level which use both factors. The case of the Cobb-Douglas function provides an affirmative answer since this function can be written in the form
$$F(V_1, V_2) = A V_1^{\alpha} V_2^{\beta} = e^{\ln A V_1^{\alpha} V_2^{\beta}} = e^{\ln A + \alpha \ln V_1 + \beta \ln V_2}.$$

If $\alpha_1 = \alpha_2 = 1$ we have a uniform distribution along each of the axes, and (5.53) corresponds to the simple case (5.38), apart from the constants A_1 and A_2.

If we have $\alpha_1 = \alpha_2 = \alpha$, but not necessarily $\alpha = 1$, then (5.53) is a production function with a scale elasticity

$$\varepsilon = \frac{\alpha}{\alpha+1}, \tag{5.54}$$

which can take any value in the interval $0 < \varepsilon < 1$. In this case we furthermore have a constant elasticity of substitution. Since we have

$$\frac{V_2}{V_1} = \frac{A_2}{A_1}\left(\frac{b}{a}\right)^{\alpha+1} = \frac{A_2}{A_1}\left(\frac{q_1}{q_2}\right)^{\alpha+1} \tag{5.55}$$

the elasticity of substitution as defined by (4.39) is

$$s_{12} = \alpha+1. \tag{5.56}$$

Since $\alpha > 0$ the elasticity of substitution can take any value $s_{12} > 1$.

By this we have obtained a class of CES-functions, viz. those where $s_{12} > 1$ and where the scale elasticity is related to the elasticity of substitution by $\varepsilon = (s_{12} - 1)/s_{12}$. By the relative values of A_1 and A_2 we can generate any "distribution parameter".

Even though the case just studied is somewhat attractive in that it generates a simple and well-known macro function, it must nevertheless be deemed unrealistic. The case of alternative one-factor processes is conceivable, but very special. The assumption about the distributions, as given in (5.51), is absolutely unrealistic since there is no limit to the efficiency of the best production units. We could however repair this by assuming f_1 and f_2 to be zero up to certain points and only from there on obey (5.51). We would then obtain a function of the form

$$X = \frac{A_1}{\alpha_1}\left\{\left[\frac{\alpha_1+1}{A_1}V_1 + s_1^{\alpha_1+1}\right]^{\frac{\alpha_1}{\alpha_1+1}} - s_1^{\alpha_1}\right\} +$$

$$\tag{5.57}$$

$$+ \frac{A_2}{\alpha_2}\left\{\left[\frac{\alpha_2+1}{A_2}V_2 + s_2^{\alpha_2+1}\right]^{\frac{\alpha_2}{\alpha_2+1}} - s_2^{\alpha_2}\right\},$$

where s_1 and s_2 are the lower limits to the domains of (5.51). The perhaps more attractive case of replacing (5.51) by $f_i(\xi_i) = A_i(\xi_i - s_i)^{\alpha_i - 1}$ ($i = 1, 2$) results in a much more complicated macro function.

5.5. *Distribution along a hyperbola*

As another example of a production function derived from a distribution along a curve, we shall consider the case of a hyperbolic curve for the capacity distribution; i.e. we assume the capacity to be distributed along the curve

$$\xi_1\xi_2 = 1. \tag{5.58}$$

There are many possibilities as to how the capacity might be distributed along this curve. The simplest case seems to be the case of a uniform distribution per unit of the angle of the ray from the origin to the ξ_1, ξ_2-point as measured by ξ_2/ξ_1.

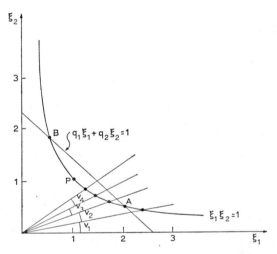

Fig. 5.3. Capacity distribution along a hyperbola $\xi_1\xi_2 = 1$.

The situation is depicted in Figure 5.3. The assumption is that there is the same capacity along the parts of the curve confined within each of the angles v_1, v_2, v_3, v_4 etc., which all raise ξ_2/ξ_1 by the same amount. Per unit of length along the curve the density is clearly low in the south-eastern part and increasing as one moves towards the left.

The integration should now be carried out along the curve between A and B, i.e. along the curve south-west of the line $q_1\xi_1+q_2\xi_2 = 1$. Let $\lambda = \xi_2/\xi_1$ and let $\underline{\lambda}$ and $\bar{\lambda}$ denote ξ_2/ξ_1 at A and B respectively. If the capacity is 1 per unit of λ, then we have

$$X = \int_{\underline{\lambda}}^{\bar{\bar{\lambda}}} d\lambda = \bar{\bar{\lambda}} - \underline{\lambda}, \tag{5.59}$$

$$V_1 = \int_{\underline{\lambda}}^{\bar{\bar{\lambda}}} \xi_1 \, d\lambda = \int_{\underline{\lambda}}^{\bar{\bar{\lambda}}} \lambda^{-\frac{1}{2}} \, d\lambda = 2\,(\bar{\bar{\lambda}}^{\frac{1}{2}} - \underline{\lambda}^{\frac{1}{2}}), \tag{5.60}$$

$$V_2 = \int_{\underline{\lambda}}^{\bar{\bar{\lambda}}} \xi_2 \, d\lambda = \int_{\underline{\lambda}}^{\bar{\bar{\lambda}}} \lambda^{\frac{1}{2}} \, d\lambda = \tfrac{2}{3}(\bar{\bar{\lambda}}^{\frac{3}{2}} - \underline{\lambda}^{\frac{3}{2}}). \tag{5.61}$$

In (5.60) we have replaced ξ_1 by $\lambda^{-\frac{1}{2}}$ in the integration because we have $\lambda = \xi_2/\xi_1 = 1/\xi_1^2$ along the curve $\xi_1\xi_2 = 1$. A similar substitution is done in (5.61).

It is a matter of convenience that we introduce $\underline{\lambda}$ and $\bar{\bar{\lambda}}$ directly in the expressions above instead of having the limits expressed in terms of q_1 and q_2. There is clearly a one-to-one correspondence between q_1, q_2 and $\underline{\lambda}, \bar{\bar{\lambda}}$. This correspondence can be set out in the following way. The values $\underline{\lambda}$ and $\bar{\bar{\lambda}}$ are defined by $\lambda = \xi_2/\xi_1$ at the intersections between the line $q_1\xi_1 + q_2\xi_2 = 1$ and the curve $\xi_1\xi_2 = 1$. From this follows that $\underline{\lambda}$ and $\bar{\bar{\lambda}}$ must satisfy

$$q_1 \frac{1}{\lambda} + q_2 = \frac{1}{\lambda^{\frac{1}{2}}}. \tag{5.62}$$

Introducing $\gamma = \lambda^{\frac{1}{2}}$ this can be written as

$$\gamma^2 - \frac{1}{q_2}\gamma + \frac{q_1}{q_2} = 0. \tag{5.63}$$

If we now let $\bar{\gamma} = \underline{\lambda}^{\frac{1}{2}}$ and $\bar{\bar{\gamma}} = \bar{\bar{\lambda}}^{\frac{1}{2}}$ these two values of γ are the roots of (5.63).[9] Accordingly the second degree expression in (5.63) can be written as $(\gamma - \bar{\gamma})(\gamma - \bar{\bar{\gamma}}) = \gamma^2 - (\bar{\gamma} + \bar{\bar{\gamma}})\gamma + \bar{\gamma}\bar{\bar{\gamma}}$ and we have the well known relations between roots and coefficients of the second degree equation:

$$\bar{\gamma} + \bar{\bar{\gamma}} = \frac{1}{q_2}, \quad \bar{\gamma}\bar{\bar{\gamma}} = \frac{q_1}{q_2}. \tag{5.64}$$

From this we obtain

$$q_1 = \frac{\bar{\gamma}\bar{\bar{\gamma}}}{\bar{\gamma} + \bar{\bar{\gamma}}} = \frac{\underline{\lambda}^{\frac{1}{2}}\bar{\bar{\lambda}}^{\frac{1}{2}}}{\underline{\lambda}^{\frac{1}{2}} + \bar{\bar{\lambda}}^{\frac{1}{2}}}, \quad q_2 = \frac{1}{\bar{\gamma} + \bar{\bar{\gamma}}} = \frac{1}{\underline{\lambda}^{\frac{1}{2}} + \bar{\bar{\lambda}}^{\frac{1}{2}}}. \tag{5.65}$$

These formulas give the marginal productivities of the macro function cor-

---

[9] It is required that $q_1q_2 < 1$ in order that there shall be two distinct roots, which is again necessary for effectively positive output.

responding to the various positions of the zero quasi rent line as expressed by λ and $\bar{\lambda}$.

In order to simplify the following expression we introduce $\bar{\gamma} = \bar{\lambda}^{\frac{1}{2}}, \bar{\bar{\gamma}} = \bar{\bar{\lambda}}^{\frac{1}{2}}$ in (5.59–5.61). We then have

$$X = \bar{\bar{\gamma}}^2 - \bar{\gamma}^2, \tag{5.66}$$

$$V_1 = 2(\bar{\bar{\gamma}} - \bar{\gamma}), \tag{5.67}$$

$$V_2 = \tfrac{2}{3}(\bar{\bar{\gamma}}^3 - \bar{\gamma}^3). \tag{5.68}$$

The production function is obtained by elimination of $\bar{\gamma}$ and $\bar{\bar{\gamma}}$ from (5.66–5.68).

From (5.67) we have $\bar{\bar{\gamma}} = \tfrac{1}{2}V_1 + \bar{\gamma}$. Inserting this in (5.66) we obtain

$$X = \left(\frac{V_1}{2} + \bar{\gamma}\right)^2 - \bar{\gamma}^2 = \frac{V_1^2}{4} + V_1\bar{\gamma},$$

which further yields

$$\bar{\gamma} = \frac{X}{V_1} - \frac{V_1}{4}, \quad \bar{\bar{\gamma}} = \frac{X}{V_1} + \frac{V_1}{4}. \tag{5.69}$$

Inserting this in (5.68) we get

$$V_2 = \tfrac{2}{3}\left[\left(\frac{X}{V_1} + \frac{V_1}{4}\right)^3 - \left(\frac{X}{V_1} - \frac{V_1}{4}\right)^3\right].$$

This can be simplified to

$$V_2 = \frac{V_1^3}{48} + \frac{X^2}{V_1}, \tag{5.70}$$

which is, for given value of X, the formula for an isoquant. The explicit form of the production function is accordingly

$$X = \sqrt{V_1 V_2 - \frac{V_1^4}{48}}. \tag{5.71}$$

Equations (5.70) and (5.71) are meaningful only for V_1, V_2-values which correspond to

$$0 \leqq \lambda \leqq \bar{\lambda}, \text{ or } 0 \leqq \bar{\gamma} \leqq \bar{\bar{\gamma}}. \tag{5.72}$$

The condition $\bar{\gamma} \geqq 0$ requires $(X/V_1) - (V_1/4) \geqq 0$, i.e. $V_1 \leqq 2\sqrt{X}$. Using (5.71) this yields

$$V_1 \leqq 2 \sqrt[4]{V_1 V_2 - \frac{V_1^4}{48}}, \text{ or } V_1^4 \leqq 16 \left(V_1 V_2 - \frac{V_1^4}{48} \right),$$

which is the same as

$$V_2 \geqq \frac{1}{12} V_1^3. \tag{5.73}$$

(It is easily seen that for V_1, V_2 satisfying (5.73) the term under the square root in (5.71) is non-negative, so that a real value for X is obtained.)

It is clear from (5.67–5.68) that the condition $\bar{y} \leqq \bar{\bar{y}}$ is automatically fulfilled when V_1 and V_2 are non-negative.

The resulting production function is illustrated in Figure 5.4. The region of substitution is the region between the border curve representing (5.73) and the V_2-axis. The reason for this asymmetric form is explained by the asymmetric nature of the distribution along the curve $\xi_1 \xi_2 = 1$ in Figure 5.3. To the right of any point on the curve $\xi_1 \xi_2 = 1$ there is a finite capacity,

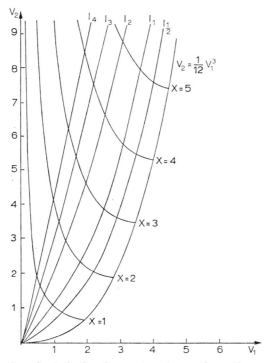

Fig. 5.4. The region of substitution, isoquants and expansion paths corresponding to a distribution of capacity along the curve in Figure 5.3.

since such a branch of the curve is confined within a finite angle as measured by ξ_2/ξ_1. Therefore there is a finite limit to the region of substitution in the V_1-direction. On the other hand, in order to capture the whole curve $\xi_1\xi_2 = 1$ in Figure 5.3 one must take the full angle between the axes, which is infinite as measured by ξ_2/ξ_1. Thus total capacity is infinite, and since there is a finite capacity to the right of any point on the curve $\xi_1\xi_2 = 1$, there must be an infinite capacity to the left of and above any such point. This implies that there is no finite limit to the region of substitution in the V_2-direction in Figure 5.4.

The isoquants are all approaching the V_2-axis asymptotically towards the north-west, whereas they are horizontal at the points where they reach the border-line towards the south-east. This is easily seen from (5.70).

The expansion paths or isocline curves are curves along which the marginal rate of substitution $dV_2/dV_1 = -q_1/q_2$ is constant. From (5.64) we have $q_1/q_2 = \bar{\gamma}\bar{\gamma}$. Using (5.69) this gives

$$\frac{q_1}{q_2} = \frac{12V_2 - V_1^3}{12V_1}, \text{ or } V_2 = \frac{1}{12}V_1^3 + \frac{q_1}{q_2}V_1.$$

For each value of q_1/q_2 the expression to the right gives the formula for the corresponding expansion path. It is seen that these paths are constructed simply as $(q_1/q_2)V_1$ added to the right boundary of the region of substitution in Figure 5.4. In the figure we have indicated expansion paths corresponding to $q_1/q_2 = \frac{1}{2}$, 1, 2, 3 and 4 by $I_{\frac{1}{2}}$, I_1, I_2, I_3 and I_4.

The asymmetric case outlined above may not be absolutely implausible. E.g., there may be production sectors where very large capacities are available with very simple techniques of production, whereas less capacity is available with more advanced techniques. If we do not take the passing to infinity along the V_2-axis too literally, such a case may be represented by the above model with V_2 representing labour input and V_1 representing e.g. some type of fuel.

However, let us also investigate a symmetric case. In order to exploit the calculations for the preceding case, we now assume that the distribution along the curve in Figure 5.3 is as given above for the branch of the curve which goes from the mid-point (P in the figure) towards the south-east while the distribution along the branch from P towards the north-west is symmetric with the distribution along the former branch.

It is clear that parts of the isoquants and the region of substitution in Figure 5.4 are still valid, namely those parts which correspond to both B and A in Figure 5.3 lying south-east of P. Correspondingly the parts corresponding to both B and A lying north-west of P are obtained as a mirror image of the former part. The more complicated parts are those which correspond to B and A not lying on the same side of P. Some results for this case can, however, also be obtained from the preceding calculations.

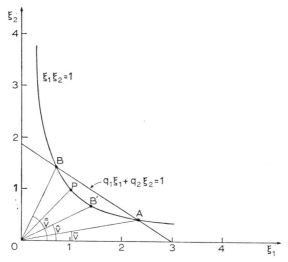

Fig. 5.5. A symmetric distribution of capacity along the curve $\xi_1\xi_2 = 1$ around point P.

Consider Figure 5.5. We now want to find X, V_1 and V_2 when all capacity between A and B is exploited. Let, as before, λ and $\bar{\bar{\lambda}}$ represent ξ_2/ξ_1 at A and B respectively, i.e. λ and $\bar{\bar{\lambda}}$ represent $\tan \bar{v}$ and $\tan \bar{\bar{v}}$, where $\bar{v}$ and $\bar{\bar{v}}$ are the angles marked off in the figure. Furthermore, let us construct an angle $\hat{v}$ in the figure which is such that along the ray corresponding to this angle we have $\xi_1/\xi_2 = \bar{\bar{\lambda}}$, i.e. we have

$$\frac{\xi_2}{\xi_1} = \tan \hat{v} = \hat{\lambda} = 1/\bar{\bar{\lambda}}.$$

This ray reaches the curve $\xi_1\xi_2 = 1$ at B'.

Total capacity between A and B can now be split in two parts; that between A and P (where $\lambda = \xi_2/\xi_1 = 1$), and that between P and B. Because of the symmetry the latter equals that between B' and P. Using (5.59) for these intervals we then have

$$X = 1-\bar{\bar{\lambda}}+1-\hat{\lambda} = 2-\bar{\bar{\lambda}}-\hat{\lambda}. \tag{5.74}$$

Next, consider the use of factor No. 1. This can be split in two parts in a similar way. First, the use of this factor by capacity between A and P will be $2(1-\bar{\lambda}^{\frac{1}{2}})$, corresponding to (5.60) with 1 as the upper limit. Next, the use of factor No. 1 between P and B will, because of the symmetry, be the same as the use of factor No. 2 between B' and P. From (5.61) we get $\frac{2}{3}(1-\hat{\lambda}^{\frac{3}{2}})$ for this part. In all we get

$$V_1 = 2(1-\bar{\lambda}^{\frac{1}{2}})+\frac{2}{3}(1-\hat{\lambda}^{\frac{3}{2}}) = \frac{8}{3}-2\,\bar{\lambda}^{\frac{1}{2}}-\frac{2}{3}\hat{\lambda}^{\frac{3}{2}}. \tag{5.75}$$

In a similar way we have

$$V_2 = \frac{8}{3}-\frac{2}{3}\bar{\lambda}^{\frac{3}{2}}-2\,\hat{\lambda}^{\frac{1}{2}}. \tag{5.76}$$

Introducing for simplicity $\bar{\gamma} = \bar{\lambda}^{\frac{1}{2}}$ and $\hat{\gamma} = \hat{\lambda}^{\frac{1}{2}}$, we have

$$X = 2-\bar{\gamma}^2-\hat{\gamma}^2 \tag{5.77}$$

$$V_1 = \frac{8}{3}-2\bar{\gamma}-\frac{2}{3}\hat{\gamma}^3 \tag{5.78}$$

$$V_2 = \frac{8}{3}-\frac{2}{3}\bar{\gamma}^3-2\hat{\gamma}. \tag{5.79}$$

These equations now replace (5.66–5.68).

The full region of substitution is shown in Figure 5.6. Consider first the right boundary. This remains as in Figure 5.4 up to the point where $X = 1$, at $V_1 = 2$, $V_2 = \frac{2}{3}$. From there on the boundary is obtained from (5.77–5.79) by putting $\bar{\gamma} = 0$. Eliminating $\hat{\gamma}$ from (5.78–5.79) for this case one obtains

$$(\tfrac{8}{3}-V_1) = \tfrac{1}{12}(\tfrac{8}{3}-V_2)^3. \tag{5.80}$$

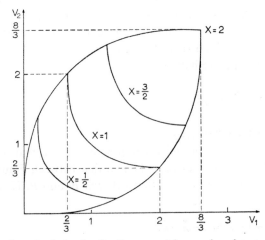

Fig. 5.6. The region of substitution for the symmetric case, based on a capacity distribution as explained in connection with Figure 5.5.

By differentiation it is easily seen that the branch where we have $V_2 = \frac{1}{12}V_1^3$ and the branch for which (5.80) is valid have the same slope at the point where they meet ($V_1 = 2$, $V_2 = \frac{2}{3}$), so that the latter part is a smooth continuation of the former part.

The upper boundary in the figure is symmetric with the lower boundary. The two boundaries meet at $V_1 = V_2 = \frac{8}{3}$, corresponding to $X = 2$. This signifies full capacity utilization, which now yields a finite amount of output in spite of the fact that the curve along which we have positive capacity extends towards infinity in both directions. The point is of course that the density becomes very thin in these tails.

The isoquants from Figure 5.4 remain valid in a region near to the first part of the right boundary of the region of substitution in Figure 5.6, and by symmetry we also have the isoquants near to the first part of the upper boundary. The isoquants corresponding to cases where capacity on both sides of the mid-point P in Figure 5.5 is used can in principle be obtained by eliminating $\bar{\gamma}$ and $\hat{\gamma}$ from (5.77–5.79).

Explicit expressions are, however, not easily obtained from (5.77–5.79). But it is a simple matter to trace the isoquants, e.g. in the following way. Consider a given value of X. A sample of (positive) values of $\bar{\gamma}$ and $\hat{\gamma}$ which yield the given value of X is easily found from (5.77), and by insertion in (5.78–5.79) the corresponding values of V_1 and V_2 are found. (This procedure is valid for $\bar{\gamma} \leqq 1$, $\hat{\gamma} \leqq 1$, otherwise the isoquants are as in the preceding case.) The isoquants in Figure 5.6 have been generated in this way.

5.6. Uniform distribution over a region bounded by a right-angled curve

Instead of assuming a distribution along a right-angled curve as in Section 5.3, we shall now assume that we have a two-dimensional distribution over a region bounded by a right-angled curve. Even the simplest case, i.e. that of a uniform distribution, gives a production function which is not too easy to handle.

In Figure 5.7 we have placed the boundary curve with the right angle at the point s_1, s_2. When the line $q_1\xi_1 + q_2\xi_2 = 1$ is placed as in the figure, integration should be performed over the fully shaded region, i.e. over the triangle with sides a and b. The formulas for output and inputs then take the following form, when we use a and b as variables instead of q_1 and q_2[10]

---

[10] The connections given in (5.28–5.29) between a and b and the marginal productivities q_1 and q_2 are valid also in the present case.

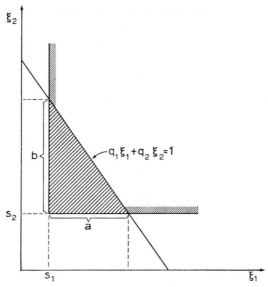

Fig. 5.7. Distribution over a region bounded by a right-angled curve.

$$X = \int_{s_1}^{s_1+a} \int_{s_2}^{s_2+b-\frac{b}{a}(\xi_1-s_1)} d\xi_2\, d\xi_1 = \tfrac{1}{2}\, ab, \qquad (5.81)$$

$$V_1 = \int_{s_1}^{s_1+a} \int_{s_2}^{s_2+b-\frac{b}{a}(\xi_1-s_1)} \xi_1\, d\xi_2\, d\xi_1 = \tfrac{1}{6}a^2 b + \tfrac{1}{2}s_1 ab, \qquad (5.82)$$

$$V_2 = \int_{s_1}^{s_1+a} \int_{s_2}^{s_2+b-\frac{b}{a}(\xi_1-s_1)} \xi_2\, d\xi_2\, d\xi_1 = \tfrac{1}{6}ab^2 + \tfrac{1}{2}s_2 ab. \qquad (5.83)$$

For simplicity we have assumed the capacity to be 1 per square unit.
From (5.81–5.83) we have

$$\frac{V_1}{X} = \tfrac{1}{3}a + s_1, \qquad (5.84)$$

$$\frac{V_2}{X} = \tfrac{1}{3}b + s_2. \qquad (5.85)$$

In this form the formulas correspond to formulas for the coordinates of the centre of gravity of a uniform triangular body. This is of some interest since it suggests a way of deriving the production function for distributions which, when they are truncated by the line $q_1\xi_1 + q_2\xi_2 = 1$, correspond to the form of bodies for which the formulas for the coordinates of the centre of gravity are known.

If we solve (5.84–5.85) for a and b and insert in (5.81) we obtain

$$X = \tfrac{9}{2}\left(\frac{V_1}{X} - s_1\right)\left(\frac{V_2}{X} - s_2\right),$$

which may be written as

$$X^3 = \tfrac{9}{2}(V_1 - s_1 X)(V_2 - s_2 X). \tag{5.86}$$

This is the production function in implicit form.

From (5.86) we can obtain the expression for an isoquant in the following form

$$V_2 = s_2 X + \frac{2X^3}{9(V_1 - s_1 X)}. \tag{5.87}$$

It is clear that we must have $V_1 > s_1 X$ and $V_2 > s_2 X$, and that the isoquants approach $V_1 = s_1 X$ and $V_2 = s_2 X$ asymptotically when V_2 and V_1 respectively tend to infinity. This is natural since we have no processes

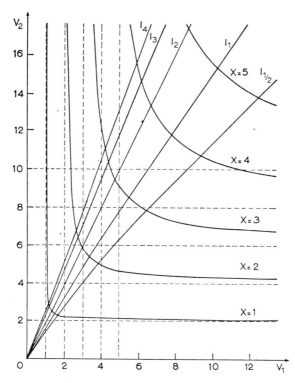

Fig. 5.8. Isoquant map (and expansion paths or isocline curves) corresponding to the capacity distribution in Figure 5.7 ($s_1 = 1$, $s_2 = 2$).

available with $\xi_1 < s_1$, and/or $\xi_2 < s_2$, while we can produce as much as we like with processes which have ξ_1 as near to s_1 as we like or with processes which have ξ_2 as near to s_2 as we like.

An isoquant map, for $s_1 = 1, s_2 = 2$, is given in Figure 5.8. The asymptotes of the isoquants are indicated by dotted lines.

It is of some interest to notice that when $s_1 = s_2 = 0$ we obtain a special case of Cobb-Douglas function, namely

$$X = (\tfrac{9}{2})^{\tfrac{1}{3}}V_1^{\tfrac{1}{3}}V_2^{\tfrac{1}{3}}. \tag{5.88}$$

This is of course also a special case of professor Houthakker's original result discussed in Section 5.2; it corresponds to the case $\alpha_1 = \alpha_2 = 1$ where his "generalized Pareto distribution" degenerates into a uniform distribution over the whole positive quadrant. As has been mentioned before this case is unrealistic since it assumes the existence of production units with infinite efficiency. But it appears difficult to obtain manageable formulas if we combine the non-uniformity of Houthakker's general distribution with the shifting of the distribution away from the origin which is represented by the parameters s_1 and s_2 in our production function (5.86).

It may appear somewhat disturbing that our production function is, by (5.86), determined implicitly by an equation of the third degree in output X. For given values of V_1 and V_2 there should in principle be three roots for X. Before proceeding further, let us dispose of this apparent difficulty.

Write (5.86) as $X^3 = g(X)$, where $g(X) = \tfrac{9}{2}(V_1 - s_1 X)(V_2 - s_2 X)$. We then have $g(X) = 0$ for $X = V_1/s_1$ and for $X = V_2/s_2$. These values are of course not necessarily distinct. There will clearly always be one and only one real, positive root of the equation $X^3 = g(X)$ for $X < \text{Min} [V_1/s_1, V_2/s_2]$. This is a meaningful root since it is, by (5.84–5.85), associated with positive values of a and b. There is evidently no real root in the interval between V_1/s_1 and V_2/s_2 (boundaries included) since here $X^3 > 0$ and $g(X) \leqq 0$. On the other hand there may be two real roots (or one double root) for $X > \text{Max} [V_1/s_1, V_2/s_2]$. These are however not meaningful since they are associated with negative values of a and b in (5.84–5.85). Finally, possible complex roots of the equation are of course not meaningful as solutions for output. All told we have thus located one real, meaningful root.

By standard methods of solving a third degree equation it is possible to write down the explicit expression for X, i.e. the production function in explicit form. This has been done, but no convenient simplification seems to be obtainable, so the formula is probably more impressive than useful. I therefore abstain from reproducing it here.

In Figure 5.8 we have also entered some expansion paths (isocline curves), i.e. curves along which the marginal rate of substitution is constant. The curves are labelled $I_{\frac{1}{4}}$, I_1, I_2, I_3, I_4, where the subscript indicates the rate of substitution, i.e. the slope of the isoquant, along the curve. It is easy to verify that all these expansion paths start out from the origin with a slope s_2/s_1, i.e. they are tangential at the origin. One expansion path (I_2 in the figure) is the straight ray with this slope. The other expansion paths are bending away from this particular path; along each of these the ratio V_2/V_1 approaches the numerical value of the marginal rate of substitution corresponding to that expansion path.

Let us finally make some observations concerning the scale properties of the production function defined by (5.86). We let k indicate the factor proportion, i.e.

$$\frac{V_2}{V_1} = k. \tag{5.89}$$

We then put $V_1 = V$ and $V_2 = kV$ along the factor ray defined by (5.89) for constant k. Inserting this in (5.86) we have the production function along this ray:

$$X^3 = \tfrac{9}{2} (V - s_1 X)(kV - s_2 X). \tag{5.90}$$

By implicit differentiation in this formula we can find the elasticity of X with respect to V expressed in terms of V and X. Using (5.90) we can furthermore arrive at an expression in terms of X alone (which seems to be simpler than an expression in terms of V):

$$\varepsilon = \frac{dX}{dV}\frac{V}{X} = \frac{8kX + 3(ks_1 + s_2)\sqrt{8kX + 9(ks_1 - s_2)^2} + 9(ks_1 - s_2)^2}{12kX + 3(ks_1 + s_2)\sqrt{8kX + 9(ks_1 - s_2)^2} + 9(ks_1 - s_2)^2}. \tag{5.91}$$

We first notice that ε is constant and equal to $\tfrac{2}{3}$ if $s_1 = s_2 = 0$, corresponding to the special form (5.88) of the production function obtaining in this case. If $s_1 > 0$ and/or $s_2 > 0$, so that the region of positive capacity is bounded away from the origin, we clearly have $\varepsilon < 1$ for all $X > 0$. If $X \to 0$ it is easy to see that $\varepsilon \to 1$ provided that $s_2 \neq ks_1$. In the special case $s_2 = ks_1$ we have $\varepsilon \to 0/0$ when $X \to 0$, but a further examination shows that $\varepsilon \to 1$ also in this case.

When $X \to \infty$ it is easily seen that $\varepsilon \to \tfrac{2}{3}$.

All this confirms the reasoning in connection with (4.38).

In the case now under consideration the distribution of marginal production units will simply be a rectangular distribution, and we have

$$M(\xi_1) = s_1 + \frac{a}{2}, \quad M(\xi_2) = s_2 + \frac{b}{2}, \tag{5.92}$$

$$\sigma_1^2 = \frac{a^2}{12}, \quad \sigma_2^2 = \frac{b^2}{12}. \tag{5.93}$$

The capacity per square unit along the zero quasi rent line in proportion to the same for the whole utilization region can also be expressed in terms of a and b. Using these facts together with (5.84–5.85) and (5.91) it is possible to write down an expression for the elasticity of substitution s_{12} according to formula (4.48). We shall here only observe that the elasticity of substitution will tend to zero when output tends to zero by $a \to 0$ and $b \to 0$, whereas it approaches 1 when X is made to increase by $a \to \infty$ and $b \to \infty$. In a way we may say that the function is "almost Leontief" for very small outputs (since also $\varepsilon \to 1$ when $X \to 0$), whereas it approaches the form of a Cobb-Douglas function with $\varepsilon = \frac{2}{3}$ for very large outputs.

5.7. *Uniform distribution over a rectangular region*

In the preceding example the region of positive capacity over which we had a uniform distribution was assumed to extend without limitation towards the north-east. Accordingly total capacity was also infinite. Let us now study

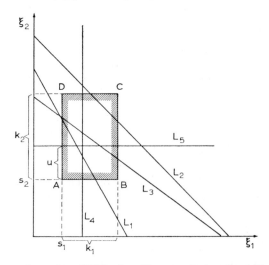

Fig. 5.9. A rectangular region $ABCD$ of positive capacity together with various possible positions (L_1, L_2, L_3, L_4, L_5) of the zero quasi rent line $q_1\xi_1 + q_2\xi_2 = 1$.

the effects of limiting this region. We shall consider the simple case obtained by limiting it in such a way that we get a rectangular region of positive capacity.

In Figure 5.9 we have shown a rectangular region $ABCD$, with sides k_1 and k_2, together with various possible positions $L_1, \ldots, L_5$ of the zero quasi rent line $q_1\xi_1 + q_2\xi_2 = 1$.

We first consider the region of substitution. The lower boundary is obtained by following the movement of V_1, V_2 as the line $q_1\xi_1 + q_2\xi_2 = 1$ moves upwards while remaining in a horizontal position like L_5 in the figure. Let the distance that L_5 has moved away from AB be u. Then we have

$$X = uk_1,$$

$$V_1 = \left(s_1 + \frac{k_1}{2}\right) X,$$

$$V_2 = \left(s_2 + \frac{u}{2}\right) X. \tag{5.94}$$

By eliminating u and X we obtain the expression for the right boundary of the region of substitution:

$$V_2 = \left(s_2 + \frac{V_1}{2k_1(s_1 + \frac{1}{2}k_1)}\right) \frac{V_1}{s_1 + \frac{1}{2}k_1}. \tag{5.95}$$

The corresponding curve starts out from the origin with the slope $s_2/(s_1 + \frac{1}{2}k_1)$, and then increases with increasing slope.

The upper boundary can be obtained in the same way from vertical positions (L_4) of the line $q_1\xi_1 + q_2\xi_2 = 1$. In Figure 5.10 the region of substitution is shown for $s_1 = 1$, $s_2 = 2$, $k_1 = 2$, $k_2 = 3$.

The mathematical formula for the production function and the corresponding isoquants will now be different for different parts of the region of substitution.

For those parts where the zero quasi rent line $q_1\xi_1 + q_2\xi_2 = 1$ cuts through AB and AD in Figure 5.9 (as L_1) the isoquants from the preceding section, i.e. based on (5.86–5.87), are still valid.

For those parts where the corresponding line in Figure 5.9 cuts through BC and DC (as L_2) the isoquants are easily obtained by the same types of formulas as (5.86–5.87). We have here instead of (5.86):

$$(\bar{X} - X)^3 = \frac{9}{2} \left[(\bar{V}_1 - V_1) - (s_1 + k_1)(\bar{X} - X) \right] \times$$

$$\times \left[(\bar{V}_2 - V_2) - (s_2 + k_2)(\bar{X} - X) \right], \tag{5.96}$$

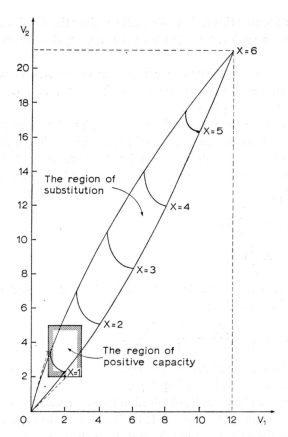

Fig. 5.10. The region of substitution and isoquants for a production function based upon a uniform distribution of capacity over a rectangular region in the ξ_1, ξ_2-diagram ($s_1 = 1$, $s_2 = 2$, $k_1 = 2$, $k_2 = 3$).

where $\bar{X}$, $\bar{V}_1$ and $\bar{V}_2$ are output and total factor inputs by full capacity utilization, i.e. obtained by integrating over the whole rectangle $ABCD$ in Figure 5.9. Total output X approaches $\bar{X}$ when V_1 and V_2 approach $\bar{V}_1$ and $\bar{V}_2$. (In Figure 5.10 we have $\bar{X} = 6$, $\bar{V}_1 = 12$ and $\bar{V}_2 = 21$.)

When V_1 and V_2 are such that the line $q_1\xi_1 + q_2\xi_2 = 1$ assumes positions like L_3 in the figure, the amount of output cannot be obtained so easily. It could best be obtained by splitting the corresponding trapezoid into a rectangle and a triangle. Then the formulas given above could be exploited. The result would however be rather messy. The isoquant map in Figure 5.10 is constructed on the basis of formulas for the boundaries of the region of substitution, such as (5.95), plus calculated values for X along these boundaries, plus formulas (5.86) and (5.96) for those subregions where these are valid, plus the fact that the isoquants are vertical at the upper and horizontal at the lower boundary of the region of substitution. This is sufficient to get a fairly complete and accurate impression of the production function.

To make the diagram comparable with Figure 4.4, which explains the general connections between the capacity distribution on the one hand and the region of substitution and the form of the isoquants on the other hand, we have also entered the region of positive capacity in the figure.

CHAPTER 6

Supply and demand functions corresponding to the short-run macro production function. Aspects of distribution

6.1. Supply and demand functions

We have touched several times previously on the price interpretation of the parameters q_1 and q_2, which are used in establishing the short-run macro production function. In Section 4.3 we established the proposition that marginal calculations on the basis of the macro function $X = F(V_1, V_2)$ yield the same results for X, V_1 and V_2 as are obtained by summation over production units capable of yielding a non-negative quasi rent, when the same prices are used in both cases. It is clear then that the supply function for output and demand functions for factor inputs corresponding to a short-run macro function of the type we are considering can be established either by starting from macro marginal balances such as (4.28) or directly on the basis of the capacity distribution by means of the formulas in (4.2). In fact, formulas (4.2) are almost directly supply and demand functions as they stand. If we use the notations P, Q_1 and Q_2 for absolute prices of output and variable inputs, where

$$\frac{Q_1}{P} = q_1, \quad \frac{Q_2}{P} = q_2, \tag{6.1}$$

the ordinary aggregate supply function and aggregate input demand functions are given by

$$X = g\left(\frac{Q_1}{P}, \frac{Q_2}{P}\right),$$

$$V_1 = h_1\left(\frac{Q_1}{P}, \frac{Q_2}{P}\right),$$

$$V_2 = h_2\left(\frac{Q_1}{P}, \frac{Q_2}{P}\right). \tag{6.2}$$

Since the forms of the functions g, h_1 and h_2 are given by (4.2), (6.2) provides explicit expressions for the supply and factor demand functions when the form of the distribution function $f(\xi_1, \xi_2)$ is known.

The zero quasi rent line $q_1\xi_1 + q_2\xi_2 = 1$ now takes the form

$$Q_1\xi_1 + Q_2\xi_2 = P \tag{6.3}$$

in terms of absolute prices.

For given input prices Q_1 and Q_2 the supply function for output is generated by varying P. This corresponds to a parallel shifting of the zero quasi rent line. By considering such a shifting in connection with the figures of Chapter 4 it is easy to visualize how output and inputs respond to changes in P. Similarly a partial change in an input price Q_1 or Q_2 corresponds to a rotation of the zero quasi rent line around one of its intersections with the V_1- and V_2-axes. The effects of this on X, V_1 and V_2 can also be easily visualized by means of such figures as we used in Chapter 4.

The mathematical examples studied in Chapter 5 will provide a sample of supply and demand functions.

The Pareto-Cobb-Douglas case. The Houthakker-Pareto-Cobb-Douglas case studied in Section 5.2 gives the following simple functions

$$X = c_0 P^{\alpha_1 + \alpha_2} Q_1^{-\alpha_1} Q_2^{-\alpha_2} = c_0 \left(\frac{P}{Q_1}\right)^{\alpha_1} \left(\frac{P}{Q_2}\right)^{\alpha_2},$$

$$V_1 = c_1 P^{1 + \alpha_1 + \alpha_2} Q_1^{-1-\alpha_1} Q_2^{-\alpha_2} = c_1 \left(\frac{P}{Q_1}\right)^{1+\alpha_1} \left(\frac{P}{Q_2}\right)^{\alpha_2},$$

$$V_2 = c_2 P^{1 + \alpha_1 + \alpha_2} Q_1^{-\alpha_1} Q_2^{-1-\alpha_2} = c_2 \left(\frac{P}{Q_1}\right)^{\alpha_1} \left(\frac{P}{Q_2}\right)^{1+\alpha_2}, \tag{6.4}$$

where c_0, c_1 and c_2 are constants depending on A, α_1 and α_2. These functions have constant elasticities which are related to the parameters of the capacity distribution (5.1) in a very simple way. Here supply and factor demands are positive as soon as $P > 0$, which is related to the fact that the underlying capacity distribution implies the existence of infinitely efficient production units. Furthermore X, V_1 and V_2 tend to infinity when P increases beyond all limits, which reflects the unlimited capacity when the capacity distribution is as given by (5.1) over the whole non-negative ξ_1, ξ_2-plane. Both these properties are unrealistic.

Distribution along a right-angled curve. The case studied in Section 5.3 is different in the first respect. We there have capacity distributed along the curve MPN in Figure 5.1. The aggregate supply function can be obtained from the first equation of (5.21). The terms a and b in this equation are related to q_1 and q_2 by equations (5.28), which give

$$a = \frac{1}{q_1}(1 - q_1 s_1 - q_2 s_2), \quad b = \frac{1}{q_2}(1 - q_1 s_1 - q_2 s_2). \tag{6.5}$$

Inserting this in $X = a + b$ and using (6.1) we get

$$X = (P - s_1 Q_1 - s_2 Q_2)\left(\frac{1}{Q_1} + \frac{1}{Q_2}\right). \tag{6.6}$$

This function is valid only for $a \geqq 0$ and $b \geqq 0$, i.e. $P - s_1 Q_1 - s_2 Q_2 \geqq 0$. Considered as a function of P, for constant Q_1 and Q_2, the function (6.6) is linear, and $P > s_1 Q_1 + s_2 Q_2$ is required for $X > 0$. The requirement is obviously that prices must be such that the most efficient production units, located in the neighbourhood of point P in Figure 5.1, shall earn a positive quasi rent.

Considered as a function of an input price, say Q_1, function (6.6) will be declining (with decreasing slope) with increasing price and reach $X = 0$ when $Q_1 = (P - s_2 Q_2)/s_1$.

Factor demand functions are somewhat more complicated. By insertion from (6.1) and (6.5) into the second equation of (5.22) we obtain for V_1:

$$V_1 = (P - s_1 Q_1 - s_2 Q_2)\left(\frac{P - s_1 Q_1 - s_2 Q_2}{2Q_1^2} + \frac{s_1}{Q_1} + \frac{s_1}{Q_2}\right). \tag{6.7}$$

A similar expression holds of course for V_2. As in the case of the supply function we must have $P - s_1 Q_1 - s_2 Q_2 > 0$ in order for V_1 to be positive.

In the particularly simple case where $s_1 = s_2 = 0$, and the production function is (5.38), we have the following supply and demand functions:

$$X = P\left(\frac{1}{Q_1} + \frac{1}{Q_2}\right), \tag{6.8}$$

$$V_1 = \frac{P^2}{2Q_1^2}, \quad V_2 = \frac{P^2}{2Q_2^2}. \tag{6.9}$$

When the distribution along PM and PN in Figure 5.1 is restricted to the stretches k_1 and k_2, then the supply and demand functions given above have a restricted validity. They will then be subjected to the limitations implied by the boundary curve $Q_1 Q_2 Q_3$ for the region of substitution in Figure 5.2. We shall omit the supplementary formulas for this case.

Pareto distributions for alternative one-factor processes. In the case of

Pareto distributions along the ξ-axes, treated by (5.51–5.56), we have the following supply and demand functions:

$$X = \frac{A_1}{\alpha_1}\left(\frac{P}{Q_1}\right)^{\alpha_1} + \frac{A_2}{\alpha_2}\left(\frac{P}{Q_2}\right)^{\alpha_2}, \qquad (6.10)$$

$$V_1 = \frac{A_1}{\alpha_1+1}\left(\frac{P}{Q_1}\right)^{1+\alpha_1}, \quad V_2 = \frac{A_2}{\alpha_2+1}\left(\frac{P}{Q_2}\right)^{1+\alpha_2}, \qquad (6.11)$$

which reduces to (6.8–6.9) for $\alpha_1 = \alpha_2 = 1$ and $A_1 = A_2 = 1$. The factor demand functions in (6.11) are reminiscent of those in (6.4) for the Pareto-Cobb-Douglas case, but failing to show cross-effects of factor prices.

It is easy to write down also the supply and demand functions for the case (5.57), where we truncated the capacity distributions along the ξ-axes away from the origin. We omit the formulas here; the main effect is of course that the supply and demand functions now require a certain minimum output price (for given input prices) in order to give positive X, V_1 and V_2.

Distribution along a hyperbola. In Section 5.5 we studied the case of a capacity distribution along a hyperbola $\xi_1\xi_2 = 1$ as explained in connection with Figure 5.3. The supply and demand functions for this case can be derived from equations (5.66–5.68) where the parameters $\underline{\gamma}$ and $\bar{\gamma}$ are related to q_1 and q_2 by (5.64). From (5.64) and the notational convention that $\bar{\gamma} > \underline{\gamma}$ we get

$$\underline{\gamma} = \frac{1 - \sqrt{1 - 4q_1q_2}}{2q_2}, \quad \bar{\gamma} = \frac{1 + \sqrt{1 - 4q_1q_2}}{2q_2}. \qquad (6.12)$$

Inserting this into (5.66–5.68), simplifying and using (6.1), we obtain the following supply and demand functions:

$$X = \frac{P\sqrt{P^2 - 4Q_1Q_2}}{Q_2^2},$$

$$V_1 = \frac{2\sqrt{P^2 - 4Q_1Q_2}}{Q_2},$$

$$V_2 = \frac{2(P^2 - Q_1Q_2)\sqrt{P^2 - 4Q_1Q_2}}{3Q_3^3}. \qquad (6.13)$$

In this case the two factor demand functions are not represented by symmetric expressions because of the unsymmetric nature of the underlying capacity distribution.

It is seen that $P^2 > 4Q_1Q_2$ is a necessary requirement for X, V_1, $V_2 > 0$.

Furthermore X, V_1 and V_2 all tend to infinity when P tends to infinity (for constant Q_1 and Q_2). The unsymmetric nature of the case under consideration is clear if we consider the effects of changes in Q_1 and Q_2. For a decreasing Q_1 supply X will increase towards a finite maximum value P^2/Q_2^2 which is reached when $Q_1 = 0$, while V_1 and V_2 reach the values $2P/Q_2$ and $2P^3/3Q_3^3$ respectively. On the other hand, if $Q_2 \to 0$ all X, V_1 and $V_2 \to \infty$. This reflects the fact explained in connection with Figure 5.3 that there is a finite capacity to the right of any point on the curve $\xi_1\xi_2 = 1$, while there is an infinite capacity to the left of and above any such point.

The symmetric case discussed in connection with Figures 5.5–5.6 gives rise to more complicated supply and demand functions which must be constructed by joining together different expressions valid for different parts of the P, Q_1, Q_2-domain. We shall not write down the formulas, but it is clear that X, V_1 and V_2 will in this case be restricted to a finite value even when $P \to \infty$ or Q_1, $Q_2 \to 0$.

Uniform distribution over a region bounded by a right-angled curve. We now consider the case discussed in Section 5.6. Supply and demand functions can here be derived from (5.81–5.85). The relationships between a and b on the one hand and q_1 and q_2 on the other hand are the same as in the case studied in Section 5.3, i.e. we can insert from (6.5) into (5.81–5.85). We obtain

$$X = \frac{1}{2Q_1Q_2}(P-s_1Q_1-s_2Q_2)^2,$$

$$V_1 = \frac{1}{2Q_1Q_2}(P-s_1Q_1-s_2Q_2)^2 \left(\frac{P-s_1Q_1-s_2Q_2}{3Q_1} + s_1\right),$$

$$V_2 = \frac{1}{2Q_1Q_2}(P-s_1Q_1-s_2Q_2)^2 \left(\frac{P-s_1Q_1-s_2Q_2}{3Q_2} + s_2\right). \qquad (6.14)$$

Like functions (6.6–6.7) these functions give positive X, V_1 and V_2 only when $P-s_1Q_1-s_2Q_2 > 0$.

If $s_1 = s_2 = 0$ the functions in (6.14) reduce to the same forms as (6.4) for $\alpha_1 = \alpha_2 = 1$. This is as it should be since the underlying capacity distribution in both cases reduces to the same, viz. a uniform distribution over the positive quadrant in the ξ_1, ξ_2-plane.

For the case of a capacity distribution only over a limited rectangle, discussed in Section 5.7, the supply and demand functions would have to be joined together from different expressions for different parts of the P, Q_1,

Q_2-domain. In this case X, V_1 and V_2 would remain finite even when $P \to \infty$ or Q_1 and $Q_2 \to 0$.

6.2. Supply and demand derivatives

For a closer examination of the supply and demand functions it is of interest to study the derivatives (or elasticities) with respect to prices. One might expect to be able to express these derivatives in terms of some characteristics of the capacity distribution function f. This is done very simply by using the expressions in (4.17). By differentiating $X = g(Q_1/P, Q_2/P)$ with respect to Q_1 we obtain

$$\frac{\partial X}{\partial Q_1} = \frac{\partial g}{\partial q_1} \frac{\partial q_1}{\partial Q_1} = -\frac{J}{P} M(\xi_1). \tag{6.15}$$

The expression for $\partial X / \partial Q_2$ is obtained in the same way.

For the derivative with respect to output price we have

$$\frac{\partial X}{\partial P} = \frac{\partial g}{\partial q_1} \frac{\partial q_1}{\partial P} + \frac{\partial g}{\partial q_2} \frac{\partial q_2}{\partial P} = -J \left[M(\xi_1) \left(-\frac{Q_1}{P^2} \right) + M(\xi_2) \left(-\frac{Q_2}{P^2} \right) \right].$$

Taking into account the fact that the relation $Q_1\xi_1 + Q_2\xi_2 = P$ holds for marginal units of production (over which the moments M are calculated) – cf. the first line of (4.20) – this reduces to

$$\frac{\partial X}{\partial P} = \frac{J}{P}. \tag{6.16}$$

The derivatives of V_1 and V_2 with respect to Q_1 and Q_2 are obtained in the same way as (6.15) by using the second and third line of (4.17). We obtain

$$\frac{\partial V_i}{\partial Q_j} = -\frac{J}{P} M(\xi_i \xi_j) \quad (i, j = 1, 2). \tag{6.17}$$

For the derivative of V_1 with respect to P we have

$$\frac{\partial V_1}{\partial P} = \frac{\partial h_1}{\partial q_1} \frac{\partial q_1}{\partial P} + \frac{\partial h_1}{\partial q_2} \frac{\partial q_2}{\partial P} = -J \left[M(\xi_1^2) \left(-\frac{Q_1}{P^2} \right) + M(\xi_1 \xi_2) \left(-\frac{Q_2}{P^2} \right) \right].$$

This formula can be simplified by taking into account the fact that since $Q_1\xi_1 + Q_2\xi_2 = P$, or $Q_1\xi_1^2 + Q_2\xi_1\xi_2 = P\xi_1$ along the zero quasi rent line we have

$$Q_1 M(\xi_1^2) + Q_2 M(\xi_1 \xi_2) = P M(\xi_1). \tag{6.18}$$

Using this the expression $\partial V_1/\partial P$ reduces to

$$\frac{\partial V_1}{\partial P} = \frac{J}{P} M(\xi_1). \tag{6.19}$$

A corresponding expression is obtained for $\partial V_2/\partial P$, now using the relationship $Q_1 M(\xi_1 \xi_2) + Q_2 M(\xi_2^2) = P M(\xi_2)$ which holds in the same way as (6.18).

Collecting the results obtained above we have the following complete matrix of supply and demand derivatives:

$$\begin{bmatrix} \dfrac{\partial X}{\partial P} & \dfrac{\partial X}{\partial Q_1} & \dfrac{\partial X}{\partial Q_2} \\[2ex] \dfrac{\partial V_1}{\partial P} & \dfrac{\partial V_1}{\partial Q_1} & \dfrac{\partial V_1}{\partial Q_2} \\[2ex] \dfrac{\partial V_2}{\partial P} & \dfrac{\partial V_2}{\partial Q_1} & \dfrac{\partial V_2}{0 Q_2} \end{bmatrix} = \frac{J}{P} \begin{bmatrix} 1 & -M(\xi_1) & -M(\xi_2) \\[2ex] M(\xi_1) & -M(\xi_1^2) & -M(\xi_1 \xi_2) \\[2ex] M(\xi_2) & -M(\xi_1 \xi_2) & -M(\xi_2^2) \end{bmatrix}. \tag{6.20}$$

It is seen that the matrix of supply and demand derivatives is closely related to the second order moment matrix of ξ_1 and ξ_2 bordered with the averages, moments and averages being calculated in the distribution of marginal production units (i.e. along $q_1 \xi_1 + q_2 \xi_2 = 1$).

The derivatives in (6.20) satisfy the following conditions, which exhibit a general property of such derivatives, valid not only on the special assumptions underlying our model:

$$\frac{\partial V_1}{\partial P} = -\frac{\partial X}{\partial Q_1}, \quad \frac{\partial V_2}{\partial P} = -\frac{\partial X}{\partial Q_2}. \tag{6.21}$$

The derivatives also satisfy the general symmetry relation

$$\frac{\partial V_1}{\partial Q_2} = \frac{\partial V_2}{\partial Q_1}. ^1 \tag{6.22}$$

The derivatives with respect to output price are related in the following simple way

---

[1] The symmetry relation (6.22) is shown by Frisch (1965), pp. 190–193. Relations corresponding to (6.21) can also be shown to hold on the basis of a general production function, i.e. a function which is not necessarily established in the way in which our $F(V_1, V_2)$ is established.

$$\frac{\partial V_1}{\partial P} = M(\xi_1)\frac{\partial X}{\partial P}, \quad \frac{\partial V_2}{\partial P} = M(\xi_2)\frac{\partial X}{\partial P}. \tag{6.23}$$

It is intuitively obvious that such relationships must hold: a partial change in output price P means a parallel shift in the zero quasi rent line $Q_1\xi_1 + Q_2\xi_2 = P$. The new production units which will then be included among those that yield a non-negative quasi rent will then on average have input coefficients $M(\xi_1)$ and $M(\xi_2)$.

The responses to changes in factor prices are not quite so simple, because a change in a factor price does not shift the zero quasi rent line in such a parallel way. In order to see why the second order moments then enter, consider first the limiting case where the region of positive capacity tends to callapse into a one-dimensional line (increasing towards the north-east in the figure). Using (4.19–4.20) and taking into account the fact that the standard deviations σ_1 and σ_2 vanish when the region of positive capacity collapses as indicated so that $M(\xi_1^2) = [M(\xi_1)]^2$, $M(\xi_2^2) = [M(\xi_2)]^2$ and $M(\xi_1\xi_2) = M(\xi_1)M(\xi_2)$ we then obtain from (6.20) the following simple structure:

$$\begin{bmatrix} \dfrac{\partial V_1}{\partial P} & \dfrac{\partial V_1}{\partial Q_1} & \dfrac{\partial V_1}{\partial Q_2} \\[2ex] \dfrac{\partial V_2}{\partial P} & \dfrac{\partial V_2}{\partial Q_1} & \dfrac{\partial V_2}{\partial Q_2} \end{bmatrix} = \begin{bmatrix} M(\xi_1)\dfrac{\partial X}{\partial P} & M(\xi_1)\dfrac{\partial X}{\partial Q_1} & M(\xi_1)\dfrac{\partial X}{\partial Q_2} \\[2ex] M(\xi_2)\dfrac{\partial X}{\partial P} & M(\xi_2)\dfrac{\partial X}{\partial Q_1} & M(\xi_2)\dfrac{\partial X}{\partial Q_2} \end{bmatrix}. \tag{6.24}$$

This characterizes V_1 and V_2 as limitational inputs with marginal input coefficients $M(\xi_1)$ and $M(\xi_2)$, since V_1 and V_2 will change in the same proportions $M(\xi_1)$ and $M(\xi_2)$ to the change in X regardless of whether the change in X is induced by change in P, Q_1 or Q_2.

For the general case we have

$$\begin{bmatrix} \dfrac{\partial V_1}{\partial P} & \dfrac{\partial V_1}{\partial Q_1} & \dfrac{\partial V_1}{\partial Q_2} \\[2ex] \dfrac{\partial V_2}{\partial P} & \dfrac{\partial V_2}{\partial Q_1} & \dfrac{\partial V_2}{\partial Q_2} \end{bmatrix} = \begin{bmatrix} M_1\dfrac{\partial X}{\partial P} & \left(1+\dfrac{\sigma_1^2}{M_1^2}\right)M_1\dfrac{\partial X}{\partial Q_1} & \left(1-\dfrac{\sigma_1\sigma_2}{M_1M_2}\right)M_1\dfrac{\partial X}{\partial Q_2} \\[2ex] M_2\dfrac{\partial X}{\partial P} & \left(1-\dfrac{\sigma_1\sigma_2}{M_1M_2}\right)M_2\dfrac{\partial X}{\partial Q_1} & \left(1+\dfrac{\sigma_2^2}{M_2^2}\right)M_2\dfrac{\partial X}{\partial Q_2} \end{bmatrix}. \tag{6.25}$$

For brevity we have here written M_1 and M_2 for $M(\xi_1)$ and $M(\xi_2)$; furthermore we have, for symmetry, introduced both σ_1 and σ_2, which are related by the equation on the second line of (4.20).

Comparing (6.25) with (6.24) we see that the existence of a standard deviation $\sigma_1 > 0$ (and then also $\sigma_2 > 0$) tends to increase the numerical values of the direct factor demand derivatives while it tends to decrease the numerical values of the cross derivatives as compared with the case of a vanishing standard deviation. In other words, larger standard deviations in the distribution of marginal production units enhance the substitution away from a factor whose price is increased.

The way in which this effect operates is illustrated in Figure 6.1. In this figure we have drawn the line $Q_1\xi_1 + Q_2\xi_2 = P$. The point $M(\xi_1)$, $M(\xi_2)$ is located on this line. We now assume that factor price No. 1 increases from Q_1 to Q_1'; the corresponding zero quasi rent line is also drawn in the figure. If all the capacity mass were located closely along a curve through the point $M(\xi_1)$, $M(\xi_2)$, as e.g. the curve KK, then all the production units "lost" by the increase in Q_1 would be approximately of the type characterized by input coefficients $M(\xi_1)$ and $M(\xi_2)$, and (6.24) would apply approximately. If on the other hand the mass is distributed over a region bordered by e.g. the curve LL in the figure, then we will loose production units in the region $ABCD$. Since this region is broader towards the south-east, we loose relatively more capacity embodied in production units which deviate from the average in the direction of high input of factor No. 1 and low input of factor No. 2 than capacity embodied in production units which deviate in the opposite direction from the average. From this the direction of the effects of the spread in the distribution of marginal production units is intuitively plausible.

One might also consider the total effect of the change in Q_1 by first reducing P, which corresponds to a parallel shift of the border-line in the figure, and then changing the ratio Q_1/Q_2, which corresponds to the effect described in Figure 4.1. For the effects of the parallel shift in the border-line it does not matter whether the region of positive capacity is wide or narrow, whereas this, represented by the standard deviations, is important for the effect of the rotation of the line. This discussion can be related to Puu's discussion of "Slutsky relations" for producers' behaviour.[2] This idea will be pursued further in Section 6.3 below.

Returning to the general formula (6.20) we see that there is a scale factor J, which enters multiplicatively in the expressions for all the supply and demand

---

[2] See Puu (1966, 1968).

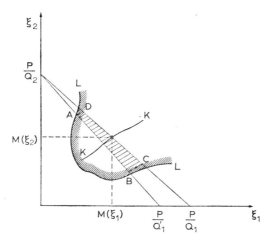

Fig. 6.1. The effects of a partial increase in factor price Q_1.

derivatives. This factor is defined by (4.15). It was demonstrated in Section 4.5, in connection with the discussion of formula (4.48) or (4.48') for the elasticity of substitution, that this factor is proportional to the average capacity per square unit along the zero quasi rent line in the ξ_1, ξ_2-diagram, which provides a natural explanation of why it appears as a factor in (6.20).

To illustrate the formulas above for the special functional forms given in Chapter 5 and partly in Section 6.1 involves very many tedious calculations. We shall therefore limit ourselves here to a few brief suggestions.

The Pareto-Cobb-Douglas case. In the Pareto-Cobb-Douglas case the distribution of marginal production units is closely related to the Beta distribution. As shown in Section 5.2 ξ_1 is distributed as η/q_1, where η follows the Beta distribution. Using this fact and the formulas for the moments of the Beta distribution[3] we obtain the following form for (6.20):

$$
\begin{bmatrix}
\dfrac{\partial X}{\partial P} & \dfrac{\partial X}{\partial Q_1} & \dfrac{\partial X}{\partial Q_2} \\[2ex]
\dfrac{\partial V_1}{\partial P} & \dfrac{\partial V_1}{\partial Q_1} & \dfrac{\partial V_1}{\partial Q_2} \\[2ex]
\dfrac{\partial V_2}{\partial P} & \dfrac{\partial V_2}{\partial Q_1} & \dfrac{\partial V_2}{\partial Q_2}
\end{bmatrix}
= \frac{J}{P}
\begin{bmatrix}
\text{The matrix} \\
\text{given in} \\
\text{formula (6.26b)}
\end{bmatrix}.
\qquad (6.26a)
$$

[3] See Cramér (1946), p. 244.

$$
\begin{bmatrix}
1 & -\dfrac{P}{Q_1}\dfrac{\alpha_1}{\alpha_1+\alpha_2} & -\dfrac{P}{Q_2}\dfrac{\alpha_2}{\alpha_1+\alpha_2} \\[2ex]
\dfrac{P}{Q_1}\dfrac{\alpha_1}{\alpha_1+\alpha_2} & -\dfrac{P^2}{Q_1^2}\dfrac{\alpha_1(\alpha_1+1)}{(\alpha_1+\alpha_2)(\alpha_1+\alpha_2+1)} & -\dfrac{P^2}{Q_1Q_2}\dfrac{\alpha_1\alpha_2}{(\alpha_1+1)(\alpha_1+\alpha_2+1)} \\[2ex]
\dfrac{P}{Q_2}\dfrac{\alpha_2}{\alpha_1+\alpha_2} & -\dfrac{P^2}{Q_1Q_2}\dfrac{\alpha_1\alpha_2}{(\alpha_1+\alpha_2)(\alpha_1+\alpha_2+1)} & -\dfrac{P^2}{Q_2^2}\dfrac{\alpha_2(\alpha_2+1)}{(\alpha_1+\alpha_2)(\alpha_1+\alpha_2+1)}
\end{bmatrix}
$$

$$(6.26b)$$

The factor J is given by Equation (5.9) by inserting $q_1 = Q_1/P$ and $q_2 = Q_2/P$.

If we consider the formula as given by (6.25) we have the following expressions for the terms causing the substitution effects of changes in input prices:

$$
\frac{\sigma_1^2}{M_1^2} = \frac{\alpha_2}{\alpha_1(\alpha_1+\alpha_2+1)}, \quad \frac{\sigma_2^2}{M_2^2} = \frac{\alpha_1}{\alpha_2(\alpha_1+\alpha_2+1)}, \quad \frac{\sigma_1\sigma_2}{M_1M_2} = \frac{1}{\alpha_1+\alpha_2+1}.
$$

$$(6.27)$$

If $\alpha_1 = \alpha_2 = 1$ (uniform distribution) all factors in (6.27) equal $\frac{1}{3}$, i.e. in this case the spread in the distribution enhances or reduces all factor demand responses to changes in factor prices by $\frac{1}{3}$ as compared with what they would be in the case of limitational inputs. More generally, if $\alpha_1 = \alpha_2 = \alpha$ all factors in (6.27) have the same value, $1/(2\alpha+1)$, which declines from 1 towards zero with increasing α. This is perhaps natural in view of the fact that the Beta distribution of the marginal production units is U-shaped when $\alpha_1 < 1$ and $\alpha_2 < 1$ and bell-shaped when $\alpha_1 > 1$ and $\alpha_2 > 1$.

Distribution along the ξ_1- and ξ_2-axes. To keep formulas simple we shall here consider only a special case of the functions from Section 5.3, namely the case where $s_1 = s_2 = 0$, i.e. there is positive capacity only along the two axes in the ξ_1, ξ_2-plane. The production function in this case is (5.38), and the supply and demand functions are (6.8–6.9).

The first order moment $M(\xi_1)$ is given for this case by (5.39) where $a = 1/q_1 = P/Q_1$ and $b = 1/q_2 = P/Q_2$. A corresponding formula holds for $M(\xi_2)$. From the reasoning in connection with (5.39–5.40) it follows that we have $M(\xi_1^2) = a^3/(a+b)$, $M(\xi_2^2) = b^3/(a+b)$ and $M(\xi_1\xi_2) = 0$. Furthermore, from the reasoning between (5.42) and (5.43) we have $J = a+b$. Collecting these expressions according to the general formula (6.20) we obtain

$$
\begin{bmatrix}
\dfrac{\partial X}{\partial P} & \dfrac{\partial X}{\partial Q_1} & \dfrac{\partial X}{\partial Q_2} \\[2ex]
\dfrac{\partial V_1}{\partial P} & \dfrac{\partial V_1}{\partial Q_1} & \dfrac{\partial V_1}{\partial Q_2} \\[2ex]
\dfrac{\partial V_2}{\partial P} & \dfrac{\partial V_2}{\partial Q_1} & \dfrac{\partial V_2}{\partial Q_2}
\end{bmatrix}
=
\begin{bmatrix}
\dfrac{1}{Q_1} + \dfrac{1}{Q_2} & -\dfrac{P}{Q_1^2} & -\dfrac{P}{Q_2^2} \\[2ex]
\dfrac{P}{Q_1^2} & -\dfrac{P^2}{Q_1^3} & 0 \\[2ex]
\dfrac{P}{Q_2^2} & 0 & -\dfrac{P^2}{Q_2^3}
\end{bmatrix}.
\tag{6.28}
$$

It is seen that this is in conformity with what can be obtained directly from the explicit supply and demand functions (6.8–6.9) for this case.

Considering the form (6.25) the terms generated by the spread in the distribution are now, by using (5.39–5.41):

$$
\frac{\sigma_1^2}{M_1^2} = \frac{Q_1}{Q_2}, \quad \frac{\sigma_2^2}{M_2^2} = \frac{Q_2}{Q_1}, \quad \frac{\sigma_1 \sigma_2}{M_1 M_2} = 1.
\tag{6.29}
$$

In a way this represents a maximum of such effects since the capacity along the zero quasi rent line is located completely at the extreme points of this line.

The other cases can be worked out in a similar way, but involve rather heavy formulae.

In the case of a *uniform distribution over a region bounded by a right-angled curve*, see Section 5.6, the distribution of marginal production units is simply a rectangular distribution with means and standard deviations given by (5.92–5.93). In this case the relative contributions of the spread in the distribution to the derivatives of factor demand with respect to the factor prices are indicated by

$$
\frac{\sigma_1^2}{M_1^2} = \frac{a^2}{12(s_1 + \tfrac{1}{2}a)^2}, \quad \frac{\sigma_2^2}{M_2^2} = \frac{b^2}{12(s_2 + \tfrac{1}{2}b)^2}, \quad \frac{\sigma_1 \sigma_2}{M_1 M_2} = \frac{ab}{12(s_1 + \tfrac{1}{2}a)(s_2 + \tfrac{1}{2}b)}.
\tag{6.30}
$$

(These formulae could be expressed in terms of P, Q_1 and Q_2 via (6.1) and (6.5).)

The terms in (6.30) are negligible when a and b are small, (and $s_1 > 0$, $s_2 > 0$), i.e. when we utilize only a small bit of the corner of the region of positive capacity in Figure 5.7. This is the case where the production function is "almost Leontief", see the final remarks of Section 5.6. On the other hand, when a and b increase so as to be large in comparison with s_1 and s_2, then all the terms in (6.30) tend to $\tfrac{1}{3}$, which is the value characterizing the Pareto-Cobb-Douglas case when $\alpha_1 = \alpha_2 = 1$, cf. (6.27). This is in agreement with the observation at the end of Section 5.6 that the production function approaches a Cobb-Douglas form for very large outputs. If we extend the consideration to the case studied in Section 5.7, i.e. distribution over a rectangular region, then the contributions of the spread in the distribution will of course decrease again towards zero when we approach full capacity utilization.

6.3. *Further observations on expansion and substitution effects in factor demand functions*[4]

In recent papers[5] Puu has shown that factor demand responses to changes in factor prices can be decomposed into "scale effects" and "substitution effects" in a way which more or less parallels the Slutsky decomposition in consumer demand theory. Working with elasticities Puu proves the following equation

$$e_{ij} = \varepsilon_{ij} - a_j E_i E_j \eta, \tag{6.31}$$

where e_{ij} is the elasticity of demand for factor No. i with respect to factor price No. j, when other prices, including output price, are constant. In our notation

$$e_{ij} = \frac{\partial V_i}{\partial Q_j} \frac{Q_j}{V_i} \ (P \text{ and } Q_h \text{ for } h \neq j \text{ constant}). \tag{6.32}$$

The symbol ε_{ij} in (6.31) represents the substitution effect. This is defined as the elasticity of demand for factor No. i with respect to factor price No. j when other factor prices are constant and output X is constant:

$$\varepsilon_{ij} = \frac{\partial V_i}{\partial Q_j} \frac{Q_j}{V_i} \ (X \text{ and other factor prices constant}). \tag{6.33}$$

We may think of this as being generated by an "experiment" in which the factor price change is "compensated" by a change in the output price which is such that producers are induced to keep output constant.

The term $a_j E_i E_j \eta$ in (6.31) is the "scale effect", or "expansion effect" as we shall prefer to call it, thus associating it terminologically with the concept of an expansion path. The component E_i of this term is the elasticity of factor No. i with respect to output X when all factor prices are constant:

---

[4] This section draws partly on Hersoug (1969b).
[5] See Puu (1966, 1968).

$$E_i = \frac{\partial V_i}{\partial X} \frac{X}{V_i} \text{ (all factor prices constant)}. \tag{6.34}$$

We may think of the variation in X as a given change, or as induced via a change in output price. In any case the elasticities defined by (6.34) characterize the expansion path. We shall call them expansion elasticities.

The component a_j in the expansion term is the share of cost component No. i in total output value, i.e.

$$a_i = \frac{Q_i V_i}{PX}. \tag{6.35}$$

Finally, η is the supply elasticity

$$\eta = \frac{\partial X}{\partial P} \frac{P}{X} \text{ (all factor prices constant)}. \tag{6.36}$$

Intuitively the composition of the expansion term can be understood in the following way. If we consider the marginal cost curve, this will shift positively by $E_j a_j$ per per cent for an increase in factor price Q_j. This will decrease output by $\eta E_j a_j \%$, and accordingly input of factor No. i by $\eta E_j a_j E_i$, which is the same as the (negative) expansion effect in Equation (6.31).

We shall now relate the decomposition shown by the "Slutsky equation" (6.31) to the discussion of supply and demand derivatives in Section 6.2, and to the expressions in (6.25) in particular since the separation of the terms depending on the standard deviations σ_1 and σ_2 from the rest of these expressions must apparently be related to "substitution effects" in the Slutsky sense.

First consider the substitution terms ε_{11} and ε_{21} in our special case. These can be obtained from (6.20) by forming the total differentials of X, V_1 and V_2 with respect to P and Q_1 for $dQ_2 = 0$ and requiring $dX = 0$. This last requirement gives $dP = M(\xi_1) dQ_1$. Inserting this in the differentials for V_1 and V_2 we obtain

$$dV_1 = \frac{J}{P} [M(\xi_1)^2 - M(\xi_1^2)] dQ_1 = -\frac{J}{P} \sigma_1^2 dQ_1,$$

$$dV_2 = \frac{J}{P} [M(\xi_1) M(\xi_2) - M(\xi_1 \xi_2)] dQ_1 = \frac{J}{P} \sigma_1 \sigma_2 dQ_1. \tag{6.37}$$

Correspondingly we may consider a variation in Q_2 for constant X. Forming elasticities we obtain

$$\varepsilon_{11} = -\frac{J}{P}\frac{Q_1}{V_1}\sigma_1^2, \quad \varepsilon_{12} = \frac{J}{P}\frac{Q_2}{V_1}\sigma_1\sigma_2,$$

$$\varepsilon_{21} = \frac{J}{P}\frac{Q_1}{V_2}\sigma_1\sigma_2, \quad \varepsilon_{22} = -\frac{J}{P}\frac{Q_2}{V_2}\sigma_2^2. \tag{6.38}$$

Using the first line of (6.20) we can write these expressions as

$$\varepsilon_{11} = \frac{Q_1}{V_1}\frac{\sigma_1^2}{M_1}\frac{\partial X}{\partial Q_1}, \qquad \varepsilon_{12} = -\frac{Q_2}{V_1}\frac{\sigma_1\sigma_2}{M_2}\frac{\partial X}{\partial Q_2},$$

$$\varepsilon_{21} = -\frac{Q_1}{V_2}\frac{\sigma_1\sigma_2}{M_1}\frac{\partial X}{\partial Q_1}, \quad \varepsilon_{22} = \frac{Q_2}{V_2}\frac{\sigma_2^2}{M_2}\frac{\partial X}{\partial Q_2}, \tag{6.39}$$

where $\partial X/\partial Q_1$ and $\partial X/\partial Q_2$ are to be interpreted as derivatives of the supply function as in Section 6.2.

Apart from the factors Q_1/V_1 and Q_2/V_2, which are due to the fact that the ε's are elasticities, we see that the substitution terms as represented by ε_{ij} according to Puu's definitions are the same as the components of (6.25) which we separated out as depending upon the standard deviations in the capacity distribution of marginal production units.

In terms of more natural proportions than in (6.38) the substitution terms can be written in the following form:

$$\varepsilon_{11} = -\frac{J}{X}a_1\left(\frac{\sigma_1}{\bar{\xi}_1}\right)^2, \quad \varepsilon_{12} = \frac{J}{X}a_2\frac{\sigma_1\sigma_2}{\bar{\xi}_1\bar{\xi}_2},$$

$$\varepsilon_{21} = \frac{J}{X}a_1\frac{\sigma_1\sigma_2}{\bar{\xi}_1\bar{\xi}_2}, \quad \varepsilon_{22} = -\frac{J}{X}a_2\left(\frac{\sigma_2}{\bar{\xi}_2}\right)^2. \tag{6.40}$$

Here $\bar{\xi}_i$ is as before the average input coefficient $\bar{\xi}_i = V_i/X$, and the factor J/X can be interpreted as discussed in connection with formulas (4.48–4.50).

The substitution effects represented by the ε's can also be expressed in terms of the elasticity of substitution s_{12} discussed in Section 4.5. Using the expressions given in Section 4.5 together with (6.38) or (6.40) we obtain

$$\varepsilon_{11} = -s_{12}\frac{a_2}{\varepsilon}, \quad \varepsilon_{12} = s_{12}\frac{a_2}{\varepsilon},$$

$$\varepsilon_{21} = s_{12}\frac{a_1}{\varepsilon}, \quad \varepsilon_{22} = -s_{12}\frac{a_1}{\varepsilon}. \tag{6.41}$$

Thus the substitution terms in (6.31) are directly related to the elasticity of substitution.[6] (ε in (6.41) is the scale elasticity.)

Examples: For the Pareto-Cobb-Douglas case from Section 5.2 (6.41) gives simply

$$\varepsilon_{11} = -\frac{\alpha_2}{\alpha_1+\alpha_2}, \quad \varepsilon_{12} = \frac{\alpha_2}{\alpha_1+\alpha_2},$$

$$\varepsilon_{21} = \frac{\alpha_1}{\alpha_1+\alpha_2}, \quad \varepsilon_{22} = -\frac{\alpha_1}{\alpha_1+\alpha_2}, \tag{6.42}$$

since $s_{12} = 1$ and $\varepsilon = (\alpha_1+\alpha_2)/(\alpha_1+\alpha_2+1)$ in this case and furthermore the relative cost components in output value are directly given by the exponents in the production function (5.2). These results can of course be checked against direct calculations from the explicit supply and demand functions given by (6.4).

For the case of distribution along the ξ_1- and ξ_2-axes, with production function given by (5.38) and supply and demand functions given by (6.8–6.9), we have $\varepsilon = \frac{1}{2}$ and $s_{12} = 2$. Further we have $a_1 = Q_2/[2(Q_1+Q_2)]$ and $a_2 = Q_1/[2(Q_1+Q_2)]$. Corresponding to (6.41) we get the following substitution effects:

$$\varepsilon_{11} = -2\frac{Q_1}{Q_1+Q_2}, \quad \varepsilon_{12} = 2\frac{Q_1}{Q_1+Q_2},$$

$$\varepsilon_{21} = 2\frac{Q_2}{Q_1+Q_2}, \quad \varepsilon_{22} = -2\frac{Q_2}{Q_1+Q_2}. \tag{6.43}$$

Whereas the substitution terms in (6.42) are constant and on average of the order of magnitude of $\frac{1}{2}$ they are in (6.43) variable with input prices and on average of the order of magnitude of 1.

In the case of a uniform distribution over a region bounded by a right-angled curve, mentioned towards the end of Section 6.2, and with factor demand functions given by (6.14), the elasticity of substitution increases from 0 towards 1 as X increases from 0 towards infinity. The substitution terms ε_{ij} will correspondingly increase from 0 towards an average order of magnitude of $\frac{1}{2}$.

---

[6] The result given in (6.41) reflects the symmetry $a_i\varepsilon_{ij} = a_j\varepsilon_{ji}$ as well as the relations $\Sigma_j\varepsilon_{ij} = 0$ shown by Puu, see Puu (1968) pp. 122–123. The factor a_i/ε can be interpreted as the share of cost component No. i, Q_iV_i, in total cost $\Sigma_jQ_jV_j$ (denoted by κ_i in Puu's exposition) since $\Sigma_jQ_jV_j$ will make up a proportion ε of output value PX, see equation (4.31).

After these illustrations of the substitution terms in the "Slutsky equation" (6.31), let us consider the expansion terms.

The elasticities E_i, defined by (6.34), are obtained from the derivitatives in (6.20) when Q_1 and Q_2 are constant. We have $dV_i = (J/P)M(\xi_i)\,dP$ and $dX = (J/P)\,dP$, and accordingly

$$E_1 = M(\xi_1)\frac{X}{V_1} = \frac{M(\xi_1)}{\xi_1}, \quad E_2 = M(\xi_2)\frac{X}{V_2} = \frac{M(\xi_2)}{\xi_2}. \tag{6.44}$$

Since the supply derivative with respect to output price is J/P, we have for the supply elasticity

$$\eta = \frac{J}{X}. \tag{6.45}$$

Using (6.44–6.45) and (6.35) we then get the following expression for the expansion effects:

$$\text{Expansion effect in } e_{ij} = -a_jE_iE_j\eta = -\frac{J}{X}a_j\frac{M(\xi_i)}{\xi_i}\frac{M(\xi_j)}{\xi_j}. \tag{6.46}$$

It is easily seen by using $\partial X/\partial Q_i = -JM(\xi_i)/P$ that these expressions, in elasticity form, are equivalent to the terms in (6.24), or those components of (6.25) which do not depend on the spread in the distribution.

Comparing (6.40) and (6.46) we see that the expansion terms and the substitution terms are, apart from signs, composed in very similar ways, the difference being that in the place where the average input coefficients for marginal production coefficients enter in the expressions for the expansion effects we have the standard deviations in the case of the substitution effects.

Examples: The substitution effects were illustrated above by (6.42–6.43). For the Pareto-Cobb-Douglas case we have from previously given formulas $(J/X) = \alpha_1+\alpha_2$, $a_j = \alpha_j/(\alpha_1+\alpha_2+1)$, $M(\xi_i) = P\alpha_i/[Q_i(\alpha_1+\alpha_2)]$ and $\xi_i = P\alpha_i/[Q_i(\alpha_1+\alpha_2+1)]$. Collecting this we obtain the following expansion effect:

$$\text{Expansion effect in } e_{ij} = -\alpha_j\frac{\alpha_1+\alpha_2+1}{\alpha_1+\alpha_2}, \tag{6.47}$$

which, in view of (5.3) can also be written as $-\alpha_j/\varepsilon$, where ε is the scale elasticity.

Now consider the case of uniform distribution along the axes in the ξ_1, ξ_2-plane, i.e. the case of Section 5.3 with $s_1 = s_2 = 0$. From previous treatments of this example we get $J/X = 1$, a_1 and a_2 as given in connection with (6.43), $M(\xi_1) = PQ_2/[Q_1(Q_1+Q_2)]$, $M(\xi_2) = PQ_1/[Q_2(Q_1+Q_2)]$ and $\bar{\xi}_i = M(\xi_i)/2$. This yields the following result:

$$
\text{Expansion effects in}
\begin{bmatrix}
e_{11} & e_{12} \\
\\
e_{21} & e_{22}
\end{bmatrix}
=
\begin{bmatrix}
-2\dfrac{Q_2}{(Q_1+Q_2)} & -2\dfrac{Q_1}{(Q_1+Q_2)} \\
\\
-2\dfrac{Q_2}{(Q_1+Q_2)} & -2\dfrac{Q_1}{(Q_1+Q_2)}
\end{bmatrix}.
$$

$$(6.48)$$

We conclude this discussion by combining the substitution and expansion effects from (6.40) and (6.46) according to the "Slutsky equation" (6.31) in order to check that it brings us back to the original expressions given in (6.20):

Full elasticity:	Substitution effect:	Expansion effect:	Total:

$$
e_{11} \quad = -\frac{J}{X}a_1\left(\frac{\sigma_1}{\bar{\xi}_1}\right)^2 \quad -\frac{J}{X}a_1\left(\frac{M_1}{\bar{\xi}_1}\right)^2 \quad = -\frac{J}{P}M(\xi_1^2)\frac{Q_1}{V_1}
$$

$$
e_{12} \quad = \frac{J}{X}a_2\frac{\sigma_1\sigma_2}{\bar{\xi}_1\bar{\xi}_2} \quad -\frac{J}{X}a_2\frac{M_1 M_2}{\bar{\xi}_1\bar{\xi}_2} \quad = -\frac{J}{P}M(\xi_1\xi_2)\frac{Q_2}{V_1}
$$

$$
e_{21} \quad = \frac{J}{X}a_1\frac{\sigma_1\sigma_2}{\bar{\xi}_1\bar{\xi}_2} \quad -\frac{J}{X}a_1\frac{M_1 M_2}{\bar{\xi}_1\bar{\xi}_2} \quad = -\frac{J}{P}M(\xi_1\xi_2)\frac{Q_1}{V_2}
$$

$$
e_{22} \quad = -\frac{J}{X}a_2\left(\frac{\sigma_2}{\bar{\xi}_2}\right)^2 \quad -\frac{J}{X}a_2\left(\frac{M_2}{\bar{\xi}_2}\right)^2 \quad = -\frac{J}{P}M(\xi_2^2)\frac{Q_2}{V_2}
$$

$$(6.49)$$

We have here used M_i for $M(\xi_i)$. In the summation so as to obtain the totals to the right we have used the relationships given in (4.19–4.20). It is seen that the totals are in full conformity with the expressions in (6.20), Q_i/V_j entering the expressions in (6.49) because these are elasticities.

In the two specific cases used as examples in this section we get the following totals of substitution and expansion effects:

For the Pareto-Cobb-Douglas case we have e.g.

$$
e_{11} = -\frac{\alpha_2}{\alpha_1+\alpha_2} - \alpha_1\frac{\alpha_1+\alpha_2+1}{\alpha_1+\alpha_2} = -1 - \alpha_1, \tag{6.50}
$$

which is seen to agree with the explicit functional form in (6.4). In the same way the other elasticities are seen to agree with (6.4).

For the case of a uniform distribution along the axes in the ξ_1, ξ_2-plane we get by adding the effects from (6.43) and (6.48) $e_{11} = e_{22} = -2$, $e_{12} = e_{21} = 0$, which agrees with the explicit factor demand functions in (6.9).

6.4. *Factor remuneration and distribution*

From previous formulas it is seen that production factors Nos. 1 and 2 are remunerated according to the marginal productivities in the short-run macro production function. The corresponding factor shares in value of total output are given by

$$a_1 = \frac{Q_1 V_1}{PX}, \quad a_2 = \frac{Q_2 V_2}{PX} \tag{6.51}$$

which can also be written as

$$a_1 = \frac{V_1}{X}\bigg|\frac{1}{q_1}, \quad a_2 = \frac{V_2}{X}\bigg|\frac{1}{q_2}. \tag{6.52}$$

In the preceding section these proportions were introduced as cost components.

On the basis of the expressions in (6.52) the factor shares can be evaluated directly from a diagram like Figure 4.2, in which point A represents the "centre of gravity" of the capacity mass in the shaded area (the utilization region).

We will in general have $a_1 + a_2 < 1$. The difference corresponds to the share of quasi rent in total value of output. Total quasi rent will be determined by

$$R = \int\int_{G(Q_1/P,\ Q_2/P)} (P - Q_1\xi_1 - Q_2\xi_2) f(\xi_1, \xi_2)\, d\xi_1\, d\xi_2, \tag{6.53}$$

where the integral is taken over the utilization region G defined by (3.14). It is easily seen from this, using (3.15), that the proportion of total quasi rent in total output value is

$$a_3 = \frac{R}{PX} = 1 - a_1 - a_2. \tag{6.54}$$

Introducing the scale elasticity ε defined by (4.29) we can write this as

$$a_3 = 1 - \varepsilon, \tag{6.55}$$

i.e. the share of quasi rent is equal to 1 minus the scale elasticity. This, of course, expresses a classical result concerning the share of profits in production at the micro level. Since we showed in connection with Figure 4.2 that the scale elasticity is equal to the proportion OA/OB in the figure, it follows that the share of quasi rent in total value of output is given by:

$$\text{Share of quasi rent} = a_3 = \frac{AB}{OB} \text{ in Figure 4.2.} \qquad (6.56)$$

The whole situation is depicted in Figure 6.2.

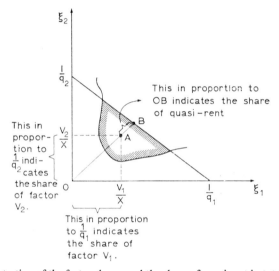

Fig. 6.2. Illustration of the factor shares and the share of quasi rent in total output value.

It is of course implicit in the logic of Figure 6.2 that the three proportions indicated in the figure add up to unity. This fact can also be proved directly by geometrical reasoning.

Consider Figure 6.3, which reproduces the relevant elements of Figure 6.2, supplemented with a line DG which is parallel with the zero quasi rent line EH and goes through the centre of gravity A. We have $OC = V_1/X$, $OF = V_2/X$, $OE = 1/q_1$ and $OH = 1/q_2$.

The factor shares according to Figure 6.2 are now $a_1 = OC/OE$, $a_2 = OF/OH$, $a_3 = AB/OB$. We want to satisfy ourselves that we have

$$a_1 + a_2 + a_3 = \frac{OC}{OE} + \frac{OF}{OH} + \frac{AB}{OB} = 1. \qquad (6.57)$$

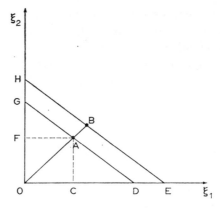

Fig. 6.3. Proof of the fact that the factor shares as indicated in Figure 6.2 add up to 1.

This can be done by transforming the proportions in (6.57) to proportions in OE. We clearly have $AB/OB = DE/OE$, since DG is parallel with EH. Next consider the term OF/OH. We will show that this is the same as CD/OE. This can be done e.g. by the following chain of equalities:

$$\frac{OF}{OH} = \frac{OF}{OG} \cdot \frac{OG}{OH} = \frac{CA}{OG} \cdot \frac{OD}{OE} = \frac{CD}{OD} \cdot \frac{OD}{OE} = \frac{CD}{OE}.$$

Altogether we have

$$\frac{OC}{OE} + \frac{OF}{OH} + \frac{AB}{OB} = \frac{OC}{OE} + \frac{CD}{OE} + \frac{DE}{OE} = 1. \tag{6.58}$$

From Figure 6.2 we see that the share of quasi rent in total value of output will be high when the region of positive capacity is wide along a ray from the origin, and the centre of gravity in the region of employed production units is located considerably closer to the origin than the boundary line corresponding to production units earning zero quasi rent. It corresponds to the situation in a production sector with much of the capacity concentrated in very modern and efficient production units, while some amount of rather inefficient production capacity must also be used in order to achieve the given total output (or the given total factor employment). In certain branches of production with restrictive business practices it has not been an unknown method of obtaining high quasi rents simply to create or sustain such a situation by deliberately avoiding closing down rather obsolete production units in order to justify claims for tariff protection etc.

In most of the explicit examples studied in Chapter 5 we derived the scale elasticity ε. Furthermore we derived the elasticity of substitution s_{12} which is closely related to the response of factor shares to changes in relative factor prices. We shall not repeat the results for ε and s_{12} here, but just refer to Chapter 5.

6.5. *A note on the generalized case*

In Section 3.6 we considered a generalization of our short-run macro production function by introducing a capacity utilization function $u(s)$ defined by (3.44), which is a more smoothly increasing function of quasi rent s than in our standard case where $u(s) = 0$ for $s < 0$ and $u(s) = 1$ for $s \geqq 0$. Total output and inputs are in this case given by (3.46), and the production function is implicitly determined by these equations. We shall briefly suggest how far the analysis for the standard case can be extended to hold also for this more general case.

The basic equations for the study of marginal productivities, supply and factor demand equations etc. for the standard case are (4.18). Similar equations can be derived for the generalized case. Differentiating the equations in (3.46) with respect to q_1 and q_2 we obtain equations which may be written in exactly the same form as (4.18), only with the factor J and the moments M redefined by

$$J = \int \int u'(1-q_1\xi_1-q_2\xi_2)f(\xi_1, \xi_2) \, d\xi_1 \, d\xi_2, \tag{6.59}$$

$$M(y) = \frac{1}{J} \int \int yu'(1-q_1\xi_1-q_2\xi_2)f(\xi_1, \xi_2) \, d\xi_1 \, d\xi_2. \tag{6.60}$$

The moments $M(\xi_1)$, $M(\xi_2)$, $M(\xi_1^2)$ etc. correspond to $y = \xi_1$, $y = \xi_2$, $y = \xi_1^2$ etc. in (6.60).

In (6.59–6.60) integration is extended over the whole region of positive capacity, and u' is

$$u'(s) = \frac{du(s)}{ds}. \tag{6.61}$$

It appears intuitively reasonable that the derivative of the capacity utilization function should enter as it does. If q_1 and/or q_2 change we will have responses in output and inputs particularly from production units with quasi rents at levels where the degree of utilization is sensitive to further changes in quasi rents, i.e. at levels where u' is big. The standard case can be identified as a limiting case where $u' \to 0$ for $s < 0$ and $s > 0$ and $u' \to \infty$ for $s = 0$. In this case all the weight in the function of the relevant moments will come from the production units along the zero quasi rent line.[7]

The analysis from Equations (4.18) onwards, and the corresponding results for supply and demand functions, cannot be reformulated so easily so as to cover the generalized case. The reason is that the relationships between the moments set out in (4.20) no longer hold, since these were based on the exact relationship $q_1\xi_1 + q_2\xi_2 = 1$. This implies, among other things, that the marginal productivities are no longer equal to q_1 and q_2. Instead we get

$$\frac{\partial X}{\partial V_1} = \frac{1}{D}[M(\xi_1)\sigma_2^2 - \sigma_{12}M(\xi_2)],$$

$$\frac{\partial V}{\partial V_2} = \frac{1}{D}[M(\xi_2)\sigma_1^2 - \sigma_{12}M(\xi_1)], \qquad (6.62)$$

where the moments M are as introduced by (6.60), σ_1, σ_2 and σ_{12} are standard deviations and the covariance corresponding to (4.19), and D is the determinant of the second order moments $M(\xi_i\xi_j)$. The simple expression to the right in (4.21) for this determinant however no longer holds since it was derived by using the exact relationship $q_1\xi_1 + q_2\xi_2 = 1$.[8]

From (6.62) it does not seem possible to extract any simple or transparent relationship between the marginal productivities and q_1 and q_2. If the correlation between ξ_1 and ξ_2 is non-positive in the distribution used in forming the moments, i.e. in the distribution with density $u'(1 - q_1\xi_1 - q_2\xi_2)f(\xi_1, \xi_2)/J$, then the marginal productivities in (6.62) are clearly positive. This case will occur if the region of positive capacity is broad and/or $u'(s)$ is large mainly in the neighbourhood of the zero quasi rent line. However, it is logically possible to conceive of cases where this correlation is positive, and to such a degree that one of the marginal productivities according to (6.62) becomes negative. (They cannot both be negative at the same time.) From this it is clear that many complicated cases may arise in the study of the properties of the short-run macro production function as well as the supply and factor demand functions based on the generalized case suggested in Section 3.6.

---

[7] This limiting process as well as some further aspects of the generalized case have been studied by Bjøntegård (1970).

[8] The expressions (6.62) are taken from Bjøntegård (1970).

6.6. *Short run and shorter run*

The supply functions and factor demand functions analysed in this chapter are "short-run" functions since they describe variations that can take place on the basis of a given stock of fixed capital represented by a given capacity distribution.

These functions will reflect the decreasing returns property of the short-run production function. If short-run variations in inputs and output take place approximately along isocline curves rather than by strong substitution due to drastic changes in relative input prices, we would expect output per unit of input to be lower at high output levels than at low output levels. This applies at the macro level. In the individual enterprises we should observe proportional variations according to the ex post functions assumed in Section 2.3. Under the generalizations discussed in Section 3.5 we might have decreasing returns even at the micro level. Increasing returns at the micro level are also permitted by the generalizations in Section 3.5, but, according to the optimization assumptions made, we would not *observe* outputs in individual enterprises at levels where increasing returns occur.

In recent years there has been a growing interest in the study of short-run fluctuations in output and demand for labour. Empirical research in this field seems to reveal a pattern which does not agree with the above-mentioned implications of our theory; in fact, it seems to be a rather universal finding that output per man increases with output in the short run, as if there were increasing returns to labour in the short run.[9]

Several models have been constructed which more or less successfully try to explain this pattern. These models take into account lags in decisions, costs of readjustment, costs of hiring and firing labour, formation of expectations etc.

Fair, in the study referred to in note 9, has constructed and implemented empirically with apparent success a model which assumes the same type of ex post technology at the micro level as we have assumed in our standard model. In his model the distinction between hours of work paid-for and hours of work actually used in the production process is essential. Only the former is observed in traditional statistics, while the latter is relevant for production. Fair shows that the one is a poor proxy for the other as far as short run variations are concerned, and constructs a model which explains

---

[9] This research, and models designed to explain these empirical findings, are surveyed by Fair (1969).

the systematic variation in the proportion between the two. The model explains why labour paid-for will fluctuate less than labour actually used, and thereby create the impression that there are increasing returns to labour in the short run.

From Fair's study we may draw the conclusion that the observed phenomena referred to do not contradict the technological assumptions underlying our model. But, in the case of labour, there is apparently a "short run" in which demand, as it is observed in the market, does not conform with the factor demand functions derived from our short-run production function by a simple and essentially static type of optimisation. The variations studied in the case of the demand for labour are monthly or even weekly variations. This is a shorter run than the one in which our short-run functions would be expected to hold good.

Perhaps the relation between the two types of short-run analysis might be expressed by saying that while the present study is concerned with short-run equilibrium, the labour demand studies referred to are concerned with short-run disequilibrium dynamics.[10]

---

[10] See in this connection also Rasche and Shapiro (1968), pp. 132–133.

CHAPTER 7

Some elements of the dynamics of production

7.1. *Introductory remarks*

Within our framework there are several factors which contribute to changes in production through time.

First there are of course changes in current inputs V_1 and V_2 generating changes in total output which we may visualize as movements along the surface corresponding to the short-run macro production function $X = F(V_1, V_2)$.

Next there are investments in new equipment. These materialize as new production units which enter the capacity distribution and create corresponding shifts in the short-run macro function. Scrapping of existing production units is a corresponding negative component.

Finally there is technological progress. There is a natural distinction between embodied and disembodied technological progress. However, there seems to be a need for a further sub-classification of disembodied progress according to how it influences capacity and/or input requirements of existing production units.

We shall consider these elements in turn. (It is, however, not necessary to devote any special section to the changes in current inputs V_1 and V_2.) For convenience we shall sometimes consider additions of new capacity and shifts in functions without relating these elements to the flow of time, but we shall towards the end of the present chapter collect all effects in a "complete growth equation" where we consider the changes in inputs, output and functional forms as taking place as a continuous process through time.

7.2. *Effects of new capacity on the short-run macro production function*

New production units are selected from among the possibilities indicated by an ex ante function as discussed in Section 2.2 and symbolized by Equation (2.1). When a new unit is ready for operation it will represent production possibilities given by an ex post production function as discussed in Section 2.3 and more specifically indicated by (2.2).

If the ex ante function has been stationary for a long time, if furthermore prices and the interest rate have been, and are expected to remain constant, and if several other factors surveyed in Section 3.1 have been absent, then the new production units might be expected to be distributed in the ξ_1, ξ_2-diagram similarly to the already existing production units.

In general one would, however, expect the new capacity to be distributed in the ξ_1, ξ_2-diagram differently from the already existing capacity. In order to link the discussion up with the theoretical study of the short-run function in Chapters 3 and 4 we again introduce a continuous formulation. We now let $f^+(\xi_1, \xi_2)$ represent *the form* of the distribution of new capacity and X^+ the total new capacity added during a certain time interval. If V_1^+ and V_2^+ represent input requirements by the new production units we have

$$\int \int f^+(\xi_1, \xi_2) \, d\xi_1 \, d\xi_2 = 1,$$

$$V_1^+ = X^+ \int \int \xi_1 f^+(\xi_1, \xi_2) \, d\xi_1 \, d\xi_2 = X^+ m_1^+,$$

$$V_2^+ = X^+ \int \int \xi_2 f^+(\xi_1, \xi_2) \, d\xi_1 \, d\xi_2 = X^+ m_2^+, \qquad (7.1)$$

where the integration covers all ξ_1, ξ_2-values. In (7.1) m_1^+ and m_2^+ are the average inputs per unit of output for the new capacity. The first integral is equal to unity because f^+ gives the *relative* distribution of new capacity, while X^+ indicates the absolute amount.

When the new capacity indicated by X^+ and the distribution function $f^+()$ is added to the capacity distribution left over from the past, then we obtain a new short-run macro function given implicitly by

$$X = \int \int_{G(q_1, q_2)} [f(\xi_1, \xi_2) + X^+ f^+(\xi_1, \xi_2)] \, d\xi_1 \, d\xi_2,$$

$$V_1 = \int \int_{G(q_1, q_2)} \xi_1 [f(\xi_1, \xi_2) + X^+ f^+(\xi_1, \xi_2)] \, d\xi_1 \, d\xi_2,$$

$$V_2 = \int \int_{G(q_1, q_2)} \xi_2 [f(\xi_1, \xi_2) + X^+ f^+(\xi_1, \xi_2)] \, d\xi_1 \, d\xi_2. \qquad (7.2)$$

These formulas correspond to (3.15) or (4.2). From (7.2) we could study the effects of X^+ and f^+ on the macro function $X = F(V_1, V_2)$. It is quite easy to see how the whole analysis through Chapters 4 and 6 could be repeated with (7.2) replacing (3.15), and how the results in terms of various moments in the distribution $f(\xi_1, \xi_2)$ would then repeat themselves in terms of moments of $f(\xi_1, \xi_2)$ and $f^+(\xi_1, \xi_2)$. We shall not consider all these aspects, but concentrate on the vertical shift in the short-run macro function and the effect upon the marginal rate of substitution corresponding to various V_1, V_2-constellations. We shall limit attention to the case of a "small" addition of new capacity so that we may be satisfied with first-order approximations.

Let us introduce in (7.2) the functions h, g_1 and g_2 defined by (4.2) and furthermore introduce similar functions defined on the basis of the distribution of the new capacity:

$$g^+(q_1, q_2) = \int \int_{G(q_1, q_2)} f^+(\xi_1, \xi_2)\, d\xi_1\, d\xi_2,$$

$$h_i^+(q_1, q_2) = \int \int_{G(q_1, q_2)} \xi_i f^+(\xi_1, \xi_2)\, d\xi_1\, d\xi_2 \quad (i=1,2). \tag{7.3}$$

These functions give additional output *realized* and additional inputs *used* per unit of new capacity *created* when the zero quasi rent line is $q_1\xi_1 + q_2\xi_2 = 1$. When q_1 and q_2 are such that all new capacity earns non-negative quasi rent, then we have according to (7.1):

$$\left.\begin{aligned} g^+(q_1, q_2) &= 1, \\ h_i^+(q_1, q_2) &= m_i^+ \quad (i=1,2) \end{aligned}\right\} \begin{aligned} &\text{when } q_1\xi_1 + q_2\xi_2 \leqq 1 \text{ for all} \\ &\xi_1, \xi_2 \text{ for which } f^+(\xi_1, \xi_2) > 0. \end{aligned} \tag{7.4}$$

Notice that h_1^+ and h_2^+ do not indicate average input coefficients for *utilized* new capacity. These average input coefficients are h_1^+/g^+ and h_2^+/g^+.

With the notation introduced above, (7.2) can be written as

$$\begin{aligned} X &= g(q_1, q_2) + X^+ g^+(q_1, q_2), \\ V_1 &= h_1(q_1, q_2) + X^+ h_1^+(q_1, q_2), \\ V_2 &= h_2(q_1, q_2) + X^+ h_2^+(q_1, q_2). \end{aligned} \tag{7.5}$$

These relationships define the new production function after the addition of the new capacity X^+.

In order to study the vertical shift in the macro production function generated by the addition of the new capacity we utilize the pre-shift functional form $F()$ given by (4.3–4.4). Since we have $F() = g(h_1^{-1}(), h_2^{-1}())$ we may clearly write, on the basis of (7.5):

$$X = F\left(V_1 - X^+ h_1^+(q_1, q_2), V_2 - X^+ h_2^+(q_1, q_2)\right) + X^+ g^+(q_1, q_2). \tag{7.6}$$

The interpretation of this relation is as follows: With given values of V_1

and V_2 there are associated parameters q_1 and q_2 through the two last equations of (7.5). The output X obtained is then given by (7.6), where $F()$ is the form of the short-run macro function before the addition of new capacity. It is seen that output is raised by the additional output from the utilized part of the new capacity represented by $X^+ g^+(q_1, q_2)$, while at the same time output shrinks because the utilization of new capacity draws current inputs from old production units. The latter component is represented by the deductions of $X^+ h_1^+(q_1, q_2)$ and $X^+ h_2^+(q_1, q_2)$ from the total inputs V_1 and V_2 under the functional symbol F in (7.6). The question now is, what is the net effect of these components, i.e. how much higher is X calculated from (7.6) than what it would have been according to the production function based only on the old capacity for constant total inputs V_1 and V_2?

In order to have a first-order approximation to this we differentiate (7.6) with respect to X^+ and evaluate the derivative at $X^+ = 0$. This gives

$$\left. \frac{\partial X}{\partial X^+} \right|_{X^+ = 0} = -h_1^+(q_1, q_2)F_1 - h_2^+(q_1, q_2)F_2 + g^+(q_1, q_2),$$

where F_1 and F_2 are the partial derivatives of F. Since q_1 and q_2 also change with X^+ the derivatives of h_1^+, h_2^+ and g^+ are in principle also involved in the expression, but they disappear when the derivative is evaluated at $X^+ = 0$.

Now at $X^+ = 0$ the derivatives F_1 and F_2 are the same as q_1 and q_2. The expression above can then be written as

$$\left. \frac{\partial X}{\partial X^+} \right|_{X^+ = 0} = \int \int_{G(q_1, q_2)} (1 - q_1\xi_1 - q_2\xi_2)f^+(\xi_1, \xi_2)\, d\xi_1\, d\xi_2$$
$$= g^+(q_1, q_2) - q_1 h_1^+(q_1, q_2) - q_2 h_2^+(q_1, q_2), \qquad (7.7)$$

where we have used the definitions (7.3) of g^+, h_1^+ and h_2^+.

The interpretation of (7.7) is simple: The net increase in total output by the addition of new capacity is measured by the quasi rent (in terms of output) earned by the utilized part of the new capacity. This conclusion is natural since quasi rents measure the superiority of new production units over marginal units from which current inputs have to be released in order to operate the new units. The conclusion is also in full conformity with the interpretation of the dual variables r^i in the discrete case studied in Section 2.4. These dual variables were associated with the capacity constraints in the ex post production functions of the individual production units and thus indicated the increase in total output by relaxation of the capacity constraints. As was pointed out towards the end of Section 2.4 these dual variables r^i were equal to the non-negative quasi rents. Investment in new production capacity is of course precisely such a relaxation of capacity constraints.[1]

In an actual growth process one would expect wages to increase relatively more than costs of capital. In the investment decision, i.e. the choice from the ex ante function, one would then tend to substitute capital for labour. This would manifest itself in a lower average input coefficient for labour in the distribution $f^+(\xi_1, \xi_2)$ of new capacity than in the distribution $f(\xi_1, \xi_2)$ of old capacity. For other current inputs the expected development would not always be quite so clear. In many cases one would perhaps expect the new production units to be located in the ξ_1, ξ_2-diagram with the centre of gravity m_1^+, m_2^+ south-west of the centre of gravity of the distribution of old capacity, but there are obvious exceptions to this. In any case, except perhaps for early phases of deep depressions, one would expect all new capacity created at any moment to be able to earn non-negative quasi rents and thus to be put in operation. In such cases (7.4) is valid and formulas (7.2) or (7.5) take the simpler form

$$X = g(q_1, q_2) + X^+,$$

$$V_1 = h_1(q_1, q_2) + X^+ m_1^+,$$

$$V_2 = h_2(q_1, q_2) + X^+ m_2^+, \tag{7.8}$$

where m_1^+ and m_2^+ are average input coefficients for all new capacity created. Correspondingly (7.6) takes the form

$$X = F(V_1 - X^+ m_1^+, V_2 - X^+ m_2^+) + X^+ \tag{7.9}$$

and (7.7) reduces to

$$\frac{\partial X}{\partial X^+} = 1 - q_1 m_1^+ - q_2 m_2^+. \tag{7.10}$$

Since the quasi rents earned on the new capacity are larger the smaller are q_1 and q_2, and since q_1 and q_2 are smaller the farther towards the north-east we are in the V_1, V_2-plane, the shift in the short-run macro function $F(V_1,$

---

[1] Compare in this connection also Solow (1962), Section 4, where the author discusses the concept of marginal productivity in a putty-clay model with only one current input (labour) and concludes that "the marginal physical product of a machine ... is precisely the quasi-rent it earns in production".

V_2) will clearly be smaller near to the origin and larger towards the north-east in the V_1, V_2-plane.

Let us next consider the effect upon the marginal rate of substitution, as given by Equation (4.26), of an addition of new capacity. We then consider the two last equations in (7.5) and differentiate these implicitly with respect to X^+ for $X^+ = 0$, keeping V_1 and V_2 fixed. This gives

$$h_{11} \frac{\partial q_1}{\partial X^+} + h_{12} \frac{\partial q_2}{\partial X^+} = -h_1^+,$$

$$h_{21} \frac{\partial q_1}{\partial X^+} + h_{22} \frac{\partial q_2}{\partial X^+} = -h_2^+, \tag{7.11}$$

where $h_{ij} = \partial h_i / \partial q_j$ for $i, j = 1, 2$. (Terms involving $\partial h_i^+ / \partial q_j$ vanish at $X^+ = 0$.)

This system is exactly the same as the one that was solved in Section 4.2, where we used the two last equations of (4.5) in order to express dq_1 and dq_2 in terms of dV_1 and dV_2. We can therefore apply the solution given by (4.22). Thus we have

$$\frac{\partial q_1}{\partial X^+} = \frac{q_2^2}{J\sigma_1^2} [M(\xi_2^2)h_1^+ - M(\xi_1\xi_2)h_2^+],$$

$$\frac{\partial q_2}{\partial X^+} = \frac{q_2^2}{J\sigma_1^2} [-M(\xi_1\xi_2)h_1^+ + M(\xi_1^2)h_2^+]. \tag{7.12}$$

We are now particularly interested in the change in q_1/q_2. We therefore use the expressions in (7.12) to evaluate

$$\frac{1}{q_1/q_2} \frac{\partial(q_1/q_2)}{\partial X^+} = \frac{1}{q_1} \frac{\partial q_1}{\partial X^+} - \frac{1}{q_2} \frac{\partial q_2}{\partial X^+}. \tag{7.13}$$

Using the relationships $q_1 M(\xi_1\xi_2) + q_2 M(\xi_2^2) = M(\xi_2)$ and $q_1 M(\xi_1^2) + q_2 M(\xi_1\xi_2) = M(\xi_1)$ which have been used on several occasions before, we obtain[2]

$$\frac{1}{q_1/q_2} \frac{\partial(q_1/q_2)}{\partial X^+} = \frac{g^+}{J} \frac{M(\xi_1)}{\sigma_1} \frac{M(\xi_2)}{\sigma_2} \left(\frac{h_1^+/g^+}{M(\xi_1)} - \frac{h_2^+/g^+}{M(\xi_2)} \right). \tag{7.14}$$

Since the addition of new capacity causes a shift in the short-run macro production function, we may apply the concepts of neutrality and bias which

---

[2] A similar formula (for the case where (7.4) is fulfilled) was first developed by Mr. Steinar Strøm in an unpublished note.

are customarily used to characterize the nature of technological progress in relation to production functions. According to traditional usage (Hicksian tradition) progress is neutral if it leaves q_1/q_2 unaffected and it is biased in the factor No. i-saving direction if it decreases the marginal productivity of factor No. i relatively to the other factor ($i = 1, 2$). We see from (7.14) that the decisive element in our context is the proportion between the average input coefficients of utilized new capacity (h_1^+/g^+ and h_2^+/g^+) as compared with the proportion between average input coefficients of the marginal production units of the old capacity ($M(\xi_1)$ and $M(\xi_2)$). We have the following results:

The shift in the short-run macro production function by the addition of new capacity is

$$\left.\begin{array}{l} \text{factor 1-saving} \\ \text{neutral} \\ \text{factor 2-saving} \end{array}\right\} \text{according as} \left\{\begin{array}{l} h_1^+/h_2^+ < M(\xi_1)/M(\xi_2) \\ h_1^+/h_2^+ = M(\xi_1)/M(\xi_2) \\ h_1^+/h_2^+ > M(\xi_1)/M(\xi_2). \end{array}\right. \quad (7.15)$$

This result is rather convenient in that new capacity which involves relatively low requirements for a certain input causes a shift in the macro function which is biased in the direction of saving the same factor as judged by the conventional criterion in terms of shifts in the marginal rate of substitution.

In Figure 7.1 we have illustrated a case of a factor 1-saving shift in the short-run macro function, i.e. a shift which increases the marginal produc-

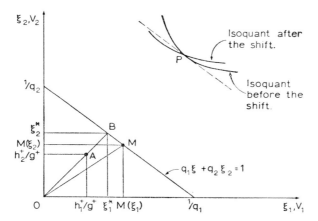

Fig. 7.1. Addition of new capacity which generates a Factor 1-saving shift in the short-run macro production function.

tivity of factor No. 2 relatively more than the marginal productivity of factor No. 1. In a similar way as in Figure 4.4 we have both the capacity distribution and the isoquants of the macro function in the same figure.

Point P in the figure represents the V_1, V_2-constellation, which corresponds to the indicated position of the zero quasi rent line. Its slope at P is the same as the slope of the zero quasi rent line. In the figure the utilized new capacity uses relatively less of factor No. 1 in proportion to factor No. 2 than the marginal units of the old capacity, i.e. $h_1^+/h_2^+ < M(\xi_1)/M(\xi_2)$, and in accordance with this the post-shift isoquant through P has a lesser slope.

The new isoquant through P does of course not represent the same output as the old isoquant through P. The difference is indicated by (7.7).

If we like, an expression pertaining to this shift can also be found in the figure. We then first rewrite (7.7) as

$$\frac{\partial X}{\partial X^+} = g^+(q_1, q_2) \left[1 - q_1 \frac{h_1^+(q_1, q_2)}{g^+(q_1, q_2)} - q_2 \frac{h_2^+(q_1, q_2)}{g^+(q_1, q_2)} \right]. \qquad (7.16)$$

Now define ξ_1^* and ξ_2^* by the requirements

$$\frac{h_1^+}{g^+} = \alpha \xi_1^*, \qquad \frac{h_2^+}{g^+} = \alpha \xi_2^*, \qquad q_1 \xi_1^* + q_2 \xi_2^* = 1, \qquad (7.17)$$

where α is a factor of proportionality; in other words, ξ_1^* and ξ_2^* are input coefficients satisfying the zero quasi rent condition and having the same proportion as the average input coefficients for the utilized new capacity. The corresponding point in Figure 7.1 is marked off as B. (The construction is the same as for $\tilde{\xi}_1$, $\tilde{\xi}_2$ in connection with the discussion of the scale elasticity, cf. Figure 4.2.) The proportionality factor α is equal to OA/OB in the figure.

Using (7.17) in connection with (7.16) we obtain

$$\frac{\partial X}{\partial X^+} = g^+(q_1, q_2) (1 - \alpha), \qquad (7.18)$$

which says that the vertical shift in the macro production function per unit of new capacity is the share of new capacity which is utilized (g^+) multiplied by the proportion $(1 - \alpha)$ which is represented by $1 - (OA/OB) = AB/OB$ in Figure 7.1. This latter proportion is a natural expression of how much more efficient the utilized new capacity is than the marginal units of the old capacity from which it draws current inputs.

Summarizing we may say that the proportion AB/OB in the figure is indicative of the size of the vertical shift in the macro production function per unit of new capacity while the angle between OB and OM is indicative of the bias of the shift. But in neither case does the geometrical illustration give a direct and complete measure since other factors are also involved, as is seen from the formulae.

For cases where (7.8–7.9) are valid, some of the results illustrated in Figure 7.1 could be derived more directly by geometric considerations based on the form (7.9).

The results given above are "local". A natural question of a "global" nature is whether it is conceivable that the addition of new capacity can shift the whole macro function in a way which can be represented in a simple parametric form. It seems to be difficult to find other such cases of general interest than the rather trivial case where the new capacity is distributed in the same way as the old capacity. However, in special cases there are of course possibilities of simple parametric shifts of the macro function. Consider e.g. the case studied in Section 5.6. Here we have a uniform capacity distribution over a region bounded by a right-angled curve with the corner located at $\xi_1 = s_1$, $\xi_2 = s_2$. New capacity may here be added below and to the left of the old capacity in Figure 5.7 in such a way that the complete capacity distribution after the new capacity has been added is of the same form as before, only with smaller values of s_1 and s_2. Then the short-run macro function would retain the form (5.86) with the parameters s_1 and s_2 shifting towards lower values.

It would be possible to follow up the discussion above by considering the effects of new capacity on supply and factor demand functions as well as distributive shares. This thread will, however, not be taken up here.

7.3. *Embodied technological progress*

Embodied technological progress can in our framework be defined as favourable shifts in the ex ante production function which leave the efficiency of already established production units unaffected.[3]

This type of technological progress affects the short-run macro production function only by influencing the distribution of the new capacity added.

In the formulae of the preceding section we indicated the amount of new capacity simply by a figure X^+ without relating it to the amount of invest-

---

[3] In professor Svennilson's terminology this is "the N-type of technical progress" where "N" indicates that it affects only New equipment. See Svennilson (1964), p. 106. It is the same type of progress which is discussed in Chs. II and III of Salter (1960).

ment. The effect of embodied technological progress cannot then be revealed explicitly. As has been suggested already new capacity will in most practical cases largely be distributed with more favourable input coefficients ξ_1 and ξ_2 than old capacity. In common language this will certainly often be called technological progress but may be the result of substitution effects whereby more capital is invested in each unit of new capacity in order to obtain lower current input coefficients. Thus, only by considering the amount of investment is it possible to distinguish between such substitutions on the basis of a given ex ante function and technological progress in the form of shifts in the ex ante function.

In Section 2.2 we introduced the ex ante function as

$$\bar{x} = \phi(\bar{v}_1, \bar{v}_2, \bar{k}), \tag{7.19}$$

where $\bar{x}$ is the capacity, $\bar{v}_1$ and $\bar{v}_2$ are current input requirements at full capacity utilization, and $\bar{k}$ is the capital invested in a new production unit. By optimization with respect to the size of new production units we derived a "technique relation"

$$\Psi(\xi_1, \xi_2, \xi_3) = 1, \tag{7.20}$$

which indicates the technological possibilities in terms of current input coefficients ξ_1 and ξ_2 and capital per unit of output capacity ξ_3. This relation was established in Section 2.5 for the purpose of discussing the concept of a long-run macro function, but it is clear that the same relation is relevant for discussing the types of investments that can be made in a certain period.

Formulae (7.19) and (7.20) have been numbered before, but have been given new numbers appropriate to this chapter for ease of reference.

When new capacity as given by (7.1) is added the technique relation (7.20) means that X^+, V_1^+, V_2^+ and the amount of new capital K^+ will have to consist of units with input coefficients ξ_1, ξ_2, ξ_3 which satisfy (7.20), or at least are not more efficient than what is implied by (7.20). If we let E be the (convex) set of possible ξ_1, ξ_2, ξ_3-combinations limited by the technique relation (7.20), then X^+, V_1^+, V_2^+ and K^+ clearly have to be such that (m_1^+, m_2^+, m_3^+) defined by

$$\frac{V_1^+}{X^+} = m_1^+, \quad \frac{V_2^+}{X^+} = m_2^+, \quad \frac{K^+}{X^+} = m_3^+ \tag{7.21}$$

belongs to this set E.

The shift in the short-run macro function generated by new capacity is measured by the quasi rent it earns. If we consider for simplicity the case where all new capacity is utilized it is measured by the expression in (7.10). Since we have $X^+ = K^+/m_3^+$, where m_3^+ is the average capital coefficient of new capacity this can instead be written as

$$\frac{\partial X}{\partial K^+} = \frac{1 - q_1 m_1^+ - q_2 m_2^+}{m_3^+}. \tag{7.22}$$

By this the output-increasing shift in the short-run macro function is expressed per unit of new capital and is seen to be equal to quasi rents per unit of new capital.

The fact that the point (m_1^+, m_2^+, m_3^+) now has to belong to the feasible set E mentioned in connection with (7.21) clearly sets a limit to the value of the expression in (7.22). For low values of capital per unit of output the numerator in (7.22) will be negative or zero; for increasing m_3^+ the numerator will get positive; if we increase m_3^+ further there will sooner or later be a less than proportional increase in the numerator and the whole expression (7.22) will again decrease.

It appears that the immediate output effect of investments would be maximized by choosing investments so as to maximize the immediate rate of quasi rent per unit of new capital. However, in an economy which aims at efficiency over some longer time rather than at one point of time, investment decisions should, with the technology assumed here, be taken on the basis of present *and future* prices (in practice of course expected future prices) rather than current prices only.[4] This point will not be pursued here. The main thing to be observed in the present context is that the technique relation sets a limit to the output effect of new investment as given by (7.22).

The effect of embodied technological progress is that it shifts the boundary (7.20) and thus tends to call forth a more favourable set of average input coefficients m_1^+, m_2^+, m_3^+ for the new capacity than what would have been possible in the absence of this shift. What will be the effect on the shift in the short-run macro function as given by (7.22) of having more favourable input coefficients for the new capacity?

Consider first, for simplicity, a case where the ex ante function is

$$\bar{x} = (1+\alpha)\phi(\bar{v}_1, \bar{v}_2, \bar{k}) \text{ with } \alpha > 0 \tag{7.23}$$

instead of (7.19). The technique relation (7.20) is then replaced by

$$\Psi((1+\alpha)\xi_1, (1+\alpha)\xi_2, (1+\alpha)\xi_3) = 1. \tag{7.24}$$

---

[4] Compare Johansen (1967).

This permits input coefficients which are reduced to $1/(1+\alpha)$ in proportion to what they would otherwise have been. Suppose now that this manifests itself in average input coefficients which are $m_i^+/(1+\alpha)$ instead of m_i^+ ($i = 1, 2, 3$). Then the shift in the short-run macro function will be given by

$$\left(\frac{\partial X}{\partial K^+}\right)^\alpha = \frac{1+\alpha-q_1 m_1^+ - q_2 m_2^+}{m_3^+} \tag{7.25}$$

instead of (7.22), where the superscript α indicates that we are considering the case of the ex ante function being improved by a proportion α.

From (7.25) and (7.22) we can calculate by what proportion the shift in the short-run macro function is increased due to the progress which is reflected by α. We obtain

$$\frac{(\partial X/\partial K^+)^\alpha - (\partial X/\partial K^+)}{(\partial X/\partial K^+)} = \frac{\alpha}{1-q_1 m_1^+ - q_2 m_2^+}. \tag{7.26}$$

It is seen that the shift is increased by more than the proportion α when $0 < (1-q_1 m_1^+ - q_2 m_2^+) < 1$. In fact, if the capital input coefficient m_3^+ alone had been reduced by a proportion α it would have been sufficient to increase $(\partial X/\partial K^+)$ by a proportion α since this would have given, as a proportion, α more of new capacity with the same quasi rent per unit of output. The additional gain in the case where all input coefficients are decreased is due to the fact that less of current inputs have to be withdrawn from marginal production units in order to exploit each new unit of capacity.

The expression in (7.26) gives the effect on the shift at a certain point on the short-run macro function, namely at the V_1, V_2-point corresponding to q_1, q_2. It is clear that the value of the expression in (7.26) is very high when q_1 and q_2 are so high that $1-q_1 m_1^+ - q_2 m_2^+$ is near to zero. In this case we are at a point where the new capacity in the case of no progress is barely profitable in operation and an improvement in input coefficients increases its net contribution to output proportionately very much. For higher values of V_1 and V_2, corresponding to lower values of q_1 and q_2, the expression in (7.26) attains a lower value, and as q_1 and q_2 tend to become smaller, which means that we approach full capacity utilization, the value of the expression in (7.26) tends to α. For this part of the short-run macro function the shift due to the new capacity is thus raised by a proportion which is nearly the same as the relative shift in the ex ante function. The addition to the full capacity of the sector as a whole is of course raised by exactly the proportion α.

The type of progress by which (7.19) and (7.20) were replaced by (7.23) and (7.24) may naturally be called neutral progress. In our context the shift in the technique relation is the essential thing. A neutral progress in the technique relation as indicated by (7.24) can of course be brought about by more general types of shifts in the ex ante function since it is irrelevant for the technique relation how the ex ante function shifts at points which are not efficient (in the sense underlaying the definition of the technique relation) or will not become efficient as a result of the shift.[5]

Various types of biases of technological progress could be defined in connection with the ex ante function and the corresponding technique relation.[6] We shall not go deeply into this, but only make some suggestions concerning the effects on the shift in the short-run macro function.

Consider first a bias in the capital-using direction which tends to raise m_3^+ and decrease m_1^+ and m_2^+ as compared with the case of neutral progress. The effect of this on the shift in the short-run macro function as expressed by (7.22) is ambiguous because less new capacity will be created per unit of capital invested while at the same time the quasi rent per unit of new capacity is increased.[7] We will definitely have a positive effect on the shift for such low values of V_1 and V_2 (high values of q_1 and q_2) that the quasi rent of new capacity is barely positive. For V_1, V_2-points nearer to full capacity utilization the effect of the capital-using bias of the progress on the shift in the short-run function may be negative. In-between there will then be a break-even region.

A bias as between the two current inputs in the form of the technological progress will also have effects on the shift in the short-run macro function which are different for different parts of the function. Let us consider a factor 1-saving bias which tends to make m_1^+ smaller and m_2^+ larger than they would otherwise be. This will cause an increase in the shift as expressed by $\partial X/\partial K^+$ in Equation (7.22) when q_1/q_2 is large, i.e. in the part of the input space where V_2/V_1 is large, and cause a decrease in the shift when q_1/q_2 is small, i.e. in the part of the input space where V_2/V_1 is small. Between these cases is a case where the shift is unaffected.

The various cases are illustrated in Figure 7.2. (We could have explained

---

[5] How the function shifts outside these points may, however, be of relevance for the average input coefficients $m_i{}^+$ ($i = 1, 2, 3$) of the new capacity when this does not consist only of similar and efficient production units.

[6] Compare the discussion in Ch. III of Salter (1960). The discussion would, however, have to be somewhat more complicated in our case than in Salter's because we recognize more factors of production than labour and capital.

[7] Per unit of new capacity created the shift in the short-run macro function will of course be larger in the capital-using case, cf. (7.10).

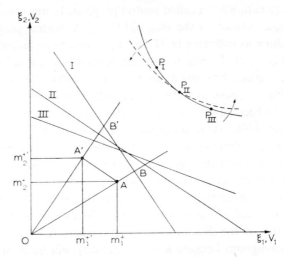

Fig. 7.2. The effect of a Factor-1 saving bias in embodied technological progress on the isoquants of the short-run macro production function.

this in connection with Figure 7.1, but prefer not to overburden it.) Let us assume that due to a factor 1-saving bias we get additional capacity with average input coefficients $m_1^{+\prime}$ and $m_2^{+\prime}$ instead of m_1^+ and m_2^+, i.e. point A' instead of point A in the figure (while m_3^+ is the same). The lines I, II and III represent three positions of the zero quasi rent line $q_1\xi_1 + q_2\xi_2 = 1$ with q_1/q_2 decreasing from I to III. In position II the zero quasi rent line is parallel with the line connecting A and A'.

The three positions of the zero quasi rent line correspond to the same total output X in the short-run macro function before the shift, i.e. they correspond to three points on the same isoquant as illustrated by the points P_I, P_{II} and P_{III} in the figure. (As in Figure 4.4 the tangents of the isoquant at the points P_I, P_{II} and P_{III} are parallel to the lines I, II and III respectively.)

Now consider first position I of the zero quasi rent line. Exploiting the reasoning in connection with Figure 7.1 we see that $A'B'/OB'$ is larger than AB/OB and accordingly the shift in the short-run macro function is larger at P_I for A' than for A, i.e. as a result of the factor 1-saving bias. For position II the corresponding proportions would be the same for A' and A and accordingly the bias in the progress would have no effect at point P_{II} on the isoquant. At P_{III} there would be a negative effect.

The effects mentioned here would clearly tend to rotate the isoquant in the direction indicated by the dotted curve through P_{II}. Applying conventional criteria for bias to this rotation of the isoquant we reach the very tidy result that a factor 1-saving bias in the ex ante function, via the effect on the average input coefficients of new capacity, tends to shift the isoquants of the short-run macro function in the factor 1-saving direction.

In the discussion above we have concentrated on the effects of embodied technological progress, via the location of the distribution of new capacity on the size of the shift and the slope of the isoquants of the short-run macro function. We could discuss also the effects on the scale properties and the elasticity of substitution in the short-run macro function. This could be done on the basis of e.g. Figure 4.2 and formulae (4.48–4.48′).[8]

Above we have talked rather vaguely about the relation between shifts in the ex ante production function, or the technique relation, and the actual manifestation of these shifts through the distribution of new capacity as represented particularly by the average input coefficients of the new capacity, m_1^+, m_2^+ and m_3^+. If all new capacity created in a period of time were efficiently chosen and of the same type, then shifts in the ex ante function would bear a direct and firm relation to the input coefficients of new capacity. If we consider the ex ante function as a sort of frontier function and admit the influence of factors which cause non-efficient choices, as we have done implicitly above, then the connection is not so firm. The improvement in input coefficients of new capacity as compared with previously constructed capacity could then be considered as a mixture of two effects: (1) Shifts in the ex ante function, and (2) better utilization of already existing technological knowledge. The first effect is embodied technological progress in the most narrow sense. The latter effect could perhaps be described as a movement of the individual subjective ex ante functions towards the frontier describing the most advanced existing technological know-how (compare the discussion towards the end of Section 2.2), i.e. improved dissemmination of existing know-how, together with improved decision-making, reduction of distortions, disturbances etc. This distinction is of course inflicted with much of the same ambiguity as the concept of the ex ante function itself, as discussed in Section 2.2. But, in an approximate way I think it can be drawn meaningfully in many practical cases. The distinction will of course have practical implications. To augment the first type of effect is a matter of research and inventiveness while the augmentation of the second type of

---

[8] For a discussion of the form of shifts in the technique relation there are many considerations in a recent paper by Atkinson and Stiglitz (1969), which are relevant within our framework.

effect is a matter of information, organisation and efficient decision-making. There is in practice much talk about the importance of the latter group of factors, and it is an attractive feature of the present approach to production studies that there is a place in the framework where such effects can be explicitly taken care of.

7.4. *The concept of disembodied technological progress*

Disembodied technological progress affects the modes of operation of existing production units in such a way as to improve their performance. Such progress will cause a shift in the short-run macro production function even in the absence of investment.[9]

Since the short-run macro function is derived from the capacity distribution of micro units it seems natural to relate this kind of progress to what happens to the micro units and derive the consequences for the macro function rather than to postulate directly the shift in the macro function.

Since each micro unit is characterized by its capacity and its input coefficients we can have different types of progress. In general all these characteristics of a micro unit may change due to disembodied progress. We shall consider the total progress as composed of two types of disembodied progress:

(1) *Capacity-increasing progress*, which increases the capacity of a production unit while leaving the input coefficients unaffected.

(2) *Input-saving progress*, which reduces the input coefficients of a production unit without affecting its capacity.

Any form of total progress can clearly be represented by a suitable mixture of these two types. This is true if we have, e.g., an improvement in organization which increases the output capacity of a production unit at constant *total* input requirements. A reason for distinguishing these two types of progress is that they have to be brought into our model in rather different ways from a formal point of view as will be shown in the two following sections where we treat the two types of disembodied progress in more detail. I think, however, that the distinction is meaningful also from a practical point of view. A more uninterrupted operation of machinery will for instance largely be of the capacity-increasing type since it will increase output capacity per unit of time (at least in many cases) while leaving energy

---

[9] This is the "F-type of technical progress" in the terminology of Professor Svennilson (1964), where "F" indicates that it affects the utilization of already existing Fixed capital.

and raw materials inputs per unit of output more or less unaffected. (What will happen to labour input per unit of output is less clear.) On the other hand reduction of waste in various forms will not increase capacity, but will bring down current input requirements per unit of output. I think enterprise managers will often know, when they try to improve efficiency, whether they are primarily after an increase in capacity or cheaper production, i.e. saving of inputs per unit of output.[10]

Before we go on to treat these two types of disembodied progress in more detail a couple of points of some general significance should be mentioned.

Firstly there is a point about the distinction between embodied and disembodied progress. We have defined embodied progress as favourable shifts in the ex ante function *which leave the efficiency of already established production units unaffected*. It does not follow from this that embodied progress is the only type of progress which influences the ex ante function. In fact it would often seem natural to think of disembodied progress as affecting both the operation of existing production units and the ex ante function. E.g., if the progress is due to organizational measures or improved quality of some inputs, then this could be taken into account in designing new production units and would thus affect the ex ante function as well as improve the efficiency of already existing production units. On the other hand there are clearly cases where the operation of old equipment can be improved on the basis of ideas which are not relevant for new production units. Then we could have disembodied progress which does not influence the ex ante function.[11]

Referring to the form of the capacity distribution, and the region of positive capacity in particular, a region which is long in the direction along rays from the origin would be an indication of embodiedness of technological progress while a region which is short in this direction is an indication of disembodiedness. These indications are not, however, sufficient indicators by themselves. The first form mentioned may also be due to substitution of capital for current inputs along a constant ex ante function, and the latter

---

[10] A treatment of disembodied technological change in a somewhat similar framework is suggested in Solow (1962). However, the suggestions given there seem to bear only upon what we have mentioned above as a special mixture of capacity-increasing and input-saving progress, viz. the case when capacity is increased under constant total inputs.

[11] In his discussion of the two types of progress professor Svennilson (1964) suggests that "most of the positive elements in the F-trend, such as increasing skill of the labour force and innovations of methods of operation, may be applied at new equipment and form part of the N-trend".

form may also occur when there is little total progress. Thus the evidence mentioned above is nearer to being sufficient if we *know* that there has been technological progress. Further indications could of course be obtained if we observe the capacity distributions at different points of time.

Secondly there is the problem as to whether there are any costs involved in the process of disembodied technological progress. We shall not bring such costs explicitly into the picture, but there may of course be costs covered by "society" involved such as for instance in the case of education. In many practical cases there may also be more specific costs incurred by the individual production unit. In the following sections we shall represent disembodied progress by some simple parameters. Formally there would probably be no difficulty involved in considering these as variables in such a way that more favourable values could be achieved at higher costs. Extended in this direction the model might be used to analyse the choice between rationalization and new investment.

Thirdly we might touch upon other changes in the efficiency of existing equipment than those called "progress". There may be normal and foreseen changes in the efficiency of a production unit as a part of the normal life cycle of equipment, perhaps first increasing and later decreasing efficiency. The time profiles may be different for efficiency as measured by capacity and as measured by input requirements per unit of output, and of course again different for different current inputs. We have already touched upon some such effects in connection with the discussion of the more general type of ex ante function (2.5) in Section 2.3. The formal expressions of disembodied technological progress which we shall introduce in the sequel can be interpreted so as to include such effects.[12]

7.5. *Capacity-increasing disembodied technological progress*

Capacity-increasing technological progress means that each production unit is able to produce more than before with the same input coefficients. If the "pre-progress" distribution is $f(\xi_1, \xi_2)$ we would now have the "post-progress" distribution $f^1(\xi_1, \xi_2)$ where

$$f^1(\xi_1, \xi_2) \geqq f(\xi_1, \xi_2), \tag{7.27}$$

---

[12] Professor Svennilson's "F-type of technical progress", mentioned before, is defined as "the net result of deterioration and technical progress".

with strict inequality holding at least over some parts of the region of positive capacity if we are to speak unreservedly about positive progress. However, even if (7.27) does not hold everywhere, it is of course possible that the short-run macro function $F^1(V_1, V_2)$ corresponding to the post-progress capacity distribution has a higher value at all V_1, V_2-points than the pre-progress short-run macro function $F(V_1, V_2)$.

Let us distinguish the pre- and post-progress function by writing

$$f^1(\xi_1, \xi_2) = [1+\alpha\kappa(\xi_1, \xi_2)]f(\xi_1, \xi_2), \tag{7.28}$$

where $\alpha\kappa(\xi_1, \xi_2)$ is the proportionate increase in capacity for production units with input coefficients ξ_1, ξ_2. The function $\kappa(\xi_1, \xi_2)$ gives the *form* of the shift and α is a parameter introduced to indicate the size of the shift. This is convenient when we come to consider the effect of a "small" shift.

In terms of the functions introduced by (7.27–7.28) the short-run macro function after the shift in the capacity distribution will be determined by

$$X = g(q_1, q_2)+\alpha \left[\int \int_{G(q_1, q_2)} \kappa(\xi_1, \xi_2)f(\xi_1, \xi_2)\, d\xi_1\, d\xi_2 \right], \tag{7.29}$$

$$V_i = h_i(q_1, q_2) + \alpha \left[\int \int_{G(q_1, q_2)} \xi_i\kappa(\xi_1, \xi_2)f(\xi_1, \xi_2)\, d\xi_1\, d\xi_2 \right] \ (i = 1, 2) \tag{7.30}$$

where g, h_1 and h_2 are the functions first introduced by (4.2). Proceeding in a similar way as in connection with the addition of new capacity, see (7.5–7.6), we can write (7.29–7.30) as

$$X = g(q_1, q_2)+\alpha g^\kappa(q_1, q_2),$$

$$V_i = h_i(q_1, q_2)+\alpha h_i^\kappa(q_1, q_2), \tag{7.31}$$

where g^κ, h_1^κ and h_2^κ are similar functions as g, h_1 and h_2, only based on $\kappa(\xi_1, \xi_2)f(\xi_1, \xi_2)$ rather than $f(\xi_1, \xi_2)$. We then have output X after the progress given by

$$X = F\left(V_1 - \alpha h_1^\kappa(q_1, q_2), V_2 - \alpha h_2^\kappa(q_1, q_2)\right)+\alpha g^\kappa(q_1, q_2) \tag{7.32}$$

and the increase in output per unit of the shift in the capacity distribution, evaluated at $\alpha = 0$, is given by

$$\frac{\partial X}{\partial \alpha}\bigg|_{\alpha = 0} = \int \int_{G(q_1, q_2)} (1-q_1\xi_1-q_2\xi_2)\, \kappa(\xi_1, \xi_2)f(\xi_1, \xi_2)\, d\xi_1\, d\xi_2 \tag{7.33}$$

in the same way as by (7.7) for the case of addition of new capacity. The interpretation is of course also the same: the effect on output is measured by quasi rents generated by the increased capacity. It does not matter for the effects of increased capacity on the short-run macro function whether this increase is based on investment in new equipment or capacity-increasing technological progress affecting the already existing equipment. (The likely forms of the shifts will of course be different since new capacity based on investment will usually be more concentrated around lower ξ_1, ξ_2-values than the disembodied technological progress. Such special cases as discussed in connection with (7.4) are therefore less interesting in the present context.)

We can also exploit the results of Section 7.2 to give the effect on the marginal rate of substitution. In the same way as by (7.14) we now have

$$\frac{1}{q_1/q_2} \frac{\partial(q_1/q_2)}{\partial \alpha} = \frac{g^\kappa}{J} \frac{M(\xi_1)}{\sigma_1} \frac{M(\xi_2)}{\sigma_2} \left(\frac{h_1{}^\kappa/g^\kappa}{M(\xi_1)} - \frac{h_2{}^\kappa/g^\kappa}{M(\xi_2)} \right). \tag{7.34}$$

Furthermore we have conclusions corresponding to (7.15). Thus we get e.g. a factor 1-saving shift in the macro function if capacity-increasing progress is particularly strong in production units using relatively little of input No. 1. As in Section 7.2, see particularly Figure 7.1, the comparison is with average input coefficients for marginal production units.

The most simple case of capacity-increasing progress is of course the case of a constant κ, i.e. all capacities increase in the same proportion. We may call this the case of *uniform* capacity-increasing progress. Then the functional forms g^κ, h_1^κ and h_2^κ in (7.31) are the same as g, h_1 and h_2 multiplied by κ so that we have (putting $\alpha = 1$):

$$X = (1+\kappa)g(q_1, q_2),$$
$$V_i = (1+\kappa)h_i(q_1, q_2) \quad (i = 1, 2). \tag{7.35}$$

We then have the post-progress macro function

$$X = (1+\kappa)F\left(\frac{V_1}{1+\kappa}, \frac{V_2}{1+\kappa}\right), \tag{7.36}$$

where F is the form of the pre-progress macro function. This type of progress projects the isoquants of the macro function proportionately away from the origin while the value of output corresponding to each of these isoquants is raised by the proportion κ. At a fixed V_1, V_2-point the value of X is increased only due to the decreasing returns to scale in the short-run macro function.

It should be observed that this simple uniform progress does not imply neutrality of the shift in the macro function as judged by (7.34).

7.6. *Input-saving disembodied technological progress*

Input-saving progress reduces input coefficients of production units without changing their capacity.

Let us consider hypothetically the situation "before" and "after" some such progress has taken place. We may formally introduce this type of progress in the following way. Let ξ_1^0, ξ_2^0 be inputs per unit of output for some type of equipment before the progress has taken place. Now assume that all equipment of similar type is improved in the same way. If we then let ξ_1^1, ξ_2^1 be the input coefficients after the progress has taken place, we could relate them to the initial position by some functions γ_1 and γ_2:

$$\xi_1^1 = \gamma_1(\xi_1^0, \xi_2^0),$$

$$\xi_2^1 = \gamma_2(\xi_1^0, \xi_2^0). \tag{7.37}$$

If the distribution of production units before the progress takes place – the "pre-progress" distribution – is given by $f^0(\xi_1^0, \xi_2^0)$ we get a "post-progress" distribution $f^1(\xi_1^1, \xi_2^1)$ which depends upon f^0 and the functions introduced by (7.37). The relationship is given by

$$f^1(\xi_1^1, \xi_2^1) = f^0(\gamma_1^{-1}(\xi_1^1, \xi_2^1), \gamma_2^{-1}(\xi_1^1, \xi_2^1)) \left| \begin{array}{cc} \dfrac{\partial \gamma_1^{-1}}{\partial \xi_1^1} & \dfrac{\partial \gamma_1^{-1}}{\partial \xi_2^1} \\[2mm] \dfrac{\partial \gamma_2^{-1}}{\partial \xi_1^1} & \dfrac{\partial \gamma_2^{-1}}{\partial \xi_2^1} \end{array} \right|, \tag{7.38}$$

where γ_1^{-1} and γ_2^{-1} are obtained by inverting the system (7.37). In general one might expect the functions γ_1 and γ_2 to be such that there is no problem about inverting the system. Equation (7.38) is well known e.g. from the theory of transformation of variables in probability distributions.

Corresponding to (3.15) the post-progress short-run macro production function will now be given by

$$X = \int \int_{G(q_1, q_2)} f^1(\xi_1^1, \xi_2^1) \, d\xi_1^1 \, d\xi_2^1,$$

$$V_1 = \int \int_{G(q_1, q_2)} \xi_1^1 f^1(\xi_1^1, \xi_2^1) \, d\xi_1^1 \, d\xi_2^1,$$

$$V_2 = \int \int_{G(q_1, q_2)} \xi_2^1 f^1(\xi_1^1, \xi_2^1) \, d\xi_1^1 \, d\xi_2^1. \tag{7.39}$$

In general there will be no simple relation between the pre-progress and the post-progress macro function. A particularly simple case occurs, however, when we have *uniform* progress in the sense that all production units are improved to the same relative degree. We then have

$$\xi_1^1 = \alpha_1 \xi_1^0, \quad \xi_2^1 = \alpha_2 \xi_2^0, \tag{7.40}$$

where α_1 and α_2 are constants. From (7.38) we have in this case

$$f^1(\xi_1^1, \xi_2^1) = f^0\left(\frac{\xi_1^1}{\alpha_1}, \frac{\xi_2^1}{\alpha_2}\right) \begin{vmatrix} \dfrac{1}{\alpha_1} & 0 \\ 0 & \dfrac{1}{\alpha_2} \end{vmatrix} = f^0\left(\frac{\xi_1^1}{\alpha_1}, \frac{\xi_2^1}{\alpha_2}\right)\frac{1}{\alpha_1\alpha_2}. \tag{7.41}$$

Inserting this in (7.39) and changing variables back to ξ_1^0, ξ_2^0 in the integrations it is easy to see that we get

$$X = g^0(\alpha_1 q_1, \alpha_2 q_2),$$
$$V_i = \alpha_i h_i^0(\alpha_1 q_1, \alpha_2 q_2) \quad (i = 1, 2),$$

where the functions g^0, h_1^0 and h_2^0 are the same as by (4.2), only based on the distribution $f^0(\xi_1^0, \xi_2^0)$. Corresponding to (4.4) we then obtain the following post-progress macro function

$$F^1(V_1, V_2) = F^0\left(\frac{V_1}{\alpha_1}, \frac{V_2}{\alpha_2}\right), \tag{7.42}$$

where F^0 is the pre-progress function. Considering e.g. Figure 4.4 it is easy to see how (7.42) moves the region of substitution and the isoquants in a direction determined by α_1 and α_2.

Although there is in general no simple relation between the pre-progress and the post-progress macro function, some simplifications obtain when we consider only a "small" amount of progress. Let us, for this purpose, introduce a parameter α, which indicates (as in the previous section) the amount of the progress, and functions $\mu_1(\xi_1, \xi_2)$ and $\mu_2(\xi_1, \xi_2)$, which indicate the direction of the progress in the following way

$$\alpha\mu_i(\xi_1^0, \xi_2^0) = \frac{\xi_i^0 - \xi_i^1}{\xi_i^0} \quad (i = 1, 2) \tag{7.43}$$

or

$$\xi_i^1 = \gamma_i(\xi_1^0, \xi_2^0) = \xi_i^0(1 - \alpha\mu_i(\xi_1^0, \xi_2^0)) \quad (i = 1, 2). \tag{7.44}$$

Here μ_1 and μ_2 are defined in such a way that $\mu_i > 0$ means positive progress (positive saving of input).

We could now develop the formulae (7.38–7.39) for the special form of γ_1 and γ_2 given by (7.44). However, for seeing the simplifications which obtain when we have a "small" amount of progress, represented by a small value of the parameter α, it is better to return to integrating over ξ_1^0, ξ_2^0 in the integrals in (7.39). We then have

$$X = \int\int_{G^*} f^0(\xi_1^0, \xi_2^0)\, d\xi_1^0\, d\xi_2^0,$$

$$V_1 = \int\int_{G^*} [\xi_1^0 - \alpha\mu_1(\xi_1^0, \xi_2^0)\xi_1^0] f^0(\xi_1^0, \xi_2^0)\, d\xi_1^0\, d\xi_2^0,$$

$$V_2 = \int\int_{G^*} [\xi_2^0 - \alpha\mu_2(\xi_1^0, \xi_2^0)\xi_2^0] f^0(\xi_1^0, \xi_2^0)\, d\xi_1^0\, d\xi_2^0, \qquad (7.45)$$

where G^* is now the region in the ξ_1^0, ξ_2^0 – plane which corresponds to $G(q_1, q_2)$ in the ξ_1^1, ξ_2^1 – plane

This is an important point to understand. After the progress has taken place we have to integrate over a triangular region $G(q_1, q_2)$ in the distribution of ξ_1^1, ξ_2^1 in order to optimize the utilization of the total inputs V_1 and V_2. By shifting back to integrating over ξ_1^0, ξ_2^0 we shall include "the same production units" in the integration, but in the ξ_1^0, ξ_2^0-plane these same units do not necessarily constitute a triangular region. This is the fact which complicates the derivation of the formal expression for the effects of input-

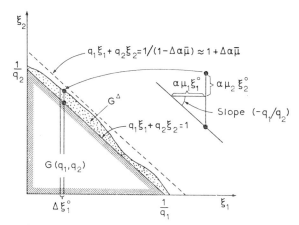

Fig. 7.3. The region G^* over which one integrates in Equations (7.45) consists of the region $G(q_1, q_2)$ plus the region G^Δ.

saving progress. (The simplification in the special case (7.40–7.42) obtains because in this case the region G^* *is* the same kind of triangle as $G(q_1, q_2)$.)

The relationship between the regions $G(q_1, q_2)$ and G^* is suggested in Figure 7.3.

$G(q_1, q_2)$ is represented by the shaded region in the figure. In ξ_1^0, ξ_2^0-coordinates this would correspond to the region G^*, which consists of $G(q_1, q_2)$ and the dotted region G^Δ. We have assumed $\alpha > 0$ and $\mu_1, \mu_2 \geqq 0$. The region G^Δ contains production units which were not profitable at prices q_1, q_2 before the progress, but which will be profitable at the same prices after the progress has taken place; i.e., they move into $G(q_1, q_2)$.

Partitioning the region G^* in the way indicated above, and using the functions g^0, h_1^0, and h_2^0 similar to g, h_1 and h_2 introduced by (4.2), we can write (7.45) as

$$X = g^0(q_1, q_2) + \int\int_{G^\Delta} f^0(\xi_1^0, \xi_2^0)\,d\xi_1^0\,d\xi_2^0 = g^0(q_1, q_2) + I(G^\Delta, f^0),$$
$$(7.46)$$

$$V_i = h_i^0(q_1, q_2) + \int\int_{G^\Delta} \xi_i^0 f^0(\xi_1^0, \xi_2^0)\,d\xi_1^0\,d\xi_2^0$$

$$-\alpha\left[\int\int_{G(q_1, q_2)} \mu_i(\xi_1^0, \xi_2^0)\xi_i^0 f^0(\xi_1^0, \xi_2^0)\,d\xi_1^0\,d\xi_2^0\right]$$

$$-\alpha\left[\int\int_{G^\Delta} \mu_i(\xi_1^0, \xi_2^0)\xi_i^0 f^0(\xi_1^0, \xi_2^0)\,d\xi_1^0\,d\xi_2^0\right]$$

$$= h_i^0(q_1, q_2) + I(G^\Delta, \xi_i^0 f^0) - \alpha I(G, \mu_i\xi_i^0 f^0) - \alpha I(G^\Delta, \mu_i\xi_i^0 f^0) \quad (i = 1, 2).$$
$$(7.47$$

Here we have introduced symbols $I(G^\Delta, f^0)$ etc. for the integrals to simplify the writing of the following formulae, the first argument in $I()$ indicating the region and the second argument indicating the integrand.

In a similar way as by (7.5–7.6) we now have

$$X = F^0\bigg(V_1 - I(G^\Delta, \xi_1^0 f^0) + \alpha I(G, \mu_1\xi_1^0 f^0) + \alpha I(G^\Delta, \mu_1\xi_1^0 f^0),$$
$$V_2 - I(G^\Delta, \xi_2^0 f^0) + \alpha I(G, \mu_2\xi_2^0 f^0) + \alpha I(G^\Delta, \mu_2\xi_2^0 f^0)\bigg) + I(G^\Delta, f^0) \quad (7.48)$$

(where there are only *two* arguments under $F^0()$).

We now evaluate the derivative of (7.48) with respect to α at $\alpha = 0$ (for constant V_1 and V_2) in a similar way as by (7.32–7.33). The derivation is however somewhat more complicated in the present case because of the dependence of the region G^Δ on α. We first obtain

$$\frac{\partial X}{\partial \alpha}\bigg|_{\alpha \,=\, 0} = q_1 \left\{ - \frac{\partial I(G^A, \xi_1^0 f^0)}{\partial \alpha} + I(G, \mu_1 \xi_1^0 f^0) \right\}$$

$$+ q_2 \left\{ - \frac{\partial I(G^A, \xi_2^0 f^0)}{\partial \alpha} + I(G, \mu_2 \xi_2^0 f^0) \right\} + \frac{\partial I(G^A, f^0)}{\partial \alpha}$$

$$= q_1 I(G, \mu_1 \xi_1^0 f^0) + q_2 I(G, \mu_2 \xi_2^0 f^0) +$$

$$+ \frac{\partial I(G^A, (1 - q_1 \xi_1^0 - q_2 \xi_2^0) f^0)}{\partial \alpha}. \tag{7.49}$$

We have here used the fact that integrals taken over the region G^A are zero when $\alpha = 0$, since G^A then collapses into the line $q_1 \xi_1 + q_2 \xi_2 = 1$. The expression to the right in the last formula contains the derivative of the following integral when we collect terms involving integration over the region G^A:

$$I^*(\alpha) = I(G^A, (1 - q_1 \xi_1^0 - q_2 \xi_2^0) f^0) =$$

$$= \int \int_{G^A} (1 - q_1 \xi_1^0 - q_2 \xi_2^0) f^0 (\xi_1^0, \xi_2^0) \, d\xi_1^0 \, d\xi_2^0 . \tag{7.50}$$

To study the derivative of this integral with respect to α we first notice that $I^*(\alpha) \leqq 0$ since $1 - q_1 \xi_1^0 - q_2 \xi_2^0 \leqq 0$ in the region G^A. Furthermore, since G^A increases with α we have $\partial I^*(\alpha)/\partial \alpha \leqq 0$. Now consider the difference $I^*(\alpha + \Delta\alpha) - I^*(\alpha)$ for $\alpha = 0$, i.e. $I^*(\Delta\alpha) - I^*(0) = I^*(\Delta\alpha)$. We shall see that this goes to zero faster than $\Delta\alpha$ when $\Delta\alpha \to 0$. Let $\bar{\mu}$ be an upper limit to $\mu_1(\xi_1, \xi_2)$ and $\mu_2(\xi_1, \xi_2)$. Then G^A is contained in the band in the ξ_1^0, ξ_2^0-plane, which is such that ξ_1^1, ξ_2^1 given by

$$\xi_1^1 = \xi_1^0 (1 - \Delta\alpha\bar{\mu}), \ \xi_2^1 = \xi_2^0 (1 - \Delta\alpha\bar{\mu}) \tag{7.51}$$

belongs to $G(q_1, q_2)$, while ξ_1^0, ξ_2^0 does not. This band will have the line $q_1 \xi_1^0 + q_2 \xi_2^0 = 1$ as the inner boundary and the parallel line

$$q_1 \xi_1^0 + q_2 \xi_2^0 = 1/(1 - \Delta\alpha\bar{\mu}) \approx 1 + \Delta\alpha\bar{\mu} \tag{7.52}$$

as its outer boundary (suggested by the dotted line in Figure 7.3). When $\Delta\alpha$ is small the size of the band will be proportional with $\Delta\alpha$. Thus the size of the region G^A will have an upper bound $c\Delta\alpha$, where c is a finite constant.

Let us next consider the factor $(1 - q_1 \xi_1^0 - q_2 \xi_2^0)$ in the integrand in (7.50). In the band which contains the region G^A we have $1 - q_1 \xi_1^0 - q_2 \xi_2^0 \leqq 0$ as noticed above. The value of $1 - q_1 \xi_1^0 - q_2 \xi_2^0$ can be bounded by

$$\left| 1 - q_1 \xi_1^0 - q_2 \xi_2^0 \right| \leqq \Delta\alpha\bar{\mu}/(1 - \Delta\alpha\bar{\mu}) \tag{7.53}$$

because of (7.51–7.52).

Finally f^0 is finite so that we have $f^0(\xi_1^0, \xi_2^0) \leq \bar{f}$, where $\bar{f}$ is a constant. Collecting these results we can put down the following bound on the value of $I^*(\Delta\alpha)$:

$$|I^*(\Delta\alpha)| \leq (c\Delta\alpha)\frac{\Delta\alpha\bar{\mu}}{1 - \Delta\alpha\bar{\mu}} \cdot \bar{f} = \frac{c\bar{\mu}\bar{f}(\Delta\alpha)^2}{1 - \Delta\alpha\bar{\mu}}. \tag{7.54}$$

Accordingly we have

$$\frac{I^*(\Delta\alpha)}{\Delta\alpha} \to 0 \text{ as } \Delta\alpha \to 0, \tag{7.55}$$

which means that

$$\frac{\partial I^*(\alpha)}{\partial\alpha}\bigg|_{\alpha = 0} = \frac{\partial I(G^{\Delta}, (1 - q_1\xi_1^0 - q_2\xi_2^0)f^0)}{\partial\alpha}\bigg|_{\alpha = 0} = 0, \tag{7.56}$$

and (7.49) reduces to

$$\frac{\partial X}{\partial\alpha}\bigg|_{\alpha = 0} = q_1 I(G, \mu_1\xi_1^0 f^0) + q_2 I(G, \mu_2\xi_2^0 f^0)$$

$$= \sum_{i=1}^{2} q_i \iint_{G(q_1, q_2)} \mu_i(\xi_1^0, \xi_2^0)\xi_i^0 f^0(\xi_1^0, \xi_2^0) \, d\xi_1^0 \, d\xi_2^0. \tag{7.57}$$

The interpretation of this result is simple. It means that, for a "small" input-saving progress, the vertical shift in the macro production function at a given V_1, V_2-point is simply measured by the amounts of inputs released from production units under operation multiplied by the marginal productivities of the pre-progress function (q_1 and q_2). The more complicated effects along the border-line of the utilization region are, for a "small" amount of progress, of a negligible order of magnitude as compared with this straight-forward effect.

The mathematical arguments presented above are of course somewhat lacking in rigour. A fully satisfactory treatment would have to involve a more precise analysis of the conditions under which the various derivatives really exist. I cannot see, however, that such a complete mathematical treatment would reveal anything new of economic significance. (The same comment holds for the following analysis of the possible biases of the shift in the macro function.)

The assumptions underlying the above treatment of input-saving progress may appear to be rather general since the amount and the direction of the progress may vary according to the initial position ξ_1^0, ξ_2^0. It should be noticed, however, that it is not absolutely general. Production units located at the same ξ_1^0, ξ_2^0-point might conceivably move differently. This might be of some importance particularly if we interpret the "progress" as reflecting not only progress in the most immediate sense, but rather as a mixture of various effects acting on existing production units, as suggested at the end of Section 7.4. Then different production units which, at a certain moment of time, are at the same ξ_1, ξ_2-position may be so as parts of different histories, i.e. the given ξ_1, ξ_2-point may be a point of intersection of different paths of movement in the ξ_1, ξ_2-plane. This problem could only be solved by considering the capacity distribution at a certain moment of time as consisting of several "layers", perhaps defined by the year of construction of equipment, but other criteria are also conceivable. Functions like μ_1 and μ_2 above would have to be introduced for each layer, and the total effect upon aggregate output would be a sum of effects like (7.57) for all layers.

Let us next consider the effect upon the marginal rate of substitution q_1/q_2 in the macro function $F(V_1, V_2)$ of input-saving disembodied progress. We then consider the equations in (7.47) and differentiate these (under constant V_1 and V_2) with respect to α for $\alpha = 0$. We have

$$h_{11} \frac{\partial q_1}{\partial \alpha} + h_{12} \frac{\partial q_2}{\partial \alpha} = - \frac{\partial I(G^A, \xi_1^0 f^0)}{\partial \alpha} + I(G, \mu_1 \xi_1^0 f^0),$$

$$h_{21} \frac{\partial q_1}{\partial \alpha} + h_{22} \frac{\partial q_2}{\partial \alpha} = - \frac{\partial I(G^A, \xi_2^0 f^0)}{\partial \alpha} + I(G, \mu_2 \xi_2^0 f^0), \qquad (7.58)$$

where h_{ij} are the derivatives $h_{ij} = \partial h_i / \partial q_j$ as in connection with Equation (7.11), now defined on the basis of the pre-progress capacity distribution f^0.

The integrals over G to the right in (7.58) are the same as those which enter into the result (7.57). Derivatives like $\partial I(G^A, \xi_i^0 f^0)/\partial \alpha$, which also appear in (7.58), vanished in (7.57) because they combined in (7.49) in a special way so that the integrand involved $(1 - q_1 \xi_1^0 - q_2 \xi_2^0)$, which is negligible near the zero quasi rent line. This is not the case in connection with (7.58). We therefore have to evaluate these derivatives.

We proceed by first establishing an expression for the integral which is a valid approximation when α is small so that the whole region G^A is thin along the zero quasi rent line – see Figure 7.3. Consider an increment $\Delta \xi_1^0$ from a value ξ_1^0. The value of the part of the integral $I(G^A, \xi_1^0 f^0)$, which is confined within the vertical strip defined by $\Delta \xi_1^0$, can be approximated by the value of $\xi_1^0 f^0(\xi_1^0, \xi_2^0)$ on the zero quasi rent line multiplied by the area of the intersection between this strip and the region G^A. The height of this region of intersection is

$$\alpha\mu_2\xi_2^0 + \alpha\mu_1\xi_1^0 \frac{q_1}{q_2} = \frac{1}{q_2}\alpha\,(q_1\mu_1\xi_1^0 + q_2\mu_2\xi_2^0). \tag{7.59}$$

This can be seen as follows, when we consider a neighbourhood small enough to permit us to consider μ_1 and μ_2 as constants. A point at the top of the strip based on $\varDelta\xi_1^0$ is by the movement $-\alpha\mu_1\xi_1^0$, $-\alpha\mu_2\xi_2^0$ brought to the zero quasi rent line, since the border points of G^A are those which will represent marginal production units after the progress has taken place. From this it follows that the vertical distance is first $\alpha\mu_2\xi_2^0$, and in addition comes the vertical distance corresponding to a horizontal component $\alpha\mu_1\xi_1^0$ by moving along the zero quasi rent line. This vertical distance is $\alpha\mu_1\xi_1^0(q_1/q_2)$ since the slope of the line is $(-q_1/q_2)$. This is illustrated to the right in Figure 7.3.

The expression in parantheses to the right in (7.59) can be interpreted as the increase in the rate of quasi rent per unit of input-saving progress as measured by α: For a production unit located at ξ_1^0, ξ_2^0 pre-progress quasi rent per unit of output value is $1 - q_1\xi_1^0 - q_2\xi_2^0$; post-progress quasi rent is $1 - q_1\xi_1^1 - q_2\xi_2^1 = 1 - q_1\xi_1^0 - q_2\xi_2^0 + \alpha(q_1\mu_1\xi_1^0 + q_2\mu_2\xi_2^0)$. Let the difference per unit of α be s_α. Then the height in (7.59) can be written as

$$\frac{1}{q_2}\alpha s_\alpha, \text{ where } s_\alpha = s_\alpha(\xi_1^0,\,\xi_2^0) = q_1\mu_1\xi_1^0 + q_2\mu_2\xi_2^0. \tag{7.60}$$

Now the integral $I(G^A, \xi_1^0 f^0)$ can (for a sufficiently small value of α) be calculated as an integral over ξ_1^0 only. For any ξ_1^0 and $\varDelta\xi_1^0$ the contribution to the value of $I(G^A, \xi_1^0 f^0)$ is

$$\xi_1^0 f^0(\xi_1^0, \frac{1}{q_2} - \frac{q_1}{q_2}\xi_1^0)\left[\frac{1}{q_2}\alpha s_\alpha\varDelta\xi_1^0\right],$$

where the term in brackets to the right is the area of the intersection region mentioned above (considered as a rectangle which is permissible as an approximation). Accordingly we have, for a small value of α,

$$I(G^A, \xi_1^0 f^0) \approx \frac{\alpha}{q_2}\int_0^{\frac{1}{q_1}} \xi_1^0 f^0(\xi_1^0, \frac{1}{q_2} - \frac{q_1}{q_2}\xi_1^0)s_\alpha(\xi_1^0, \frac{1}{q_2} - \frac{q_1}{q_2}\xi_1^0)\,\mathrm{d}\xi_1^0$$

and

$$\frac{\partial I(G^A, \xi_1^0 f^0)}{\partial\alpha} = \frac{1}{q_2}\int_0^{\frac{1}{q_1}} \xi_1^0 s_\alpha(\xi_1^0, \frac{1}{q_2} - \frac{q_1}{q_2}\xi_1^0)f^0(\xi_1^0, \frac{1}{q_2} - \frac{q_1}{q_2}\xi_1^0)\,\mathrm{d}\xi_1^0. \tag{7.61}$$

(In the variation underlying formula (7.61) q_1 and q_2 are also to be considered as variables, depending on α. But the contribution to $\partial I(G^A, \xi_1^0 f^0)/\partial \alpha$ via q_1 and q_2 vanishes at $\alpha = 0$.)

In Section 4.2 we introduced special notation for averages along the zero quasi rent line, see (4.16). Using this notation we have for (7.61) and the corresponding expression involving ξ_2^0:

$$\frac{\partial I(G^A, \xi_i^0 f^0)}{\partial \alpha} = JM(\xi_i^0 s_\alpha). \quad (i = 1, 2) \tag{7.62}$$

Introducing this in (7.58) and solving the system as we have done before for similar systems we get

$$\frac{\partial q_1}{\partial \alpha} = \frac{q_2^2}{J\sigma_1^2} \{ -M(\xi_2^2)[I(G, \mu_1\xi_1^0 f^0) - JM(\xi_1^0 s_\alpha]$$

$$+ M(\xi_1\xi_2)[I(G, \mu_2\xi_2^0 f^0 - JM(\xi_2^0 s_\alpha)]\},$$

$$\frac{\partial q_2}{\partial \alpha} = \frac{q_2^2}{J\sigma_1^2} \{ M(\xi_1\xi_2)[I(G, \mu_1\xi_1^0 f^0) - JM(\xi_1^0 s_\alpha)]$$

$$- M(\xi_1^2)[I(G, \mu_2\xi_2^0 f^0) - JM(\xi_2^0 s_\alpha)]\}. \tag{7.63}$$

We are now particularly interested in the change in the marginal rate of substitution as expressed by q_1/q_2. We proceed in a similar way as by (7.12–7.14) and obtain

$$\frac{1}{q_1/q_2} \frac{\partial(q_1/q_2)}{\partial \alpha} = \frac{1}{J} \frac{M(\xi_1)}{\sigma_1} \frac{M(\xi_2)}{\sigma_2} \left[\frac{I(G, \mu_2\xi_2 f)}{M(\xi_2)} - \frac{I(G, \mu_1\xi_1 f)}{M(\xi_1)} \right]$$

$$+ \frac{M(\xi_1)}{\sigma_1} \frac{M(\xi_2)}{\sigma_2} \left[\frac{M(\xi_1 s_\alpha)}{M(\xi_1)} - \frac{M(\xi_2 s_\alpha)}{M(\xi_2)} \right]. \tag{7.64}$$

(In this final formula we have dropped the superscript ^{0} previously used to indicate the pre-progress situation.)

Let us now interpret this formula. Consider first the contribution of the first bracket. This is concerned with the effect of reduced input requirements on capacity in use since $I(G, \mu_i\xi_i f)$ is the integral over the utilization region of the reduction in input No. i for all ξ_1, ξ_2-positions. We see that the effect on q_1/q_2 is negative, i.e. we have a factor No. 1-saving shift in the macro function $F(V_1, V_2)$, if

$$I(G, \mu_1\xi_1 f)/I(G, \mu_2\xi_2 f) > M(\xi_1)/M(\xi_2). \tag{7.65}$$

This condition means that the *relative* saving of factor No. 1 in proportion to factor No. 2 is greater than the input of factor No. 1 in proportion to factor No. 2 at marginal production units. This is explained by the following consideration. We are concerned with the change in the marginal rate of substitution q_1/q_2 at a given V_1, V_2-point. When there is a shift due to the type of technological progress represented by μ_1 and μ_2 we should therefore readjust the zero quasi rent line so that V_1 and V_2 remain the same as before. If the progress causes factor savings in the same proportion as $M(\xi_1)/M(\xi_2)$, a parallel shift in the zero quasi rent line would do, and q_1/q_2 would remain constant. If we save relatively more of V_1, the zero quasi rent line must be rotated to a flatter position so as to include relatively more production units with higher inputs of factor No. 1 and fewer of those using much of factor No. 2 in order for V_1, V_2 to remain the same as before the shift. Since q_1/q_2 measures the slope of the isoquant of the macro function this implies a factor No. 1-saving progress as judged by the effect on $F(V_1, V_2)$ according to Hicksian definitions. This is a tidy and convenient connection between indicators of the direction of progress at the micro and the macro level.

Next consider the term in the second bracket in (7.64). Here only averages along the zero quasi rent line are involved. The effect expressed by this term clearly has to do with the movement of previously unused capacity into the utilization region. Consider first the case of a constant s_α as defined by (7.60). A constant s_α means that all production units along the zero quasi rent line improve their profitability to the same degree as a result of input-saving progress. This clearly obtains if $\mu_1(\xi_1, \xi_2) = \mu_2(\xi_1, \xi_2) = \mu = $ constant along the zero quasi rent line. Then we have $s_\alpha = \mu$. In this case the term in the second bracket in (7.64) vanishes because $M(\xi_1 s_\alpha) = s_\alpha M(\xi_1)$ and $M(\xi_2 s_\alpha) = s_\alpha M(\xi_2)$.

Considering the case where μ_1, μ_2 and s_α vary with ξ_1, ξ_2 along the zero quasi rent line we see that the second bracket in (7.64) contributes to a factor No. 1-saving shift in the macro production function (a reduction in q_1/q_2) if

$$M(\xi_2 s_\alpha)/M(\xi_1 s_\alpha) > M(\xi_2)/M(\xi_1). \tag{7.66}$$

This condition is fulfilled if production units which use relatively much of factor No. 2 experience a particularly large increase in profitability (high value of s_α). The explanation is that this brings relatively much of capacity which requires large inputs of factor No. 2 into the region of utilization if q_1 and q_2 were constant. In order to bring us back to the same V_1, V_2-point as before the shift q_2 must be increased relatively to q_1 so as to shift V_1/V_2

back to the old proportion, which means that the marginal rate of substitution q_1/q_2 at the given V_1, V_2-point will be reduced – i.e. we get a factor No. 1-saving shift in $F(V_1, V_2)$.

For this component of the bias in the shift in $F(V_1, V_2)$ there is no clear connection with the possible biases at the micro level as indicated by μ_1 and μ_2. For the sign of the second bracket in (7.64) it is only the increase in profitability at various points along the zero quasi rent line which matters, not whether it comes about through a high value of μ_1 and a low value of μ_2, or vice versa.

This last effect may in certain cases appear somewhat paradoxical. Consider e.g. the case of a constant $\mu_2 > 0$ and $\mu_1 = 0$ along the zero quasi rent line, i.e. the case where the progress at the micro level takes the form of reduced inputs of factor No. 2 only. Then the condition given above by (7.66) for a factor No. 1-saving contribution to the shift in the macro function is clearly satisfied since $s_\alpha = q_2\mu_2\xi_2$ will now be large where ξ_2 is large in the formation of the average $M(\xi_2 s_\alpha)$, while s_α will be small where ξ_1 is large in the formation of the average $M(\xi_1 s_\alpha)$. However, this is natural in view of the fact that such a reduction in input requirements for factor No. 2 causes a substitution of factor No. 2-intensive production units for units which use much of factor No. 1 and thus creates a factor No. 1-saving tendency. (The full effect of course also includes the effect expressed by the first bracket in (7.64).)

7.7. A special combination of capacity-increasing and input-saving disembodied technological progress

In Section 7.5 we introduced a function $\kappa(\xi_1, \xi_2)$ to indicate the form of capacity-increasing progress. In Section 7.6 we introduced two functions $\mu_1(\xi_1, \xi_2)$ and $\mu_2(\xi_1, \xi_2)$ to indicate the form and direction of input-saving progress. In both cases we have introduced the parameter α to indicate the scale of the progress. Let us now consider the special case where all three functions κ, μ_1 and μ_2 are the same:

$$\kappa(\xi_1, \xi_2) \equiv \mu_1(\xi_1, \xi_2) \equiv \mu_2(\xi_1, \xi_2). \tag{7.67}$$

The interpretation of this special case is clear from a consideration of total input requirements at full capacity utilization of production units within a "cell" $\Delta\xi_1\Delta\xi_2$ in the ξ_1, ξ_2-plane. Total input requirement of factor No. 1 in such a cell can be written as

$$v_1^0(\varDelta\xi_1, \varDelta\xi_2) \approx \xi_1 f(\xi_1, \xi_2)\varDelta\xi_1\varDelta\xi_2 \tag{7.68}$$

before the progress takes place. When the progress has taken place the input requirement of the same production units at full capacity will be

$$v_1^1(\varDelta\xi_1, \varDelta\xi_2) \approx (1-\alpha\mu_1(\xi_1, \xi_2))\xi_1(1+\alpha\kappa(\xi_1, \xi_2))f(\xi_1, \xi_2)\varDelta\xi_1\varDelta\xi_2$$
$$= (1-\alpha\mu_1(\xi_1, \xi_2))(1+\alpha\kappa(\xi_1, \xi_2))v_1^0(\varDelta\xi_1, \varDelta\xi_2)$$
$$\approx v_1^0(\varDelta\xi_1, \varDelta\xi_2), \tag{7.69}$$

where the last approximate equality holds when α is small so that α^2 can be neglected. A similar conclusion holds of course for input No. 2. Thus the case (7.67) is, for a small value of α, a type of progress by which total capacity of a production unit is increased by the proportion $\alpha\kappa(\xi_1, \xi_2)$ while total input requirements remain constant.[13]

In this case we get the total vertical shift in the macro function $F(V_1, V_2)$ by combining formulas (7.33) and (7.57). This gives

$$\left.\frac{\partial X}{\partial\alpha}\right|_{\alpha=0} = \int\int_{G(q_1, q_2)} \kappa(\xi_1, \xi_2)f(\xi_1, \xi_2)\, d\xi_1\, d\xi_2, \tag{7.70}$$

which is an obvious result.

For the bias in the shift in $F(V_1, V_2)$ we may combine formulae (7.34) and (7.64). In the case of (7.67) it is clear that $h_i^\kappa(q_1, q_2)$ in (7.34) (introduced by (7.31)) is the same as $I(G, \mu_i\xi_i f)$ in the notation used in (7.64). The term from (7.34) then cancels against the first term in (7.64). Furthermore, in the term in the second bracket in (7.64) the factor s_α, which is defined by (7.60), reduces to $s_\alpha = \kappa(\xi_1, \xi_2)$, so that we have

$$\frac{1}{(q_1/q_2)}\frac{\partial(q_1/q_2)}{\partial\alpha} = \frac{M(\xi_1)}{\sigma_1}\frac{M(\xi_2)}{\sigma_2}\left[\frac{M(\kappa\xi_1)}{M(\xi_1)} - \frac{M(\kappa\xi_2)}{M(\xi_2)}\right]. \tag{7.71}$$

This means that the only effect upon the marginal rate of substitution of the type of progress now under consideration stems from the movements of production units across the border of the utilization region. The interpretation and comments given in connection with the second term of (7.64) are valid also in the present case.

If $\kappa(\xi_1, \xi_2)$ is constant, then (7.70) gives

$$\frac{\partial X}{\partial\alpha} = \kappa X = \kappa F(V_1, V_2), \quad \text{(for constant } \kappa) \tag{7.72}$$

---

[13] If we replace (7.67) by the condition $\mu_1(\xi_1, \xi_2) \equiv \mu_2(\xi_1, \xi_2) \equiv \kappa(\xi_1, \xi_2)/[1+\alpha\kappa(\xi_1, \xi_2)]$, then we have the type of progress mentioned in the text for any value of α, not necessarily "small".

while the expression in (7.71) vanishes, i.e. we have a neutral shift.

In the case of constant κ and constant μ_1 and μ_2 with $\mu_1 = \mu_2$ the shift in $F(V_1, V_2)$ can of course easily be given in a "global" form, not only as derivatives with respect to a shift parameter, by combining formulae (7.36) and (7.42). We now use (7.42) for $\alpha_1 = \alpha_2 = 1 - \mu$, where $\mu_1 = \mu_2 = \mu$. We then get

$$X = (1+\kappa)F\left(\frac{V_1}{(1+\kappa)(1-\mu)}, \frac{V_2}{(1+\kappa)(1-\mu)}\right), \tag{7.73}$$

and if

$$(1+\kappa)(1-\mu) = 1, \text{ i.e. } \mu = \frac{\kappa}{1+\kappa}, \tag{7.74}$$

then this reduces to

$$X = (1+\kappa)F(V_1, V_2), \tag{7.75}$$

i.e. a neutral shift in the macro function not only locally, but globally.

Condition (7.74) means that input requirements in a "cell" $\Delta\xi_1, \Delta\xi_2$ under full capacity utilization remain constant under a finite amount of progress. For a "small" amount of progress the condition is approximately the same as $\kappa = \mu \ (= \mu_1 = \mu_2)$.

Since the type of progress discussed in this section has some simplifying implications for the shift in the macro function, and since it has also a simple interpretation at the micro level, it might be a candidate for being listed as a basic type of progress rather than a combination of the two types which we have introduced. This would of course be perfectly all right. But since there are definitely types of progress which save inputs without augmenting capacity to the same degree, or increase capacity without reducing ξ_1 and ξ_2 to the same degree, the "complement class" of progress necessary to cover the full range of types of progress would then have to include shifts which are not naturally thought of as "progress". The distinction which we have introduced has the advantage that almost any conceivable type of disembodied progress can be described as a mixture of positive (or at least non-negative) progress components in the form of the two basic types. Furthermore, our distinction is analytically convenient in that the consequences for the macro function $F(V_1, V_2)$ of each of these types of progress follow from one special type of change in the equations which implicitly define $X = F(V_1, V_2)$.

7.8. *A complete growth equation*

In the preceding sections we have discussed the introduction of new capacity and various forms of technological progress mainly without referring explicitly to the passing of time. Let us now consider continuous time and collect the various effects into a growth equation for total output, i.e. an expression for $dX/dt = \dot{X}$. Notationally we may think of it as being evaluated for $t = 0$. In such an expression for the differential of X with respect to time the various effects will operate in an additive manner. (We may convince ourselves on this point by starting out from Equations (7.6), (7.32) and (7.48) and combine all the effects, which are introduced separately in these equations, into one equation of a similar type before we carry out the differentiation with respect to time.)

The effect of increased current inputs will clearly be $q_1 \dot{V}_1 + q_2 \dot{V}_2$, where $\dot{V}_i = dV_i/dt$ $(i = 1, 2)$.

For the introduction of new capacity we shall, for simplicity, write down the equation now only for the case where all new capacity is able to earn a non-negative quasi rent. Since it is natural to express this component in its relation to the amount of investment, we may use Equation (7.22), where K^+ is the amount of new capital introduced. We now consider the addition of new capital K^+ as generated by a flow of investment so that $dK^+ = I\,dt$.

In a similar way we use Equation (7.33) for capacity-increasing disembodied progress and Equation (7.57) for input-saving disembodied progress. We now let the parameter α, which indicated the scale of the progress, represent time so that $d\alpha$ can be replaced by dt. This means that we now have progress represented by $\kappa(\xi_1, \xi_2)$, $\mu_1(\xi_1, \xi_2)$ and $\mu_2(\xi_1, \xi_2)$ per unit of time (at $t = 0$).

In this way we establish the following "complete" growth equation (omitting superscripts [0], which were introduced in some of the derivations above):

$$\dot{X} = q_1 \dot{V}_1 + q_2 \dot{V}_2$$

$$+ \frac{1 - q_1 m_1^+ - q_2 m_2^+}{m_3^+} I$$

$$+ \int\int_{G(q_1, q_2)} (1 - q_1\xi_1 - q_2\xi_2)\kappa(\xi_1, \xi_2)f(\xi_1, \xi_2)\, \mathrm{d}\xi_1\, \mathrm{d}\xi_2$$

$$\left.\begin{array}{l} + q_1 \displaystyle\int\int_{G(q_1, q_2)} \mu_1(\xi_1, \xi_2)\xi_1 f(\xi_1, \xi_2)\, \mathrm{d}\xi_1\, \mathrm{d}\xi_2 \\[2ex] + q_2 \displaystyle\int\int_{G(q_1, q_2)} \mu_2(\xi_1, \xi_2)\xi_2 f(\xi_1, \xi_2)\, \mathrm{d}\xi_1\, \mathrm{d}\xi_2 \end{array}\right\}$$

(increase in current inputs)

(new capital, including effects of embodied technological progress)

(capacity-increasing dis-embodied technological progress)

(input-saving disembodied technological progress) (7.76)

The interpretations of the various terms are indicated to the right. They have been extensively interpreted and discussed in the previous sections and it is not necessary to repeat this here. Let it only be noticed that embodied technological progress works through the term on the second line of (7.76) as discussed in Section 7.3, and that the effect of better utilization of already existing technological knowledge etc. can also be included here as discussed towards the end of Section 7.3. Furthermore, if there is disembodied progress as represented by the functions κ, μ_1 and μ_2, there will probably also be a corresponding shift in the ex ante function and thereby an effect through the term on the second line of (7.76) also on this account as discussed in Section 7.4.

These elements which operate through the establishment of new capacity have in a way a dimension with respect to time which is different from the other components in the growth equation. If there is a continuous shifting of the ex ante function going on at $t = 0$, then this in itself does not influence the value of the term on the second line of (7.76). Only progress that has taken place over some finite time interval counts. Thus we can only say that the value of the term on the second line is higher than it would otherwise have been due to progress that has taken place over some interval in the past. (Cf. the discussion in connection with Equations (7.25–7.26).)

The expression in (7.76) explains total growth in a way which may be considered partly as a movement along the short-run macro function and partly as a shift in the function. The term $q_1 \dot{V}_1 + q_2 \dot{V}_2$ represents a movement along the surface of the function $X = F(V_1, V_2)$, whereas the other terms all represent shifts in $F(V_1, V_2)$.

If we have the same rates of capacity increasing and input saving progress, i.e. the case given by (7.67), then the growth equation (7.76) simplifies into

$$\dot{X} = q_1 \dot{V}_1 + q_2 \dot{V}_2 + \frac{1 - q_1 m_1^+ - q_2 m_2^+}{m_3^+} I$$

$$+ \int \int_{G(q_1, q_2)} \kappa(\xi_1, \xi_2) f(\xi_1, \xi_2) \, d\xi_1 \, d\xi_2. \tag{7.77}$$

If furthermore $\kappa(\xi_1, \xi_2) = \kappa = $ constant, then the last term can be written as κX, which corresponds to the traditional expression of disembodied progress at a rate κ. (Cf. Equation (7.72).)

An equation of a similar nature as (7.76) above could also be written down for the changes in the marginal rate of substitution q_1/q_2. Such an equation would be relevant e.g. for the development of distributive shares. First we would have the effect of changes in V_1 and V_2. Here the expression for the elasticity of substitution developed in Section 4.5 would be relevant. Other components in the total rate of change of q_1/q_2 could be included by means of Equations (7.14), (7.34) and (7.64). From the formulae in Section 4.5 we see that we could replace the factor $\sigma_1 \sigma_2$ in all these components by the elasticity of substitution s_{12} and otherwise simple (first-order) averages. Thus the elasticity of substitution is crucial to all the components of change in the marginal rate of substitution q_1/q_2.

Since no possibility of simplification seems to appear when we combine all these elements, the full expression will be omitted here.

It should be observed that there is a limit to the validity of the growth Equation (7.76). This has to do with the fact that production equipment within our framwork has a limited capacity to absorb current inputs. If we are already (at $t = 0$) at a point of full capacity utilization in the V_1, V_2-plane, i.e. a point like Q in Figure 4.4, then V_1 and V_2 can only be increased at rates which do not exceed the absorption at new production units plus the net (positive or negative) effect of disembodied progress affecting the capacity and mode of operation of existing production units. (V_1 and V_2 are interpreted as actually consumed inputs, not as available amounts.)

Consider first the case of no disembodied progress. Then only the first two lines of Equation (7.76) are relevant. If we now have full capacity utilization, then marginal productivities q_1 and q_2 are not meaningful for increases in inputs on existing production equipment. For the validity of (7.76) V_1 and V_2 must not increase more than corresponding to what is absorbed by new production units, i.e. we must have

$$\dot{V}_1 \leqq \frac{m_1^+}{m_3^+} I, \quad \dot{V}_2 \leqq \frac{m_2^+}{m_3^+} I, \tag{7.78}$$

where m_i^+/m_3^+ is input requirement for current input No. i per unit of capital invested ($i = 1, 2$).

If strict inequalities hold in (7.78), then we move into a situation of less than full capacity utilization. Then we have

$$\dot{X} = \frac{1}{m_3^+} I - q_1 \left(\frac{m_1^+}{m_3^+} I - \dot{V}_1\right) - q_2 \left(\frac{m_2^+}{m_3^+} I - \dot{V}_2\right) \tag{7.79}$$

with positive terms in the parantheses. Here I/m_3^+ is the increase in output capacity while the following terms reflect the fact that some current inputs have to be withdrawn from old production units in order to operate the new capacity. (q_1 and q_2 must in this case be interpreted as marginal productivities by *reductions* of V_1 and V_2 in $F(V_1, V_2)$ from the point of full capacity utilization.)

If strict equalities hold in (7.78), then we continue to have full capacity utilization. The growth process is then described by the following three conditions:

$$\dot{X} = \frac{1}{m_3^+} I, \quad \dot{V}_1 = m_1^+ \dot{X}, \quad \dot{V}_2 = m_2^+ \dot{X}. \tag{7.80}$$

One might of course also discuss the case where we are on the border of the region of substitution in the V_1, V_2-plane without being at the point of full capacity utilization. This will not be further pursued here.

Let us now reintroduce disembodied progress. Then old production units are able to absorb increased current inputs to the extent that there is capacity-increasing progress. At the same time they will push out current inputs to the extent that there is input-saving progress. For the validity of the growth equation, in a situation where there is already full capacity utilization, we must accordingly have

$$\dot{V}_i + \int \int \mu_i(\xi_1, \xi_2) \xi_i f(\xi_1, \xi_2) \, d\xi_1 \, d\xi_2 \leqq \frac{m_i^+}{m_3^+} I +$$

$$+ \int \int \xi_i \kappa(\xi_1, \xi_2) f(\xi_1, \xi_2) \, d\xi_1 \, d\xi_2, \quad (i = 1, 2) \tag{7.81}$$

where the integration is performed over the whole domain of $f(\xi_1, \xi_2)$, i.e. the region of positive capacity. When (7.81) is fulfilled as an equality, i.e. when we have growth by continual full utilization of all existing equipment, then (7.76) reduces to

$$\dot{X} = \frac{1}{m_3^+} I + \int \int \kappa(\xi_1, \xi_2) f(\xi_1, \xi_2) \, d\xi_1 \, d\xi_2. \tag{7.82}$$

The whole process will then be governed by (7.82) and (7.81) as equalities, while m_1^+, m_2^+ and m_3^+ are restricted by the ex ante function.

By (7.82) growth of output appears to be determined by growth of capacity through new investment plus capacity-increasing progress affecting old equipment. One might ask, where are the effects of the growth of current inputs, embodied technological progress and input-saving disembodied progress – or are these elements irrelevant under full capacity growth?

The answer is that they are relevant, but that they all operate through the capital-output ratio of new investment m_3^+ in Equation (7.82).

Compare a higher value of $\dot{V}_i$ with a lower value. In the case of the higher value Equation (7.81) can be fulfilled, as an equality, with a higher value of the coefficient m_i^+/m_3^+, which is achieved by exploiting the substitution possibilities in the ex ante function so as to make m_3^+ smaller and m_i^+ larger. Through (7.82) this will contribute to a faster growth of output. In the same way input-saving progress contributes to making possible a lower value of m_3^+ and thereby a faster growth of output.

Embodied technological progress operates through m_1^+, m_2^+ and m_3^+. Suppose that we, due to such progress, have the possibility of making m_1^+, m_2^+, m_3^+ lower than they would otherwise be. For given values of $\dot{V}_1$ and $\dot{V}_2$ and of investment I, we would have to choose the new values of m_1^+, m_2^+ and m_3^+ so that the proportions m_1^+/m_3^+ and m_2^+/m_3^+ remain the same in order that (7.81) be fulfilled. The lower value of m_3^+ contributes through (7.82) to making $\dot{X}$ larger than it would otherwise be.

We should perhaps also reconsider the effect of capacity-increasing disembodied progress. In order to find the net contribution of this type of progress under full capacity growth we should not only consider the immediate effect in Equation (7.82), but also take into account the conditions (7.81). For given values of $\dot{V}_1$, $\dot{V}_2$ and I it is clear that the presence of capacity-increasing progress makes it necessary to have lower values of m_1^+/m_3^+ and m_2^+/m_3^+. This must under the constraint of a given ex ante function, imply a higher value of m_3^+ and thereby a smaller contribution by the term I/m_3^+ in (7.82). Thus the net effect of the presence of capacity-increasing disembodied progress is smaller than the gross contribution represented by the second term in (7.82).[14]

In the discussion above we have disregarded the possibility of retirement of production equipment while it is still able to earn positive quasi rent. If there is a technologically determined limited durability of capital equipment we could supplement the analysis above by another element, viz. a distribution $f^-(\xi_1, \xi_2)$ of production units which are retired at any moment of time. This would then of course be related to the distribution f^+ of capacity added θ periods earlier if θ is the technologically determined durability, or obey a more complicated connection with the distributions f^+ at various earlier moments of time if there is a distribution rather than a fixed value for the physical durability.

7.9. Further considerations of full capacity growth and the connections with the long-run macro function

This section offers some supplementary considerations concerning a growth process in which total capacity is always fully utilized, i.e. a growth process satisfying (7.80). Technological progress will be disregarded until the end of the section. This type of process could alternatively be interpreted as the growth of total capacity, whether it be fully utilized or not[15]; this means that we could interpret the symbols X, V_1, V_2 in the following as referring to total capacity and current inputs necessary to exploit this capacity rather than actual output and inputs, while K and I refer to total capital stock (utilized or not) and its derivative with respect to time. Referring to Figure 4.4 we might say that V_1, V_2 and X represent point Q in the figure, and the corresponding value of X, while $\dot{V}_1$, $\dot{V}_2$ and $\dot{X}$ refer to the movements of this point.

In Section 2.5 we introduced a "technique relation" in the form

$$\Psi(\xi_1, \xi_2, \xi_3) = 1, \tag{7.83}$$

---

[14] In the discussion above of the role of disembodied progress we have only considered its effect on the old production units under a given ex ante function (in which substitution may be induced). As suggested in Section 7.4, it might sometimes be natural to think of disembodied progress as affecting both existing production units and the ex ante function. We could then interpret the discussion in the text above as referring to the additional gain by disembodied progress which derives from its disembodiedness.

[15] The capacity concept which is relevant in this context is of the plant variety, cf. case 3 in the table on pp. 64–65 of my paper (1968).

where ξ_1, ξ_2 and ξ_3 are inputs per unit of output of the two current inputs and capital per unit of output on new production units of optimal size, see Equation (2.17). The function $\Psi()$ in (7.83) could be chosen so that it is homogeneous of degree 1, see the discussion in connection with Equations (2.22–2.23). When Ψ is chosen in this way it also represents what we called the long-run macro production function

$$\Psi\left(\frac{V_1}{X}, \frac{V_2}{X}, \frac{K}{X}\right) = 1, \text{ or } X = \Psi(V_1, V_2, K), \tag{7.84}$$

see Equations (2.19) and (2.24).

In order to exploit the possibility of using simple geometrical illustrations I shall now consider only two inputs and let them be V_1 and V_2. It is, however, clear that the reasoning and the conclusions apply equally well in the case of three (or more) inputs.

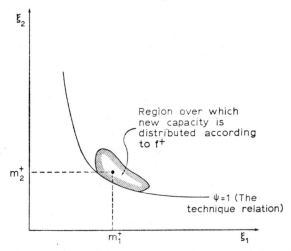

Fig. 7.4. The technique relation, distribution of new capacity, and average input coefficients for new capacity.

Consider now Figure 7.4. We have here drawn the curve corresponding to the technique relation (7.83) and indicated it by $\Psi = 1$. New capacity must consist of production units with input coefficients on or north-east of the technique curve $\Psi = 1$ in the figure. In other words, the distribution of new capacity, the form of which has previously been indicated by $f^+()$, attains positive values only in this part of the ξ_1, ξ_2-plane, e.g. over a region as suggested in the figure. The average input coefficients m_1^+ and m_2^+, defined on the basis of $f^+()$ by (7.1), must correspond to a point in the convex hull of the region over which f^+ is positive. When the attainable region delimited by $\Psi = 1$ is itself convex, it follows that the point m_1^+, m_2^+ must be on or north-east of the technique curve $\Psi = 1$.

In general the process under study will now be governed by equations

$$\dot{V}_1 = m_1^+ \dot{X}, \quad \dot{V}_2 = m_2^+ \dot{X}, \tag{7.85}$$

where m_1^+ and m_2^+ are determined by the distribution f^+ which is limited as explained in connection with Figure 7.4. The distribution f^+ and thereby the coefficients m_1^+ and m_2^+ may vary with time, but the bounding curve given by the technique relation

$$\Psi(\xi_1, \xi_2) = 1 \tag{7.86}$$

is constant since we have for the moment assumed that there is no technological progress. An interesting question now is what relation there will be between the actually realized input and output constellation V_1, V_2 and X under such a process and the long-run macro function, which in two dimensions is given by

$$\Psi\left(\frac{V_1}{X}, \frac{V_2}{X}\right) = 1, \text{ or } X = \Psi(V_1, V_2). \tag{7.87}$$

In studying this we will focus attention particularly on the movements in the inputs per unit of output V_1/X and V_2/X since these should, if the long-run macro production function be satisfied, correspond to points on the technique curve in Figure 7.4. For this purpose it is useful to consider the derivatives with respect to time of V_1/X and V_2/X, i.e.

$$\frac{d\,(V_i/X)}{dt} = \left(\frac{\dot{V}_i}{X} - \frac{V_i}{X}\right)\frac{\dot{X}}{X} \quad (i = 1, 2), \tag{7.88}$$

which may also be written as

$$\frac{\dot{V}_i}{X} = \frac{V_i}{X} + \frac{1}{\dot{X}/X}\frac{d\,(V_i/X)}{dt} \quad (i = 1, 2). \tag{7.89}$$

It is assumed that there is some growth going on so that $\dot{X} > 0$.

Several types of movement are now possible. We first consider the case where all new capacity at any moment of time is efficient and similar. The whole distribution f^+ and accordingly also the point of average input coefficients for new capacity m_1^+, m_2^+ in Figure 7.4 then collapse into a point on the curve $\Psi = 1$. From (7.85–7.86) we then have

$$\Psi\left(\frac{\dot{V}_1}{\dot{X}}, \frac{\dot{V}_2}{\dot{X}}\right) = 1, \text{ or } \dot{X} = \Psi(\dot{V}_1, \dot{V}_2). \tag{7.90}$$

This means that the *increments* in V_1, V_2 and X will satisfy what we have called the long-run macro function.

Let us consider a development where we are initially on the long-run macro function, i.e. we have $X(0) = \Psi(V_1(0), V_2(0))$. It is then easy to see that we will remain on this long-run function under the movement satisfying (7.90) if Ψ is a linear function. If Ψ is not linear, then this will not hold in general. It will hold only in the special case where V_1, V_2 and X grow in such a way that

$$\frac{\dot{V}_1}{\dot{X}} = \xi_1 = \frac{V_1(0)}{X(0)} \text{ and } \frac{\dot{V}_2}{\dot{X}} = \xi_2 = \frac{V_2(0)}{X(0)}, \tag{7.91}$$

with fixed ξ_1 and ξ_2 for all times t, and these values ξ_1 and ξ_2 are again, as indicated, equal to the ratios between the levels at the initial point of time $t = 0$. Then at any time t we also have

$$\frac{V_1}{X} = \xi_1 \text{ and } \frac{V_2}{X} = \xi_2, \tag{7.92}$$

and the fact that (7.90) is fulfilled implies that also the levels V_1, V_2 and X satisfy the long-run macro function (7.87).

In the introductory chapter we have referred to the long-run function also as the "steady state function". This term indicates a somewhat too narrow interpretation. It is clear that condition (7.91) is valid, and accordingly that V_1, V_2 and X obey the long-run function, if we have proportional growth in V_1, V_2 and X (constant and equal growth rates), but the condition also holds for more irregular growth paths where the growth rate is not constant.

We may say that the long-run function is valid when we have a homogeneous capital stock; it is not necessary that this capital stock has been generated by a path with a constant growth rate.

Alternative points on the long-run macro function can be reached by alternative growth paths of the type just described. But this of course does not imply that one can in practice move from one such point on the long-run function to another through a suitable investment path without cancelling the history already experienced (i.e. abandoning all existing capital equipment) and starting anew. Let us now consider actual movements of V_1, V_2, X when previously invested equipment is with us all the time, and when we do not necessarily adhere to conditions like (7.91) all the time so

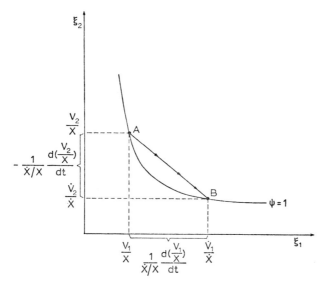

Fig. 7.5. Illustration of possible movements of V_1/X and V_2/X. Cf. Equations (7.88–7.89).

that the capital stock may be heterogeneous. Equations (7.88–7.89) are then useful.

Consider Figure 7.5, where we have drawn the technique curve $\Psi = 1$ as in Figure 7.4. As explained above this curve has a twofold interpretation: In the first place it is the possibility curve for $\dot{V}_1/\dot{X}$ and $\dot{V}_2/\dot{X}$ when new investments establish efficient production units; in the second place it represents the long-run production function in terms of factor inputs per unit of output.

We first assume that the point V_1/X, V_2/X is initially on the curve $\Psi = 1$; let the point be A in the figure. In which directions is it now possible to move from A? The answer follows from Equations (7.88) in conjunction with the requirement that $\dot{V}_1/\dot{X}$, $\dot{V}_2/\dot{X}$ shall satisfy the equation $\Psi = 1$. Let point B in the figure represent $\dot{V}_1/\dot{X}$, $\dot{V}_2/\dot{X}$. Then it follows from (7.88) that the point V_1/X, V_2/X moves in the direction indicated by the straight line from A to B, since the proportion between the components of the movement is

$$\frac{\dfrac{\mathrm{d}\,(V_2/X)}{\mathrm{d}t}}{\dfrac{\mathrm{d}\,(V_1/X)}{\mathrm{d}t}} = \frac{\dfrac{\dot{V}_2}{X} - \dfrac{V_2}{X}}{\dfrac{\dot{V}_1}{X} - \dfrac{V_1}{X}}. \qquad (7.93)$$

The speed of the movement will be directly proportional to the relative rate of creation of new capacity $\dot{X}/X$.

Since the line $\Psi = 1$ is curved as indicated in the figure, it follows that the point V_1/X, V_2/X always moves into a region which is, from an efficiency point of view, inferior to points on the line $\Psi = 1$, unless B is chosen so as to coincide with A, i.e. unless we have the kind of growth process mentioned in connection with (7.91).

If point B is located as indicated in Figure 7.5, and if we keep this point fixed, then the movement will continue along the straight line from A to B. For this case $\dot{V}_i/\dot{X}$ in (7.88) can be replaced by a constant ξ_i. Defining

$$u_i(t) = \xi_i - \frac{V_i(t)}{X(t)} \quad (i = 1, 2) \text{ and } x(t) = \frac{\dot{X}(t)}{X(t)} \tag{7.94}$$

we have from (7.88)

$$\dot{u}_i = - u_i x \quad (i = 1, 2) \tag{7.95}$$

with the solution

$$u_i(t) = u_i(0) e^{-\int_0^t x(\tau) d\tau} \quad (i = 1, 2) \tag{7.96}$$

or

$$\frac{V_i(t)}{X(t)} = \xi_i + \left(\frac{V_i(0)}{X(0)} - \xi_i \right) e^{-\int_0^t x(\tau) d\tau} \quad (i = 1, 2). \tag{7.97}$$

From this follows first that $V_i(t)/X(t)$ starts out from $V_i(0)/X(0)$ (point A in the figure) and approaches the value ξ_i (point B in the figure) gradually if $x = \dot{X}/X$ is always positive. The speed of the movement depends on $x(t)$.[16] Secondly, combining Equations (7.97) for $i = 1$ and 2 it follows that

$$\frac{\dfrac{V_2(t)}{X(t)} - \xi_2}{\dfrac{V_1(t)}{X(t)} - \xi_1} = \frac{\dfrac{V_2(0)}{X(0)} - \xi_2}{\dfrac{V_1(0)}{X(0)} - \xi_1}, \tag{7.98}$$

which means that $V_1(t)/X(t)$, $V_2(t)/X(t)$ moves along the straight line between A and B in the figure.

---

[16] For $V_i(t)/X(t)$ to converge to ξ_i it is necessary that $x(t)$ does not approach zero in such a manner that the integral $\int_0^t x(\tau) d\tau$ converges to a finite value.

The type of movement here discussed implies that if V_1/X, V_2/X has moved away from the long-run function $\Psi = 1$, then one is never able to return to a point on this long-run function in finite time. The only possibility is to make V_1/X, V_2/X converge towards such a point as shown by (7.97).[17]

Let us next consider cases where point B in the figure is not kept fixed, but moves all the time. Then even convergence towards obeying the long-run macro function does not hold (unless the movement of point B converges towards a point on $\Psi = 1$). Two cases are suggested in Figure 7.6. (The

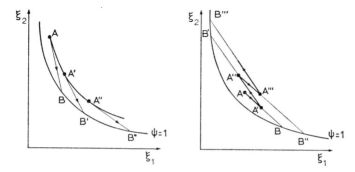

Fig. 7.6. Movements of V_1/X, V_2/X not converging towards the long-run production function.

cases are only meant to illustrate the mechanism, they are not suggested as particularly realistic cases.) In the figure to the left the movement of the point V_1/X, V_2/X starts in point A in the direction of point B. However, point B is moving along the curve $\Psi = 1$ through B', B'', ... The actual point V_1/X, V_2/X will then follow a curve like A, A', A'', ..., i.e. a curve with a tangent always pointing towards some point on the curve $\Psi = 1$, but itself never reaching this curve. In the figure to the right the movement also starts in a point A in the direction of B, which is on the curve $\Psi = 1$. However, when V_1/X, V_2/X has reached A', then $\dot{V}_1/\dot{X}$, $\dot{V}_2/\dot{X}$ is chosen at B', and V_1/X, V_2/X starts moving in the direction of B'. Then at A'' the direction is again changed, now towards B''. In this way the actual point V_1/X, V_2/X will follow the path A, A', A'', A''', ..., moving itself into more and more inefficient points as compared with points on the long-run production function.

_____

[17] These statements do, of course, not hold when old capital equipment disappears in finite time by depreciation or scrapping.

Comparing with Figure 4.4, the case to the right in Figure 7.6 will correspond to the creation of a very wide region of positive capacity, with a correspondingly wide region of substitution in the short-run production function; on the other hand, as we have observed before, points on the long-run production function would only be reached if the region of positive capacity degenerates into a point and correspondingly the region of substitution in the short-run production function collapses into a factor ray.

In connection with the illustrations in Figure 7.6 it is not essential that we started out from a point A, which is not on the curve $\Psi = 1$. Even with point A on the curve one could get into such types of movements as are illustrated in the figure.

Also in such cases where point B is moving we could solve differential equations so as to find expressions for the movements of V_1/X and V_2/X, using (7.88) in a similar way as by (7.94–7.97). Now $\dot{V}_1/\dot{X}$ and $\dot{V}_2/\dot{X}$ could not be replaced by constants however, but rather by functions of time t.

In the reasoning above we have assumed that the new capacity created at any moment of time consists of similar and efficient production units. There are, however, as suggested in previous sections, many reasons why this would not be so in practice. If we assume instead that new capacity created at some point of time consists of production units which are not necessarily equal, but corresponding to different points on the ex ante production function, then Equations (7.85) hold and we may write (7.88) as

$$\frac{d\,(V_i/X)}{dt} = \left(m_i^+ - \frac{V_i}{X}\right)\frac{\dot{X}}{X}. \quad (i = 1, 2) \tag{7.99}$$

Visualizing this again in a figure, we could repeat the whole reasoning in connection with Figures (7.5–7.6), now however with point B representing m_1^+, m_2^+. If the new capacity created at the point of time considered is distributed along the curve $\Psi = 1$, then the average point m_1^+, m_2^+ will be located not on the curve $\Psi = 1$, but in the region north-east of this curve. The situation is illustrated in Figure 7.7. The starting-point for V_1/X, V_2/X is again point A. The new capacity created is now distributed along the heavily drawn part of the curve $\Psi = 1$, with average point B. (This point must be located within the segment indicated.) Point A then moves in the direction of B. If the relative distribution of new capacity created is kept constant over time, then B will remain constant and the movement converges towards this point. Otherwise similar types of movements to those which are indicated in Figure 7.6 could also be generated now, only with points B, B', B'', ... lying north-east of the line $\Psi = 1$ rather than on this line.

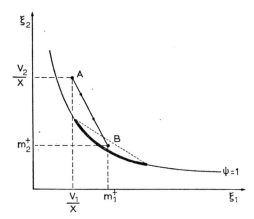

Fig. 7.7. The movement of V_1/X, V_2/X when the new capacity created is distributed along the ex ante curve.

Nothing essentially new is added when the new capacity is distributed over the region delimited by the curve $\Psi = 1$ (as illustrated in Figure 7.4), rather than along this curve, but it tends of course to keep the point V_1/X, V_2/X farther away from points representing the long-run macro production function.

Up till now we have, in this section, disregarded technological progress. Let us briefly suggest how such progress will influence the types of movement illustrated by the figures of this section.

Consider first embodied progress. This will act so as to move the ex ante function and accordingly also the long-run macro function $\Psi = 1$ continually towards the origin. In the cases studied above the actual V_1/X, V_2/X-point might converge towards a point on the long-run macro function if point B in the figures was kept fixed somewhere on the curve $\Psi = 1$. Now this will no longer be so. If B now moves with the curve $\Psi = 1$ the actual V_1/X, V_2/X-point may "chase" point B, but will in general not be able to come in the neighbourhood of it. The only possibility would be such a fast increase in the growth rate of total capacity $\dot{X}/X$ that there is a convergence towards a situation where the amount of older equipment is negligible as compared with the amount of brand-new equipment.[18]

---

[18] The point V_1/X, V_2/X would be nearer to the long-run function the higher is the growth rate $\dot{X}/X$ since a higher growth rate contributes to making the proportion of new to old equipment larger. But an *increasing* growth rate is necessary in order to make V_1/X, V_2/X *converge* towards the (moving) long-run macro function.

The case of disembodied progress is different. In this case the V_1/X, V_2/X-point moves not only as a result of investment in new equipment, but also as a result of technological progress. This could be worked out on the basis of Equations (7.81–7.82) combined with (7.88). If we think of disembodied progress as affecting both the efficiency of old equipment and the ex ante function to the same extent (compare Section 7.4), then the effect of this type of progress would be to shift all elements of our figures gradually towards the origin without changing the relative position of the actual V_1/X, V_2/X-point and the long-run macro function $\Psi = 1$ at any moment of time. The types of movements which we have discussed in connection with the preceding figures would be added to this gradual shifting towards the origin.

The relationship between the analysis of this section and the analysis in previous sections where we did not assume full capacity utilization is that the history of investments as studied in this section generates the capacity distribution which exists at any moment of time. If there should at some moment of time be less than full capacity utilization, then the general growth Equation (7.76) is relevant. The fact that there is less than full capacity utilization tends to bring the actual V_1/X, V_2/X-point closer to the long-run macro function as represented by the curve $\Psi = 1$ since there are decreasing returns to scale in the short-run function along which V_1, V_2, X contract when capacity utilization is decreased so that, roughly speaking, V_1 and V_2 are decreased relatively more than X.

CHAPTER 8

Empirical approaches to production studies

8.1. *Introductory remarks*

In Chapter 1 I referred to the rather unsatisfactory results of empirical studies on production functions as part of the background for the development of the approach reported in this book. Traditional approaches are based on one type of production function. There are of course references to the distinction between short run and long run and between micro level and aggregate level, but these distinctions represent different interpretations rather than different formulations. In our approach there are clearly different formulations of the various types of production functions. It is clear therefore that empirical analyses based on our framework must specify explicitly what type of functions they are after, and there is no reason why different types of data should yield similar empirical production functions since they may be relevant to basically different concepts of production functions.

A complete econometric study of the structure of production of a sector according to our approach would require a body of data which is rarely available. It would be necessary to have data for individual enterprises over time, or, in other words, a time series of cross sections. By suitable stratifications, or more refined techniques, it might then be possible to estimate both the ex ante and the ex post production functions at the micro level as well as the various types of technological progress discussed in Chapter 7. On this basis the short-run and long-run macro functions could be constructed. However, under perfect market conditions and similar price expectations in various quarters there might not be sufficient variation to reveal the ex ante function even on the basis of such a body of observations so that even more information, e.g. of direct technical or engineering type, might be necessary. We shall not be able to carry out any such complete empirical study in the following sections and chapters.

The nearest I have seen to such a complete study is given by Belinfante (1969). His study is based on time series – cross section data for the American steam power generating industry. He assumes that there are ex ante substitution possibilities. Ex post he assumes no substitution possibilities, but the model is slightly more flexible than our standard putty-clay model in that there is some variation in ex post factor proportions related to the degree of capacity utilization. (Compare Section 3.5 of this book.) Factor proportions are given for fuel, capital, operation labour and maintenance. The author comments that "there is a considerable amount of variation in these proportions from plant to plant", which suggests that studies along the lines analysed in this book might be interesting. The author is able to separate embodied and disembodied technological progress partly because there are observations available for plants during the periods between the time when they first got into operation and the time when the first additional investments were made, thus yielding almost direct observations of disembodied progress (similarly to the case of the well-known "Horndal effect" reported by Lundberg 1961). Disembodied progress seems to be of the type which we have designated as input-saving. The author observes that "disembodied technical change is significant for each input".[1]

In the following sections of this chapter I shall proceed by discussing various more traditional approaches to empirical production studies. The main purpose of the discussion will be to find out if or to what extent the results of such studies can be expected to yield results that are meaningful within our theoretical framework, and to which concepts of production functions they may be relevant. Econometric literature abounds in time series and cross section estimation of neo-classical production function, and I shall only discuss these types of studies in rather general terms without giving many references.[2] On the other hand I shall be more explicit in referring to some studies which may perhaps be said not to belong to the mainstream of econometric studies of production functions, but which gain particular relevance within our framework.

In Chapter 9 I shall report on some empirical analyses carried out on the basis of data from Norwegian tanker shipping along lines suggested by the present theoretical framework. They will however not illustrate all aspects of the theory.

8.2. *Production functions based on direct technological information*

The most obvious way of establishing production functions should be to

---

[1] Dr. Belinfante's study was available to me only at the final stage of the preparation of the manuscript for this book, so that I have not been able to take full advantage of it and refer to it at all relevant places in the text.

[2] Surveys are found in Walters (1963) and Brown (ed.) (1967).

utilize technological information. Nevertheless, this approach – often referred to as the engineering approach – has not been very widely used. In his survey from 1963 Walters commented that "the use of engineering and technical data for production functions is still in its infancy". This seems to be a valid observation even now after several years. There are of course several reasons for this. One important reason is probably that the engineering approach will give production functions for the very micro level while economists have generally been more interested in production functions at higher levels of aggregation.

The engineering approach to establishing production functions can take several forms. Chenery in his early contributions (1949, 1953) pointed out two forms: The experimental approach, and the analytical approach. The latter works by mathematical deductions from basic physical, chemical and technological principles. The dividing line is not always clear, and combinations of these two forms are of course also possible. In any case the function arrived at describes the relationship between inputs and outputs according to known possible ways of designing equipment and organizing production, i.e. it refers to the ex ante function at the micro level according to the terminology of this study. Since an ex ante function describes the possible ex post functions and how to establish them – see the general formulation (2.6) – a complete study would also give us the ex post functions. However, the task is often simplified to describing the full capacity point of the ex post function rather than the full function which is of course not necessarily of the form which we have assumed in our standard model.

Some more recent studies have used approaches which cannot easily be classified as belonging to the experimental or analytical approach.

Let me discuss the engineering approach to establishing production functions somewhat further by referring to some of the rather few examples of applications of this approach which are found in the literature.[3]

A very early example of a production function based on engineering types of information is a not very well known paper by Frisch (1935). It is concerned with chocolate production and considers two inputs: fat and "moulding-cooling-work". There are substitution possibilities between these two factors, because a certain number of castings must be scrapped and thrown back into the liquid mass and remoulded, thereby entailing additional work in moulding and cooling – and the proportion of scrapping is lower the

---

[3] I omit discussions of production functions based on experiments in agricultural production. In most cases these describe production processes where fixed equipment does not play the part which we have assumed.

higher is the fat content. According to the findings this generates a sufficiently wide scope for substitution to be of economic interest. This substitution possibility is apparently not rigidly embodied in the type of equipment used so that the case does not fit strictly into our standard model. This study may be indicative of other processes where raw materials and labour may be substitutable inputs because waste material can be recovered by means of more work. But there are certainly also cases where such a recovering, or the exploitation of the recovered materials, requires specific equipment so that the implied substitution possibility is of the ex ante, but not of the ex post type.

Classical and well-known studies in the field are Chenery (1949, 1953), referred to above. A concrete example given by Chenery is a production function for the process of gas transmission. There are two forms of the production function. One gives output (gas transmitted) as a function of physical inputs: "horsepower" and "tons of pipe", and the other form gives output as a function of "capital" and "current inputs" in dollars at fixed prices. Substitution between pipe and horsepower in pumping stations is here made possible particularly by the fact that smaller compressor capacity is needed the greater is the pipe diameter. This substitution possibility is clearly of the ex ante type which we have assumed; the mode of operation of the equipment is embodied in the types of pipes and compressors installed. Substitution possibilities between "capital" (comprising both pipes and pumping stations) and "current inputs" (labour, maintenance, materials, etc.) are clearly present, but rather limited because variations in the pipe/compressor proportion do not entail great changes in labour and other current inputs. As remarked by Vernon Smith[4], Chenery's production function is somewhat incomplete in that it does not include an explicit analysis of the energy input to the compressor process. If the analysis had been extended in this direction it might have revealed substitution possibilities between current inputs. These substitution possibilities would clearly be of the ex ante type, with ex post input proportions embodied in the type of equipment installed.

Chenery concludes that "a purely statistical analysis of the relation of output of all pipelines to the diameter, pressure, and horsepower, for example, would be a hopeless task because the observed range of variation in their proportions is small and it could not adequately take into account the different operating conditions for which the lines were designed. A correla-

---

[4] Smith (1961), p. 36.

tion among capital, labour, and output would probably be even further from the true form of the production function".[5] This conclusion is probably valid for a wide range of cases where one might attempt to establish ex ante micro production functions.

Similar processes for electricity and heat transmission and some chemical processes have been studied by Vernon Smith.[6] The main purpose of Smith's study is to expose the extent and importance of input substitution in industrial production processes to empirical verification. For this purpose he finds the engineering approach most powerful. The results are summarized in the following way: "The fundamental hypothesis growing out of this empirical examination is that of the stock-flow production function. ... Furthermore, the capital inputs are freely variable in considering hypothetical alternative production design plans, but once such stock inputs are installed, they can no longer be varied except by installing parallel facilities or by replacement".[7] Thus the production functions arrived at, called "long-run production functions" by Smith, are clearly of our ex ante type. Unfortunately there is also in Smith little of empirical evidence concerning substitution possibilities between various current inputs such as labour, energy, etc.

A recent study related to the production rather than transmission of energy is MacAvoy (1969). MacAvoy derives production functions for electricity production by nuclear breeder reactors on the basis of a number of highly detailed "design studies", which describe equipment as well as plant operations which reflect "today's views on technology for the 1980's and 1990's". The output variable is "maximum sustainable capacity for producing electricity" and inputs are capital and fuel. The technological factors accounting for the substitution possibilities between these inputs are described and seem to be well reflected by production functions of the Cobb-Douglas type. However, different such functions are established for different ranges of capacity and for different main types of reactors.

It is clear that the functions derived reflect only ex ante substitution possibilities, whereas there will be little scope for varying the way of operating the plants after they have been constructed.

Another very interesting recent example of the engineering approach to establishing production functions is DeSalvo (1969). He studies the linehaul process of rail freight transportation. Output is defined in terms of ton-miles

---

[5] Chenery (1953), pp. 321–322.
[6] Smith (1961), Chapter II.
[7] Smith (1961), p. 5.

transported per hour. This output may be considered as the product of cargo-tonnage and average speed of the train. DeSalvo studies how these two components are in turn determined by a number of factors such as size, type and number of cargo-carrying units in the case of tonnage, and motive power of the vehicle, drag-force characteristics and a number of delay-causing factors in the case of the speed component. Newton's second law of motion and a number of technical relationships known from railroad engineering are invoked. The isoquants are derived for a production function which expresses ton-miles per hour transported by one train as a function of horse-power used and number of cars in the train, showing a fairly high degree of substitutability. Substitution here comes about by compensating for a reduction in the number of cars by using a more powerful locomotive. We shall encounter a similar type of substitution, through compensation for smaller load capacity by higher speed so as to obtain the same number of ton-miles *per unit of time*, in the following chapter, where we shall give some empirical evidence concerning tanker ships. We should notice already here, however, that there is an important difference between the two cases. The substitution possibilities described by DeSalvo's production function are, if I understand it correctly, a type of ex post substitution possibility, which exists because cars and locomotives of different types can be combined freely in forming a train. In the case of conventional tanker ships engine and load capacity are rigidly determined and combined by the building of the ship so that the trade-off between speed and load capacity mainly generate ex ante substitution possibilities.

The model which forms our standard case would be more relevant to a production function with some expression for the capacity of the locomotive as output and labour, fuel and capital as inputs, substitution possibilities then existing in the ex ante sense as a reflection of the range of possible designs. DeSalvo's study does not explicitly bear on this aspect.

Above I have referred to two different forms of engineering approaches to production functions – the experimental and the analytical form. The MacAvoy study, based on "design studies", does perhaps not easily fall within these forms. There is a well-known study by Kurz and Manne (1963), which can quite clearly not be classified in this way although it is called "Engineering Estimates of Capital-Labor Substitution in Metal Machining". The empirical basis for this study consists of observations of the modes of operation for a large number of different general-purpose machine-tools in performing certain well-defined tasks. The main figures given are the value of the machines, labout input and daily output in performing each task on each machine. This type of study might be considered as an example of cross section studies or efficiency studies to be discussed in Sections 8.3 and 8.7 below, but may also with some justification be considered as an example of the engineering approach since it is based on detailed technical description of the tasks and the operation of the equipment. The substitution between labour and capital involved is due to various degrees of automation and is thus clearly of the ex ante type.

For each task output per worker is plotted against capital investment per worker, each point representing the performance of one machine tool at this task. In processing these data Kurz and Manne first eliminated all inefficient points, the criterion being that "if, in the performance of that task, one machine tool had a higher investment cost and not a higher output than a second machine tool, the first was said to be "inefficient" and was deleted from our analysis". (Since there is one worker at each tool, investment cost and output will here be per worker.) Next Cobb-Douglas functions and CES-functions were fitted, by least squares methods, to the remaining (efficient) points. The fits were very good, the elasticity in the case of the CES-function came out very close to 1, and the elasticities in the Cobb-Douglas functions were reasonable as viewed against distributional shares. (I omit some interesting technical points concerning the estimations.)

Within the framework outlined in this book I think the results of the Kurz-Manne study can be clearly interpreted as giving estimates of the ex ante function, or rather as estimates of the technique relation which represents the efficient points on the ex ante surface in terms of output per unit of input. For the fitted functions our technique relation would correspond to the isoquants representing 1 unit of output.

With this interpretation in mind one might perhaps have proceeded differently from Kurz and Manne in two respects.

In the first place, one might have plotted the observations in a diagram giving labour per unit of output and capital per unit of output (magnitudes of the ξ-type) rather than in the diagram mentioned above. It is not clear that the same points would be eliminated as being inefficient in both cases. Consider Figure 8.1, which corresponds to the Kurz-Manne diagram, i.e. we measure capital per unit of labour – say k/v – along the horizontal axis and output per unit of labour – say x/v – along the vertical axis. Suppose there is an observation corresponding to point P in the figure. According to the Kurz-Manne criterion this point would rule out all observations in the region south-east of APB' in the figure as inefficient since we have here higher investment cost and not higher output per tool or per worker. Other points would not be ruled out as inefficient by the observation corresponding to P.

Now assume that we are concerned with capital and labout input per unit of output, i.e. v/x and k/x, rather than capital and output per unit of labour. These proportions can be expressed as

$$v/x = \frac{1}{x/v}, \quad k/x = \frac{k/v}{x/v}.$$

It is now reasonable – and it would agree with our definition of the technique relation – to declare a point to be inefficient if there is another point for which both input coefficients v/x and k/x are lower, or at least one is lower and the other one is the same. In Figure 8.1 v/x is higher than at P for all points below BB', and k/x is higher than at P for all points to the right of the ray OQ from the origin through point P. Accordingly all points in the shaded region below and to the right of the broken line OPB' in the figure (boundaries included) are dominated by point P, whereas Kurz and Manne according to their criterion let a point P dominate only points to the right of and below the broken line APB'.

In practice I do not think this alternative way of discriminating between efficient and inefficient points would make much difference to the overall

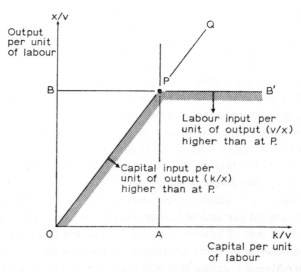

Fig. 8.1. According to the Kurz-Manne criterion points south-east of APB' are dominated by point P, while points south-east of OPB' are dominated by point P if we seek efficiency in the v/x, k/x-plane.

results obtained by Kurz and Manne with regard to the scope for capital-labour substitution.[8]

The other point announced on which one might have proceeded differently on the basis of our interpretation is the method of fitting the production function. As mentioned above, Kurz and Manne employed the least squares method. By this procedure one will necessarily obtain a fitted curve which is such that some *actually observed* points appear to be more efficient than points on the curve. This is hardly reasonable if the curve is to be interpreted as an ex ante curve or technique relation in our sense. Fitting a frontier function, with all observed points on the one side of the curve or on it, would seem to be more appropriate.[9] However, the Kurz-Manne procedure might perhaps be defended on the assumption that there are errors of measurement. As discussed in Section 2.2, the concept of an ex ante function is not an unambiguous one, and the method of fitting may also be chosen differently according to which interpretation one prefers.

Again I do not think that alternative methods would yield significantly different conclusions with regard to the scope for capital-labour substitution.

A third point of some importance, which has been raised in the discussion following Kurz and Manne's article, is concerned with the measurement of capital. Particularly if different tools have different durability the capital input measure used by Kurz and Manne may be inappropriate and distort the discrimination between efficient and inefficient points. The arguments concerning this aspect might be related to the role played by t in our general ex post function (2.5), but we shall not pursue this further here.[10]

Within our framework the type of data used by Kurz and Manne could also be processed for another purpose, namely for the construction of a short-run macro production function. It would then, however, be necessary to have not only the technical information on the efficiency of each type of machine, but also on the number of machines of each type existing in the sector under consideration so as to be able to construct the full capacity

---

[8] In the diagrammatic illustration offered by Kurz and Manne for one of the tasks considered all points which are efficient according to their criterion remain efficient also according to the criterion proposed in the text, but one of them seems to be on the brink of being declared inefficient by our criterion, while it is on the efficient side by a large margin according to the Kurz-Manne criterion.

[9] Compare Farrell (1957) and Aigner and Chu (1968), to be further discussed in following sections.

[10] See Furubotn (1965) and Lave (1966). A correction for different durabilities might be carried out along lines proposed in Johansen and Sørsveen (1967), pp. 191–194, following a suggestion by Haavelmo (1960), pp. 100–101.

distribution. In this case not only the efficient machines, but all machines should be included in the basis for the construction of the production function. This task would of course be much more interesting if other current inputs in addition to labour, perhaps energy in some form, were taken explicitly into account.

The machines in Kurz and Manne's data are "general purpose tools" which can be used for a variety of tasks. It would then be possible to establish one macro function for each task, but these would not together reveal the full production possibilities embodied in the existing stock of machines. There would seem to be two possibilities open. Firstly, one could try to define a sort of aggregate output by weighting the various tasks. I do not know enough about the technical aspects to say how meaningful this would be, but some of the coefficients estimated by Kurz and Manne on the basis of the pooled data, referring to the various characteristics of the tasks, might perhaps be useful for this purpose. Secondly, one might try to construct the multi-dimensional production set for all tasks, i.e. without any aggregation of the various tasks. This would go beyond the types of analysis otherwise discussed in this book, but could be seen as a multi-product generalization of our concept of a short-run macro function.

We may conclude this discussion of the engineering approach to establishing production functions by the following summarizing observations.

(1) The engineering approach demands very much detailed work and is feasible only for rather narrowly defined types of output. But there is a wide range of possible applications. The examples discussed above refer to production of energy, transmission of energy, goods transport and material production.

(2) It is generally rather easy to interpret the results of such studies within our framework: They give information on the ex ante function at the micro level. Since the long-run function at the macro level can be derived from the ex ante function at the micro level, the engineering studies are of course also relevant for this type of production function.[11] As suggested in connection with the discussion of the Kurz-Manne study, engineering data combined with a machine census might also form the basis for the construction of a short-run macro function. (Our study of tankers in the following chapter can perhaps be seen as an example of this.)

---

[11] It may be observed, however, that many of the engineering studies show increasing returns to scale over the whole range of output capacities covered by the studies and that other considerations than the type of optimization underlying the construction of the long-run macro function in the sense of Section 2.5 seem to limit the scale of each individual unit in practice.

(3) There are various forms of information which can be classified as engineering data. While they all give information relevant for the ex ante production function, the degree of "ex-anteness" may be different. E.g., the design studies underlying the MacAvoy study of nuclear breeder reactors are explicitly future-orientated, and the production function established aims at describing possibilities at a more or less distant future. On the other hand, the Kurz-Manne study uses data for existing machines and will therefore give a more conservative ex ante function even if inefficient machines are disregarded in the final estimation, perhaps a function already surpassed by new technology when the study is completed. The other studies discussed are probably of an intermediate type. However, nothing of this changes the ex ante nature of the production functions established, it only affects the date to which the functions refer. (Repeated studies for the same type of output, frontier functions of the Kurz-Manne type for different vintages of tools, or design studies aiming at the estimated technology for different years would reveal the movement of the ex ante function, i.e. technological progress.)

(4) Most of the engineering studies available in the literature indicate such a degree of substitutability between capital and labour that one is justified in treating substitution as an essential aspect in economics. In most cases the substitution possibilities revealed are clearly of the ex ante type while the mode of operation ex post is firmly embodied in the equipment, machinery or plant constructed. But some studies also reveal some ex post substitution possibilities, pointing to the need in some cases for a more general model than our standard model.

(5) Most of the studies available in the literature are concerned primarily with the substitution between labour and capital, which is of course of central importance. However, they would have been of greater interest in connection with the theories outlined in this book if they had been more explicit in the treatment also of other current inputs in addition to labour.

8.3. *Cross section studies*

The Kurz-Manne study referred to in the previous section is of course a sort of cross section study. The more "orthodox" cross section studies which we shall comment upon in this section do however differ from the Kurz-Manne study in several respects. The data are of a more traditional type, based on economic statistics rather than technical information about individual pieces of equipment. Naturally they then correspond to a higher level of aggregation. We may distinguish between two rather different types: cross section data for enterprises within an industry, and cross section data giving aggregate data for the same industry in different regions, states or countries.[12] The more "orthodox" cross section studies also fit the production function to *all* observations, i.e. without eliminating inefficient units before the function is fitted to the data.[13]

It is difficult to draw definite conclusions from cross section studies. Nerlove summarizes his recent survey (1967) by pointing out the striking diversity of the results and the many apparent inconsistencies. He discusses these mainly in terms of biases of estimation, as does e.g. also Mayor (1969), referred to in Chapter 1. I shall not discuss these aspects here, but rather consider the problem of how such cross section studies could be interpreted under rather ideal statistical circumstances.

If we have a cross section of enterprises using capital and, say, two current inputs as we have usually assumed, we would clearly be able to estimate the ex ante function as defined by (2.1) on this basis if the following conditions were met:

(a) The enterprises are established on the basis of the same technological information, i.e. on the basis of the same ex ante function.

(b) All observations correspond to full capacity utilization.

(c) There is sufficient spread in the observations to make estimation possible.

In connection with formula (2.1) we commented that we might expect the ex ante function to have "classical" properties. Econometric research on the basis of cross section data usually proceeds in conformity with this e.g. by allowing for non-constant returns to scale.

---

[12] For the first class of cross section studies we might furthermore distinguish between data for individual plants and data for firms comprising several plants (and a plant may again contain several technical units). This will of course be of importance for the interpretation of the results, since an ex ante function for a firm will take into account the possibility of choice between e.g. several small plants and one bigger plant and thus exhibit different scale properties from the ex ante function at the plant level. (Compare e.g. Komiya (1962) and Nerlove (1963).) We might also refer to a third category of cross section studies, viz. cross sections of different industries within a country which are also sometimes found in the literature. I find it hard, however, to interpret production functions based on such cross sections in any very meaningful way, and shall accordingly omit further considerations of them here.

[13] A study by Aigner and Chu (1968), to be discussed further on, is, with some reservations, an exception.

There may, however, be serious difficulties in connection with all the three conditions (a)–(c) given above. I shall comment on them in turn.

(a) If all enterprises covered by the data have been established at the same point of time we may perhaps not have serious difficulties about point (a). Of course this does not guarantee that all observations reflect the same technological knowledge since "knowledge" is a relative and subjective concept, as discussed in Section 2.2. However, having chosen which sort of ex ante function we are after we might adapt the way of processing data accordingly. E.g., if we are after some sort of average ex ante function a function fitted to data by the least squares method might be appropriate; on the other hand, if we are after some sort of efficient ex ante function a function fitted to data as a frontier function might be the appropriate thing to construct. In either case the precise form of fitting the function should of course depend on the further specification of the statistical aspects of the model (particularly related to point (c) above).

The most serious difficulties concerning point (a) stem of course from embodied technological progress. To the extent that such progress has been operating in the past the observations of inputs and outputs of enterprises of different vintages will represent different levels of technological knowledge, and a function fitted to all these observations by least squares or some similar technique will have only descriptive value. In other words, it will give a sort of summary information about the sector studied, but it will not yield a structural equation which indicates possible variations in a meaningful way. There seem to be two or three ways out of this.

One way is to assume that embodied technological progress has taken place in a smooth, parametric way while the *form* of the ex ante function has remained essentially the same. With some data concerning the age of the enterprise, average age of equipment or some similar indicator one might then try to estimate the ex ante function by utilizing all observations in the cross section material.[14]

The other way to proceed is to estimate a sort of frontier function on the basis of the given observations. This can be done in several ways, e.g. as suggested by the Kurz-Manne study discussed in the preceding section, i.e. by first eliminating "inefficient" points according to some criterion and fitting a function to the remaining points.

---

[14] Some such variables have been included in some econometric studies, but apparently not always with great success. However, in Hildebrand and Liu (1965) the ratio of net (depreciated) value to gross value of the capital stock seems to work reasonably well when introduced in a special way.

Aigner and Chu (1968) have fitted production functions of the Cobb-Douglas form (with unrestricted scale elasticity) as a frontier to cross section observations. Their approach is, however, not a two-step procedure like the Kurz-Manne approach, but rather a programming method (linear or quadratic), where the function is fitted to data (in logarithmic form) in one step by minimizing the sum of deviations (simple or squared) subject to the constraint that all deviations are of one sign so that the function is an efficiency frontier.

It may be difficult to choose between these two approaches to fitting a frontier function. The following consideration may perhaps indicate the most appropriate choice. In the Kurz-Manne approach the fitted function will be insensitive to changes in the inefficient observations as long as they remain inefficient. In the Aigner-Chu approach the fitted function may shift between various possible positions as a result of changes in observations which are not (before as well as after the change) on the frontier because the function is fitted so as to minimize the total of distances to all points. Which case is the more attractive on the basis of our technological assumptions? To the extent that the inefficient observations are inefficient because they represent past rather than present technological knowledge, and to the extent that we are not willing to say anything about the speed of (embodied) technological progress, it seems clear that inefficient points should not influence the position of the fitted function (interpreted as our ex ante function). On the other hand, we may argue that "technological progress" is a sort of residual which we know little about and that we like a fitted function more the smaller is the "total amount of technological progress" which it implies. This "total amount of technological progress" may be measured by the sum of distances (simple or squared) from each and every observation to the fitted production surface, i.e. this consideration leads to something like the Aigner-Chu approach.[15]

Combining such alternative assumptions as mentioned above with different assumptions about presence or absence of errors of measurement, different assumptions about other random elements[16] and different interpretations of the concept of ex ante function (as discussed in Section 2.2) a

---

[15] If we go one step further and say that (embodied) technological progress can be represented by a regular parametric shifting of the ex ante function, then we are back to the case where it may be most appropriate not to fit a frontier function at all, but rather to include the age of equipment or some similar indicator in the regressions.

[16] See particularly the distinction between "embodied" and "disembodied random elements" under point (14) in Section 3.1.

great variety of methods of fitting the function can clearly be imagined. The considerations given above only illustrate the kind of circumstances that may be of relevance in making the choice.

Before leaving Aigner and Chu's study it should be mentioned that their idea about the meaning of the production function does not necessarily coincide with ours, although they recognize limited abilities to make adjustments and to some degree also the embodiedness of technological progress. However, their approach is felt to be less provocative within the framework of the present study than within the neo-classical framework.[17]

Between the two methods of coping with embodied technological progress mentioned above (using age of plant or some similar variable as an additional variable in regressions over the whole material, or in some way or other fitting a frontier function) there is a middle course which might be taken if there is a sufficient number of observations, viz. to divide the whole material into subsamples according to vintages and fit separate functions to each subsample (again "through" each subsample or as a frontier to it according to which interpretation of the ex ante function one prefers). Such a fitting to separate subsamples defined by vintages has been done by Komiya (1962) in his study of the U.S. steam power industry.[18] If successful this procedure would be the best one to estimate the rate and type of embodied technological progress without making unduly restrictive assumptions a priori.

Komiya tried to fit a traditional production function with substitution between capital, labour and fuel. This attempt was unsuccessful. Komiya then fell back upon a limitational formulation of the production function with input functions relating inputs to output in a linear logarithmic form, a formulation which seemed to work satisfactorily. For fuel input Komiya reached the conclusion that reduction in fuel inputs per unit of output has been generated by increased scale of plants rather than shifts in the input function; there is a rather similar result for capital input, or even more: "the shift, if any, is in the direction of requiring more capital for plants of the same size"; for labour the picture is somewhat complicated, but there seems to have taken place a rather strong negative shift in the labour input function.

---

[17] The authors state, in the introduction to the paper, that it "aims towards a primarily provocative goal".

[18] Komiya divided the plants into groups constructed in the periods 1930–45, 1946–50, 1951–53, 1954–56. Within each group he used data for the year when the plant was new, a procedure which may also help to isolate effects which have to do with the ex ante function from other effects.

These conclusions taken in conjunction may suggest – as pointed out also by Komiya – that there has taken place some substitution of capital for labour (and perhaps for fuel) after all, although the statistical material is too weak to reveal the parameters of a production function with substitution possibilities.[19]

(b) The second problem in the list above was concerned with the problem of capacity utilization. The ex ante function is defined in terms of capacity output, current inputs at full capacity utilization and capital *invested* in the production unit – see (2.1). Ideally we would then like to have observations directly on these variables, but the most frequent case is that there are observations of actual current inputs and output on the one hand and capital invested (whether fully utilized or not) on the other hand.[20] To the extent that unutilized capacity is of a significant order of magnitude it is hardly meaningful to fit a function to such data directly. The fitted function would reflect a mixture of properties of the ex ante function and the ex post function in a rather intractable way. It would be more intractable the more complicated is the ex post function. Let us assume for the remainder of this discussion that the ex post function is of the simple type with fixed proportions which we have made our standard case – see (2.2).[21] Then some corrections might help in exploiting the type of data where there is not necessarily full capacity utilization.

First of all, if we take the approach of fitting a sort of frontier function, then we might reasonably expect to get what we are after since production units which are operated at less than full capacity would show up as inefficient when they are represented by actual current inputs and output, but total capital, while there will be some units operated at full capacity that will show up as being efficient. However, there may be difficulties for the part of the domain where there are production units with little capital per unit of output since here quasi rents may be negative or around zero so that we may get only few observations corresponding to full capacity utilization in this region. Accordingly the fitted function may be of lesser significance over this part of the domain.

In essence this argument means that we do in fact only use information

---

[19] For a discussion and critizism of Komiya's study, see Galatin (1968), pp. 61–68.

[20] There are of course many problems connected with the measurement of capital which we shall not go into here. They are discussed in many of the references given in this chapter.

[21] Most of the theory of this book is not dependent on this special assumption, see the generalizations in Sections 2.3 and 3.5.

contained in the data for fully utilized production units without, however, having recorded a priori which units these are.

Now suppose we have, in addition to figures for actual current inputs and output and total capital, also an indicator of capacity utilization. Then we might, on the simple assumption about a Leontief type of ex post function, simply correct the data so as to get constructed figures representing output and inputs at full capacity. We could, from then on, proceed along one of the lines discussed above on the basis of these figures. The results would of course be rather sensitive to the assumption about the ex post function.

Labour input poses a particular problem. This was discussed to some extent in Section 6.6 and we shall not repeat it here. The discussion of Section 6.6 suggests, however, that it would be essential to distinguish between labour paid-for and labour actually used in production.[22]

(c) The third problem mentioned above is the one about sufficient variation as between the units in the cross section material. This problem is of course well known, and it is partly resolved in more advanced econometric studies by simultaneous equations estimation, where observed prices and wages are exploited and the production function parameters estimated alongside parameters of demand and supply equations.

On the assumptions which are adopted through most of this book such supplementary equations, derived mainly from profit maximization conditions on the part of the producers, would be more complicated than in the pure neo-classical case. Estimations which are sensitive to the specification of such behavioural equations should therefore be viewed with some scepticism. On the other hand, since expectations about future prices, trends of technological progress etc. play a more crucial role, there might be hope for a wider spread in the decisions in our case than in the neo-classical case; and, if embodied technological progress has not been too fast, then the fact that previous decisions cannot be re-done by ex post substitution also helps to produce spread in the observations, which is useful for estimation purposes. In fact, many of the points reviewed in Section 3.1 in connection with the discussion of the capacity distribution are equally relevant in the present context.

---

[22] In Komiya (1962) there are used data for output capacity. Furthermore, data for fuel inputs are corrected so as to correspond to full capacity level of operation, while data for labour input were not so corrected because of the practical difficulties involved.

Many relevant points in connection with the correction for non-full utilization of capacity are raised by Hickman, Jorgenson and Eisner in the discussion of a paper by R. Eisner in Brown (ed.) (1967).

Some cross section studies include fuel, raw materials and/or intermediate goods inputs explicitly as factors of production besides labour and capital. However, the majority of such studies include only labour and capital as inputs and account for other inputs indirectly by measuring the product by value added rather than gross output.

This procedure is in need of more explicit justification than that usually given.[23] The procedure can be defended along two lines. First, one may assume that inputs other than labour and capital are limitational inputs, related to output in fixed proportions. Calculating value added at the same prices for all observations will then make value added proportional to gross output and only a multiplicative constant term of the production function will be affected.

The second line of defence is to assume that inputs other than labour and capital are substitutable inputs, but that they are instantaneously adapted to current prices so as to minimize costs of production or maximize profits. Under suitable assumptions about functional forms one can then derive a sort of "reduced form" production function which explains value added in terms of labour and capital. This value added production function will however represent a less autonomous relationship than the original gross output production function, and the procedure will affect not only a multiplicative constant term of the production function, but also the more interesting parameters. This has been clearly spelled out by McFadden (1967) in a review of Hildebrand and Liu (1965), for the case of Cobb-Douglas functions.

This latter basis for working with a value added function seems to be less satisfactory on the assumptions of our model than in the neo-classical case with ex post substitution. When there is no ex post substitution possibility we can hardly assume that fuel, raw materials or intermediate goods inputs are adjusted in such a systematic way to output and prices that we can derive a meaningful "reduced form" or value added production function. It might be possible to argue that such assumptions are tenable if we restrict the analysis to newly established or efficient production units. It should be remembered, however, that in the case of no ex post substitution expectations about the future, which may vary among investors, and not only current prices, are relevant for the choice of input proportions.

In the discussion above we have more or less tacitly assumed that we are concerned with cross section material consisting of data for individual pro-

---

[23] See the remarks by E.D. Domar in Brown (ed.) (1967), pp. 471–472.

duction units within a sector. As mentioned in the introduction to this section there are, however, also other types of cross section data used for
establishing production functions, viz. data giving inputs and output at the
sector level for a sample of states or countries. On the basis of our model
it seems to be necessary, in this connection, to specify more carefully than
usual which type of production function one is after. The relevant distinction
is the one between the ex ante function at the micro level and the long-run
function at the macro level. Although these functions are closely related, as
explained in Section 2.5, they are distinct. In particular, the long-run macro
function is homogeneous of degree 1, while the ex ante micro function is
generally not of this form.

The well-known study by Hildebrand and Liu (1965), to which we have
already referred, uses cross section data over the American states. The
authors are in this case rather explicit in explaining that they are primarily
after micro functions. Since census data were only available in the form of
sums of inputs and outputs they calculated arithmetic averages per establishment for inputs and output, arguing as follows: "If establishment data are
lacking, the closest approximation to the required micro data perhaps can
be obtained ... by using census figures for a given industry across the
states. ... The reason for preferring this approach is that statistics for the
average value added, labour and capital per establishment in a given state,
then may be taken as a rough indication of the 'representative establishment'
in that state, and that the observations for such representative establishments
in the different states for the same industry furnish a reasonable basis for
estimating the production surface for firms in that industry."[24] The authors
are aware of the serious aggregation problems involved. It is obvious that
such average points may fail systematically to satisfy the micro production
function when this is not linear. However, if establishments within a state
are much more similar than establishments in different states, then one may
be lucky and get reasonable results out of such a cross section study. It
would, for the purpose of revealing the ex ante function, be more useful to
have data for enterprises on the efficiency frontier, but lacking this a procedure like the one employed by Hildebrand and Liu – including the proportion between net and gross capital stock to take care of vintage effects – may
be a rough substitute.

Other cross section studies for the same industry between states or countries are often less explicit, but fail to reduce the totals for inputs and output

---

[24] See Hildebrand and Liu (1965), pp. 23–24. See also pp. 132–133.

to a per enterprise basis and accordingly seem to aim at an industry production function. This must then, in our framework be what we have called the long-run macro function. As we have discussed at various places in the theoretical chapters, this would best be revealed if individual production units were rather similar and of optimal size. In such cases the region of substitution in the short-run macro function would be long and narrow, and the point of full capacity would (supplemented with the capital input component) approximate a point on the surface of the long-run production function. Different wages and other prices might be responsible for spanning out a sufficiently wide range of variation between states.

A contrast between these two cases is that, whereas we, when we aim at estimating a micro function, would like to have observations also for enterprises of non-optimal sizes, we must, when we are after the long-run macro function, assume that the totals for an industry in a state are composed of a number of firms of optimal size. Correspondingly, if we have estimated the micro function over its full domain, then we can derive the long-run macro function, while, on the other hand, if we have estimated the long-run macro function, then we can only say something about the form of the ex ante micro function to the degree that it is reflected in what we have called the technique relation which forms the link between the ex ante micro function and the long-run macro function (see (2.17) and (2.22)).

If we have cross section material of observations from the micro units of production, then we clearly prefer observations corresponding to full utilization of capacity as discussed before. If we are after the long-run macro function and if we have cross section material consisting of aggregate data for the same sector for different states or countries at our disposal, then this is no longer necessarily so. The reason is the following. The long-run macro function is based logically on the ex ante micro function. If there has been significant embodied technological progress, then only the more recently established enterprises reveal information about the present ex ante function. In conditions of full capacity utilization all production units are fully employed and included in the aggregate figures, and they will create a negative bias in the fitted function relatively to the long-run macro function. On the other hand, when there is less than full capacity utilization, then the newer and more efficient units will count relatively more heavily in the aggregate figures and a production function fitted to such observations will be a better approximation to the long-run macro function corresponding to present technological knowledge (assuming that the decision whether or not to operate a plant is taken on the basis of obtainable quasi rents).

There is also another factor pointing in the same direction. Even if all production units are established on the basis of the same ex ante function figures for total inputs and output will not directly correspond to the long-run function unless the technique relation is linear.

These points may be illustrated, e.g., by referring to the mathematical example discussed in Section 5.5. We there studied the short-run macro function corresponding to a special capacity distribution along a hyperbola $\xi_1 \xi_2 = 1$. Now suppose this hyperbola represents the technique relation derived from the ex ante function at the micro level for a given capital input per unit of output (in order not to complicate the illustration with a third dimension). Then the long-run macro function given this amount of capital per unit of output is given by

$$\frac{V_1}{X} \frac{V_2}{X} = 1, \text{ or } X = \sqrt{V_1 V_2}, \tag{8.1}$$

cf. (2.19). The actual observations must obey the short-run macro function which is in this case given by

$$X^* = \sqrt{V_1 V_2 - \frac{V_1^4}{48}}. \tag{8.2}$$

This formula is reproduced from (5.71); we have only supplied X with an asterisk to indicate that this is the observed value as distinct from the "ideal" value X corresponding to the long-run function (8.1).

For every given pair of values $V_1, V_2 > 0$ we see that $X^* < X$, i.e. the observed values will be biased downwards. But, considering the proportion

$$\frac{X^*}{X} = \sqrt{1 - \frac{V_1^3}{48 V_2}} \tag{8.3}$$

we see that the relative bias is smaller the smaller are the amounts of inputs, i.e. the lower is the degree of capacity utilization. (E.g., let V_1 and V_2 diminish proportionately.) Inspecting Figure 5.4 it is also easy to see that the isoquants are more similar to hyperbolas (and exist over a wider range of factor proportions) the smaller is output X. Similar observations can be made in connection with other examples discussed in Chapter 5, but the technique relations would appear less attractive in these cases. In Section 5.3 we may consider the right-angled curve in Figure 5.1 as representing the technique relation (for a given capital input per unit of output); correspondingly the isoquants in Figure 5.2 – if we extend them by vertical and horizontal sections outside the region of substitution – are more like right-angled curves the smaller is output X. In Section 5.6 we may consider the boundary (towards south and west) of the region of positive capacity as representing the technique relation; thus in this case we also have capacity which is less efficient than what corresponds to the "present" technique relation. Correspondingly we again see from Figure 5.8 that the isoquants are more like right-angled curves the smaller is output X.[25]

The points discussed here are perhaps of a logical and theoretical rather than practical significance since we may hardly expect to observe such low rates of capacity utilization that these points will influence the outcome of the analysis very much.

The conclusions to be drawn from the above discussion are not very definitive, but we may tentatively put down the following points by way of a summary.

(1) Cross section studies with micro data (plants, firms or some other definition of micro units) may under favourable circumstances reveal the ex ante function at the micro level. Data representing full capacity utilization are preferable.

(2) Cross section studies on the basis of aggregate data for the same industry in various states or countries may reveal the ex ante function at the micro level or the long-run macro function according to the further assumptions that can be adopted and the way of treating the data.

(3) If there is embodied technological progress there are special problems which must be solved, e.g. by fitting a frontier function rather than a function through the middle of the scatter, or by including some variable representing vintage. (A frontier function may be the most appropriate type of function to establish even if there is no embodied progress.)

(4) On the basis of our assumptions (particularly the assumption of no ex post substitution) there are reasons to expect more variation between observations from various enterprises than in the case of neo-classical production functions; this contributes to making estimation on the basis of cross section data a more promising task. On the other hand, there is less hope of obtaining additional useful information by taking into account

---

[25] This statement about similarity holds, in the last two cases, not only in an absolute sense as it must do since we are to remain within the positive quadrant, but it also holds in a relative sense so that if we project an isoquant corresponding to a small value of X radially from the origin to a position farther towards the north-east, then we get a curve which is more like a right-angled curve than the isoquant corresponding to a larger output X which is originally in that position.

e.g. cost minimization conditions and observations of prices and wages.

(5) On the basis of our assumptions the practice of fitting a value added function with only labour and capital as specified inputs appears to be a more dubious procedure than in the case of production functions with ex post as well as ex ante substitution (unless fuel, raw materials and intermediate goods inputs are limitational factors related to output in fixed proportions also ex ante).

8.4. *Production functions based on time series studies*

Estimation of production functions on the basis of time series data are usually carried out at a very high level of aggregation, perhaps mainly because time series for inputs and outputs are usually available only for crude aggregates. I shall not discuss the general aggregation problems here, but rather assume that we have observed time series for inputs V_1, V_2, K and output X for a sector with a rather homogeneous output so as to concentrate on the problems which are more specific to our model. I shall also not comment further on the fact that most studies adopt a value added function rather than a gross output function, since the relevant considerations in the case of time series studies seem to be the same as those already adduced in connection with the cross section studies.

Suppose that we have time series observations of current inputs V_1, V_2 and output X at rather frequent points of time, and over a period in which no scrapping and investment of any significant order of magnitude have taken place. If there has been sufficient variability, we would then be able to estimate the short-run macro production function $X = F(V_1, V_2)$. There are, however, several difficulties involved. In the first place it is hardly likely that we should observe sufficient variability over a short period of time so as to span out enough of the surface of the short-run production function. In this connection it should be remembered that the short-run macro function cannot be expected to take any relatively simple mathematical form, a fact which is brought out by the excercises of Chapter 5, where even oversimplified capacity distributions tended to generate more complicated short-run macro functions than those which are in current econometric use. We would of course be satisfied with approximations over limited ranges, but within our theoretical framework decreasing returns to scale, limited capacity and a limited region of substitution are among the obligatory and most interesting characteristics of the short-run function so that mathematical forms which fail to express these characteristics will miss much of the point.

Next, even if we should have sufficiently large variability, we must remember that our short-run macro function is a sort of equilibrium concept, based on the assumption that we have a "correct" sorting out of production units which earn non-negative quasi rents and which should be operated on the one hand, and units which are only able to earn negative quasi rents and which should not be operated on the other hand. Large variation over a short span of time would probably mean that many of the observations of V_1, V_2, X would represent disequilibrium situations.[26] Since this would mean a lower value of X for the given V_1, V_2-constellation than what would follow from the function $X = F(V_1, V_2)$, something can be said for fitting a frontier function also in this case.

Altogether it seems unlikely that we should get anything useful out of attempts to construct the short-run macro function on the basis of time series over such a short time that the short-run function remains reasonably constant.

What we could try then is to use longer time series, and perhaps hope to have less violent variations so that the observations would represent something more like short-run equilibria (but not so little variation that estimation is futile for *that* reason). But, in this case the short-run macro function will probably shift to such a degree that it cannot be neglected.

We could then follow standard practice and introduce time as an argument in the short-run macro function, i.e. setting $X = F(V_1, V_2; t)$, where t generates a parametric shift in the relationship between X and V_1, V_2. However, it might be better to enter an indicator of total capital stock, i.e. writing $X = F(V_1, V_2; K)$ since the short-run relationship between X and V_1, V_2 is likely to change more or less according as total capital stock changes more or less. By this line of thought we are back at a formulation of the short-run macro function where total capital stock enters into the function. The interpretation should, however, be borne in mind. The symbol K is in this case a parameter, not a variable input like V_1 and V_2. This means that the set of (efficient) production possibilities existing at a certain moment of time consists of all constellations V_1, V_2, X which satisfy $X = F(V_1, V_2; K)$ for a given value of K, where K stands for total capital stock in existence. If we think of alternative constellations V_1, V_2, X, then each such constellation will imply a certain utilization of capital equipment. As we have discussed before, there will, to each pair of values V_1, V_2, cor-

---

[26] Cf. the discussion in Section 6.6.

respond a certain utilization region in the domain of the capacity distribution, and we could accordingly in principle observe utilization or non-utilization of the various pieces of equipment in which the capacity is embodied. On the basis of the method of aggregation used in developing a measure of the total capital stock we could then also measure the utilized part of the capital stock. Thus, we could visualize the utilized part of capital stock as a function of V_1 and V_2 (with total existing capital stock as a parameter). For the interpretation of the function $X = F(V_1, V_2; K)$ it is important to realize that it is not the utilized part of the capital stock which enters into the function.

Would capital stock be a "good" parameter for representing the shifts in the short-run macro function? I think it would only under very special assumptions. The most obvious case is the case where all investments give rise to new capacity which is distributed in exactly the same form as the already existing capacity. We have touched upon this question already towards the end of Section 7.2. The discussion of capacity-increasing disembodied technological progress in Section 7.5 is also relevant in this connection; in fact, if new capacity is always distributed in the same way as already existing capacity, then we can simply use formula (7.36). Now letting $F(V_1, V_2)$ conventionally represent the short-run macro function corresponding to a capital stock $K = 1$, we have

$$X = KF\left(\frac{V_1}{K}, \frac{V_2}{K}\right). \tag{8.4}$$

In connection with (8.4) there are now two types of variations conceivable:

(1) Hypothetical variations at a given moment of time, to generate the set of alternative (efficient) possibilities. These correspond to variations in X, V_1 and V_2 in (8.4) for a given value of capital stock K, while *utilized* capital stock varies with V_1 and V_2.

(2) Actual variations through time, in which all V_1, V_2, X and K in (8.4) vary. Again it is total existing capital stock which is the relevant variable in the function. It is seen from (8.4) that X in this case is homogeneous of degree 1 when considered as a function of V_1, V_2 and K.

Reviewing some of the examples of Chapter 5 for illustration we get first for Houthakker's Pareto-Cobb-Douglas case

$$X = CV_1^{\frac{\alpha_1}{\alpha_1 + \alpha_2 + 1}} V_2^{\frac{\alpha_2}{\alpha_1 + \alpha_2 + 1}} K^{\frac{1}{\alpha_1 + \alpha_2 + 1}} \tag{8.5}$$

instead of (5.2).[27]

For the case of capacity distribution along a right-angled curve we get from (5.25) the implicit function

$$X = \sqrt{2K} \ (\sqrt{V_1 - s_1 X} + \sqrt{V_2 - s_2 X}), \tag{8.6}$$

which for $s_1 = s_2 = 0$ simplifies to the explicit form

$$X = \sqrt{2K} \ (\sqrt{V_1} + \sqrt{V_2}) \tag{8.7}$$

corresponding to (5.38).

For the case of a capacity distribution along a hyperbola we get from (5.71)

$$X = \sqrt{V_1 V_2 - \frac{V_1^4}{48K^2}}. \tag{8.8}$$

Finally, in the case of positive capacity evenly distributed over a region bounded by a right-angled curve we get from (5.86), again in implicit form

$$X^3 = \tfrac{9}{2} K(V_1 - s_1 X)(V_2 - s_2 X), \tag{8.9}$$

which reduces to the Cobb-Douglas form

$$X = \sqrt[3]{\tfrac{9}{2}} \ V_1^{\frac{1}{3}} V_2^{\frac{1}{3}} K^{\frac{1}{3}}$$

when $s_1 = s_2 = 0$.

In all cases K enters in such a way as to make X homogeneous in V_1, V_2 and K, as it should according to the general formula (8.4).

The case given by (8.5) is of course well known from attempts at estimating production functions on the basis of time series. As discussed in Chapter 5, this form is, however, not very realistic as a short-run macro function. The other illustrations given above may be more realistic in some respects, but less realistic in others. In any case, the illustrations show that if new capacity is always distributed in the same way as existing capacity, then total capital stock can be introduced as a parameter to take account of the shifts in the short-run macro function over time, and time series data for X, V_1, V_2 and

---

[27] Compare the similar formula (9) in Houthakker (1955–56). Houthakker characterizes this formula as misleading "since the distribution of the fixed inputs between cells is an essential element of the problem; aggregating the fixed inputs is therefore not legitimate". However, if (8.5) is established in the way indicated in the text above, then this objection is not valid. When the capacity distribution is always of the same form, then there is no problem in constructing a measure of total existing capital stock. (Another and more dubious matter is the construction of a measure of utilized capital stock, since varying utilized capital stock implies different compositions of heterogeneous capital.)

K can form the basis for estimation of the short-run macro function. If this is the aim, then one should use realized output X, actually consumed current inputs V_1 and V_2, and total existing capital stock, K, i.e. not corrected for capacity utilization. Furthermore, the function should be restricted so as to make X homogeneous of degree 1 in V_1, V_2 and K.

There would be serious problems of variability involved in such a venture. On the one hand, we would like rather large variability in V_1 and V_2 in order to make estimation possible or reliable. On the other hand, we need a non-changing form of the distribution of new capacity. To the extent that variation in inputs are induced by price changes it seems hard to reconcile these two wishes.

Theoretically we could, however, imagine a process in which prices change in the short run and influence actual decisions about utilization in accordance with our theory, while at the same time average prices over the longer run remain fairly constant so that investment decisions – which should be based on expected prices over the period of utilization of equipment – are not subject to similar variations.

Disembodied technological progress could be accounted for in such an analysis by introducing time in addition to K as a parameter in the moving short-run function provided that it is of a simple parametric type. (See e.g. (7.36), (7.42) and (7.75).)

Embodied progress, however, makes things much more complicated. First, the distribution of new capacity will no longer be of the same form as the distribution of old capacity. (Even in the absence of embodied technological progress this is of course a very special assumption.) Next, the construction of a concept of "total capital stock" is much less meaningful in this case. These two complications are of course related. Perhaps reasonably simple examples in terms of parametric variations could be constructed, e.g. along the lines suggested towards the end of Section 7.2. But these would clearly require extremely special types of variation.

Thus the above discussion of the theoretical possibility of estimating short-run macro production functions on the basis of time series data should not be taken to mean that I consider it likely that such attempts will be successful. The discussion shows, I think, that we would get something meaningful (in relation to the short-run macro function) out of this only under very special circumstances. However, the theoretical possibility of such estimation, particularly when total capital stock K is introduced as a "parameter" to take care of the shifting of the short-run function, may be of importance in interpreting the results of production function estimations which are actually carried out on the basis of time series data. It suggests that there may be traces of the short-run macro function left in the results of such estimations, though mixed with many other things. I shall return to this point with a few remarks towards the end of this section.

To the extent that a distinction is at all recognized I think it is fair to say that most econometricians working with time series estimation of production functions aim at a sort of long-run macro function rather than a short-run macro function. The reasoning in connection with (8.4) immediately shows that one does not necessarily obtain the long-run function by regressing actual output on current inputs and capital stock. Function (8.4), which may be obtained by such regressions under certain circumstances, is a "moving short-run function" and not a long-run function. These two functions answer very different questions about possible variations in inputs and output, and the conceptual difference between the two types of functions is formally brought out by, among other things, the fact that function (8.4) depends upon the form of the capacity distribution, whereas the long-run function depends only upon the ex ante function at the micro level.

An actual observation of X, V_1, V_2 and K will approximate a point on the surface corresponding to the long-run macro function more closely the more concentrated are the micro production units in the neighbourhood of the point in the input coefficient space (ξ_1, ξ_2, ξ_3), which satisfies the technique relation $\Psi(\xi_1, \xi_2, \xi_3) = 1$ (see (2.17), (2.22) and (7.83)). This was discussed in Section 7.9. Although it helps, it is not sufficient (unless the technique relation is linear) that all ξ_1, ξ_2, ξ_3-points representing individual production units are located on the surface corresponding to the technique relation – they must also be closely concentrated. This is clear e.g. from the reasoning in connection with Figure 7.7.

Thus, for a single observation of X, V_1, V_2 and K to represent a point on the long-run macro function we would need a situation in the sector in which we have a very narrowly confined capacity distribution and correspondingly a short-run macro function, which is characterized by a narrow region of substitution around a ray from the origin in the V_1, V_2-plane and with nearly constant returns to scale. (Compare Figure 4.4 for the connections between the form of the capacity distribution and the form of the short-run macro function, and Sections 4.4 and 4.5 for the relationships between characteristics of the capacity distribution on the one hand and the returns to scale and the elasticity of substitution on the other hand.)

In principle it might be possible to obtain one such observation. But, for a time series estimation of the long-run function to be successful, we need a sequence of observations of different such points. With no ex post substitution we cannot pass from one such situation to another without abandoning all existing equipment and creating a completely new capital stock. In practice, i.e. when we do not abandon the existing capital stock, we are bound to create a capacity distribution which is, in the most favourable case, located along the surface representing the technique relation. If we add to this the effects of embodied technological progress and other factors which tend to render production units less efficient than what corresponds to the current technique relation, then the observations of X, V_1, V_2, K will be moved farther away from what they should be if they were to represent the long-run function. Much of the reasoning in Section 7.9 is relevant in this connection.

Factors tending to create less unfavourable circumstances for estimation of the long-run function on the basis of time series data for X, V_1, V_2 and K are perhaps the following:

(1) No or only very slow embodied technological progress. (Disembodied progress is less dangerous, but must of course be taken care of explicitly in the formulation of the function.)

(2) Short durability of capital equipment so that the capital stock existing at any moment of time will be relatively homogeneous. (Passing to the limit with vanishing durability the whole point of the distinction between ex ante and ex post aspects disappears and with it the estimation problems under discussion.)

(3) Fairly unanimous price expectations among investors so that rather similar investment choices from the ex ante function are made at each moment of time.

(4) Some changes in prices and price expectations over time so that we get some variation in factor proportions over time. But the changes should not be too dramatic because then we would get a very non-homogeneous capital stock. Long time series in proportion to the durability of capital so that we could trace out various sections of the long-run function in a rather slow way giving rise to a reasonably homogeneous capital stock at each moment of time would be the best thing to have (under otherwise favourable circumstances).

(5) The problem of varying capacity utilization has two aspects. It would clearly be best to have conforming observations of V_1, V_2 and capital input. E.g. actually consumed inputs V_1, V_2 and total existing capital stock would not be an appropriate trio of input observations if there is in fact some

unutilized capacity. The practice, often adhered to in time series studies, of adjusting capital data so as to give utilized capital stock seems to be justified if one is after the long-run function (in contrast to the case where one is after the short-run function).[28] Apart from this – i.e. if we are able to correct capital figures so as to make them conform with the actually used current inputs V_1, V_2 – it can be argued here, as in the case of some types of cross section studies, that observations from situations of low capacity utilization are better than observations from periods of high capacity utilization since production units close to the surface of the technique relation will then count relatively more in the totals.[29]

All these problems suggest that we should not expect much by way of firm results of time series studies of macro production functions. (In addition to the problems listed above come aggregation problems and the problems related to the wide-spread use of value added as an output indicator.) This pessimism is strongly substantiated by the available record of published studies. Presumably there is a much larger body of unpublished failures. Walters sums up his impressions in the following words: "It would be patently dishonest not to suggest that the simple production function has failed to prove itself a useful tool for the analysis of the time series of inputs and outputs for particular industries."[30]

A promising way to find out which are the most serious problems or sources of bias in trying to estimate production functions on the basis of time series data would seem to be simulation studies. One such study which is particularly relevant in our context is conducted by Solow (1963).

Professor Solow here constructs an economy consisting of two sectors: one sector producing consumer goods by means of machines and labour, and a capital goods sector producing machines by means of labour. We are

---

[28] However, such tricks as to assume the unutilized proportion of the capital stock to be the same as the rate of unemployment are quite arbitrary, and may probably introduce systematical biases (and it is of course defended only as being better than no adjustment). On the basis of our theory we would expect labour requirements to be higher and capital input to be lower in production units which are idle than in production units which are operated, since the decision whether or not to operate a micro unit is taken on the basis of quasi rents.

[29] In practice one should remember the distinction previously touched upon between labour hired and labour used in production. This distinction is probably more important, and accordingly the observational problems bigger, when we have low capacity utilization (or perhaps worst in intermediate situations). This practical aspect suggests that observations from situations of high capacity utilization are better.

[30] Walters (1968), p. 335. Professor Walters goes on to suggest that recognition of lagged adjustment and vintage effects might help to improve the performance of time series studies.

mainly interested in the former sector. There is a technological choice ex ante in that we may choose more or less labour intensive techniques in the consumption goods sector. All machines are assumed to have a capacity of one unit of consumables per period and a given technical durability of N periods. Let ξ_1 (λ in Solow's notations) be labour input per unit of output (or per machine per unit of time) and let ξ_2 be the value of the machine. We let this be measured by the labour needed to produce a machine.[31] Then the assumption is that

$$\xi_2 = c\xi_1^{-\gamma}, \tag{8.10}$$

where c and γ are constants (in Solow's notations $c(\lambda) = c_0\lambda^{-\gamma}$). This then is simply the technique relation, with only one current input represented by ξ_1 and capital input represented by ξ_2 (usually ξ_3 in this text when we assume two current inputs).

Solow assumes labour input requirement ξ_1 to remain constant for a machine once it has been constructed and installed, in accordance with the assumptions of our standard model.

We have generally written the technique relation in the form $\Psi(\xi_1, \xi_2) = 1$ where Ψ is homogeneous of degree one, see (2.17) and (2.22–2.24). Written in this form (8.10) appears as

$$\Psi(\xi_1, \xi_2) = c^{\frac{-1}{1+\gamma}} \xi_1^{\frac{\gamma}{1+\gamma}} \xi_2^{\frac{1}{1+\gamma}} = 1. \tag{8.11}$$

Correspondingly the long-run macro function should be, cf. (2.24):

$$X = AV^{\frac{\gamma}{1+\gamma}} K^{\frac{1}{1+\gamma}}, \text{ where } A = c^{\frac{-1}{1+\gamma}}. \tag{8.12}$$

V and K are total labour input and capital stock respectively. This conforms with Solow's production function (10′), which is "defined across long-run equilibria".[32]

Now Solow sets such an economy moving in the simulations by prescribing a given initial stock of capital, distributed over vintages with different

---

[31] Solow also considers the case where capital is measured in terms of consumer goods, but it is unnecessary to go into this here.

[32] Solow shows that such a function is valid also in "golden age" conditions where labour force and capital stock grow proportionately at a constant growth rate. It follows from our reasoning in connection with (7.91–7.92) that the constancy of the growth rate is not essential. What is essential is that the capital stock is homogeneous, and this may come about without a constant growth rate.

In connection with the interpretation of (8.10–8.12), see also Liviatan (1966).

ξ_1-values. There is a given growth path of total investment and labour force. Each sequence runs 20 periods beyond those that establish the initial situation; this should be compared with the technical durability of $N = 10$ periods.

In each period there is a surplus capacity, and wages are set so that machines able to earn non-negative quasi rent absorb the full labour force. (In the first year the 8 periods old vintage of machines is the marginal vintage.) At the same time, in each period new investments are chosen from among the possibilities delimited by the technique relation so as to maximize present value of future quasi rents under the expectation that wages will remain constant (which in fact they do not).

Many runs are generated with different values of the parameters and different growth paths for investment and labour force. However, there were no runs with fluctuations in the variables.

For every run it was pretended that there was an econometrician believing in a neo-classical production function of the Cobb-Douglas form, fitting such a function to the observed time series for V, K and X. The question then is: Would this econometrician, in spite of the fact that the observations are generated by short-run equilibria which do not obey the long-run function, obtain results which approximate this long-run function? On the basis of the discussion summarized in points (1)–(5) above, I think we would expect fairly good results in this respect: (1) There is no technological progress. (2) Durability of capital is not too long compared with the extension of the time series. (3) All investments made in one period represent the same technological choice. (4) There seem to be sufficient changes in the wage rate to span out a fairly wide range of technological choices through time, while there are no business cycle-like fluctuations. (5) There is unutilized capacity, and estimations are done on the basis of *utilized* as well as on the basis of total existing capital stock.

According to this we would expect the result of the fitting of the Cobb-Douglas function to the time series for V, K and X to yield a function not too different from the long-run function (8.12). And indeed, this is what comes out of professor Solow's experiment.

The conclusion is not without reservations. When a Cobb-Douglas function with unrestricted returns to scale was fitted, one generally came up with a scale coefficient far above unity. This effect was particularly strong when *total* capital stock was used, but it still remains, though to a lesser degree, when *utilized* capital stock is used in the regressions. In the case where a constant returns to scale Cobb-Douglas function was fitted the results for

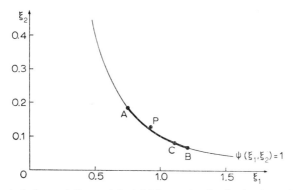

Fig. 8.2. The technique relation and the initial capacity distribution in Professor Solow's simulations ($c = 0.10$, $\gamma = 2$).

the elasticities of the fitted function were invariably very near to the elasticities of the long-run function (8.12), i.e. $\gamma/(1+\gamma)$ and $1/(1+\gamma)$ respectively for labour and capital.

The situation can be discussed on the basis of figures like those of Section 7.9. In Figure 8.2 we have depicted approximately the technique relation for one of Solow's cases, with $c = 0.10$ and $\gamma = 2$. In the initial capital stock we have capacity distributed along the curve between the points A and B, corresponding to $\xi_1 = 0.75$ and $\xi_1 = 1.20$. (Actually the capacity is discretely distributed at $\xi_1 = 0.75, 0.80, 0.85, \ldots, 1.20$ with the same capacity at each point.) At any moment of time capacity is now utilized from the left (low labour input) and extending as far towards the right as necessary for absorbing the available labour force. Initially the marginal vintage has $\xi_1 = 1.10$ so that only capacity between A and C in the figure is actually utilized. The observed V/X, K/X, where K is utilized capital, will accordingly lie in the convex hull formed by the curve segment AC, in fact somewhere in the neighbourhood of point P since capacity is so evenly distributed. It is clear that this observation approximately obeys the long-run function.

Now, as time passes new investments are made corresponding to lower values of ξ_1 (labour input per unit of output), i.e. point A moves up towards the left. Point B follows since there is a finite technical durability. Point C, representing the marginal machines, also moves towards the left as wages rise and previously marginal machines are only able to earn negative quasi rents. It is clear that point P, representing the observed V/X, K/X, will move along a curve rather similar to the curve of the technique relation $\Psi(\xi_1, \xi_2) = 1$, so that a fitted production function will approximate the true long-run function.

Some of the slight biases observed by Solow can, I think, be understood by inspecting the movements in Figure 8.2. It is e.g. observed by Solow that a more rapidly growing labour force tends to increase the capital elasticity in the fitted production function. Consider this case in Figure 8.2. A more rapidly growing labour force implies that wages do not increase as rapidly as they would otherwise do. This again means that point A in the figure, representing the position of the newest investments, does not move so rapidly towards the north-west. The capacity distribution will then tend to become narrower along the technique relation curve, and point P will accordingly tend to approach this curve. The path traced by point P will then tend to be flatter than the technique relation curve. This means that a function fitted to the observed P-points will show up with a higher capital elasticity (lower value of γ, higher value of $1/(1+\gamma)$).

Similarly I think some of the other biases shown by Solow's simulations can be understood.[33] A full discussion of all aspects of Solow's simulation study would take us too far.

Rather than summarizing the above discussion in a few brief points I shall comment on some comparisons between cross section and time series studies of production functions. Such comparisons have become particularly interesting after the CES-function has been introduced and widely used, and interest centres of course mainly upon the elasticity of substitution. Comparisons are difficult for many obvious reasons, and the picture which emerges from such comparisons is not absolutely clear. But there now seems to be consensus that on the whole time series studies tend to come up with lower estimated values of the elasticity of substitution than those from cross section studies.[34]

This picture is consistent with what we should expect if our model is approximately true. In the previous section it was concluded that aggregate cross section studies might give results approximating the long-run macro function, while cross section studies at the micro level might yield the ex

---

[33] Solow performs the fitting of the function by regressing $\log X/V$ on $\log K/V$. On the basis of our considerations it might seem more natural perhaps to work with the proportions V/X and K/X. The former approach is, however, the more common one. In any case I do not think that the choice of regression will affect the general conclusions significantly since standard errors of regression slopes are, according to Solow, usually quite small.

[34] This has been observed e.g. by Brown (1966), pp. 129–130 and Brown (ed.) (1967), pp. 7–8; this pattern was confirmed by Katz (1969), see pp. 66–67. See also Mayor (1969) and Eisner (1970), p. 747.

ante function at the micro level. Both these functions are closely related and involve an elasticity of substitution reflecting the ex ante substitution possibilities. On the other hand, in the present section it has been argued that time series studies may under certain conditions give something approximating the short-run macro function with capital stock acting as a shift parameter in this function, while they may under other conditions give results more relevant for the long-run macro function. Let us say, roughly, that we come up with a sort of compromise function between these two types. Then this function will probably imply a lower value of the elasticity of substitution since this will clearly in most cases be relatively low in the short-run macro function. Thus the observed tendency seems to be consistent with our theory.

There is, however, a snag here. The argument given above is directly applicable to the problem of substitution between two current inputs V_1 and V_2. However, most time series studies are concerned with the substitution between one current input – labour – and capital. This case is not so clear on the basis of the above arguments, so let us consider this somewhat more closely.

Let there be a short-run macro function with one current input V with capital stock acting as a parameter just as in the function (8.4). This is now

$$X = KF\left(\frac{V}{K}\right). \tag{8.13}$$

The function F is established on the basis of a one-dimensional capacity distribution $f(\xi)$.

The problem now is whether we can say anything about the *apparent* elasticity of substitution in the function (8.13). For the derivatives of (8.13) we have

$$\frac{\partial X}{\partial V} = F'\left(\frac{V}{K}\right) \tag{8.14}$$

$$\frac{\partial X}{\partial K} = F\left(\frac{V}{K}\right)(1-\varepsilon), \tag{8.15}$$

where F' is the derivative of F, and ε is the scale elasticity in the short-run function, i.e.

$$\varepsilon = \frac{\partial F}{\partial(V/K)} \frac{V/K}{F(V/K)}, \tag{8.16}$$

in general a function of V/K. This corresponds to ε in Section 4.4, where there were two current inputs.

Now the apparent elasticity of substitution in (8.13) would be

$$s = \frac{d\,(V/K)}{d\,((\partial X/\partial K)/(\partial X/\partial V))} \cdot \frac{(\partial X/\partial K)/(\partial X/\partial V)}{V/K}. \tag{8.17}$$

Inserting here this reduces to

$$s = \frac{d\,(V/K)}{d\,((1-\varepsilon)/\varepsilon \cdot V/K)} \frac{(1-\varepsilon)/\varepsilon \cdot V/K}{V/K}. \tag{8.18}$$

Writing $\mathrm{el}_{V/K}$ for an elasticity with respect to V/K (8.18) can be written as

$$s = \frac{1}{1 + \mathrm{el}\,_{V/K}((1-\varepsilon)/\varepsilon)}. \tag{8.19}$$

In the special case where ε is constant we have $s = 1$. This corresponds to the case of a short-run macro function in one current input which is of the form $F(V) = AV^{\varepsilon}$, so that (8.13) gives

$$X = KA\left(\frac{V}{K}\right)^{\varepsilon} = AV^{\varepsilon}K^{1-\varepsilon}. \tag{8.20}$$

This is of course the Pareto-Cobb-Douglas-Houthakker case reduced to only one current input. We have argued before that this is not a very realistic case, particularly in that it assumes a capacity distribution where there is no limit to the efficiency of the most efficient micro production units. If there is such a limit, then the arguments advanced at the end of Section 4.4 applies which means that ε will decline from 1 when V increases from zero. Although ε will not necessarily decline in a monotonic way, there are reasons to believe that it will on the whole be a declining function as we saw in some of the two-dimensional examples in Chapter 5. Then (8.19) implies that the apparent elasticity of substitution will be less than 1.

An illustration is given in Figure 8.3, where we have constructed the contour curves ("isoquants") of (8.13) on the basis of a given function F. The function F is drawn in quadrant IV to represent $X/K = F(V/K)$, where X/K is measured towards the left and V/K towards the north. In quadrant III we have drawn hyperbolas to represent constant values of X with X/K measured towards the left and K towards the south. We have drawn such curves for $X = 4$ and $X = 8$. Quadrant II is only used to transfer values of K to the horizontal axis towards the right. The contour lines of $X = KF(V/K)$ in a K,V-plane can then be constructed in quadrant I. Let us take one point

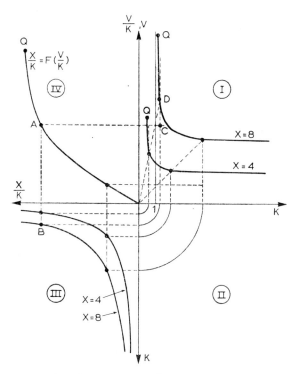

Fig. 8.3. The construction of contour curves for $X = KF(V/K)$ in the K, V-plane from a given function F.

as an example. We start out from point A on the curve representing F in quadrant IV and want a point on the apparent isoquant corresponding to $X = 8$. We then move vertically into quadrant III until we intersect the hyperbola corresponding to $X = 8$, i.e. to point B. We thus find the value of K and transfer this to the horizontal K-axis. In quadrant I we draw a vertical line corresponding to this value of K. We also draw a horizontal line from A in quadrant IV into the first quadrant. These two lines intersect at point C. This point now gives K and V/K corresponding to the given point A and the value $X = 8$. In order to find the corresponding K,V-point we use the vertical line through $K = 1$. At D, now considered as a point in the K,V-plane, we clearly have the correct values of K and V. This point is obtained as the intersection between the vertical at the given value of K and a ray from the origin through the crossing point of the horizontal line through A and the vertical line through $K = 1$.

In the same way other points on the contour curves in the V,K-plane are constructed. (In the figure we have suggested the construction of one more point on the isoquant $X = 8$ and two points on the isoquant $X = 4$. The two isoquants are of course similar since X by (8.13) is homogeneous of degree 1 in V and K.)

The short-run production function F in Figure 8.3 is drawn so as to be more realistic than the constant elasticity curve underlying the Cobb-Douglas form (8.20) in two respects. First, we have a limited total capacity corresponding to point Q in quadrant IV for any given value of K. There is correspondingly a terminal point, also marked Q, on each contour curve in quadrant I. Secondly, the curve representing F in quadrant IV starts out with a finite slope from the origin. This reflects the fact that even the most efficient micro production units have a limited efficiency, and implies that the elasticity of the F-function as defined by (8.16) is 1 at the origin and declines by increasing V. In the figure the elasticity gets very low when we approach full capacity utilization, which means that the last micro units to be utilized are much less efficient than the most efficient ones.

It is clear that if the family of contour curves in quadrant I in Figure 8.3 should be approximated by a CES-function, then it would be a CES-function with an elasticity of substitution less than one, in agreement with (8.19).

The crucial role played by the finiteness of the efficiency of all micro units can perhaps be seen most clearly if we assume that we have a finite amount of capacity with a certain efficiency indicated by the input coefficient ξ (and no more efficient capacity). Then F will be linear as long as we do not produce more than corresponds to this capacity. For the corresponding part of the V,K-plane we will simply have $X = Ka(V/K) = aV$, where $a = 1/\xi$, i.e. the contour curves will be parallel and equidistant horizontal lines like the asymptotes of the isoquants of the CES-function in the case of an elasticity of substitution less than one.[35]

Returning to the main point of this discussion it seems plausible that we may get a macro function with a relatively low value of the elasticity of substitution if we try to fit a function to time series for X, V and K in cases where we, by this procedure, reveal the moving short-run function (with total capital stock as a parameter) rather than the real long-run function. Such a short-run function with K as a parameter can be derived in an exact way only when new investments are always distributed in the same way as

---

[35] These arguments could be further illustrated by using the results obtained by Levhari (1968).

existing capacity. This is of course not a realistic assumption, but it may still be true that some properties of such short-run functions are reflected to some extent in the results of attempts to fit production functions to time series of aggregate data so that this procedure may tend to yield apparent elasticities of substitution less than one.

8.5. *Estimation on the basis of cost functions, cost minimizing conditions or profit maximizing conditions*

In recent years there have been many attempts to estimate production functions indirectly via cost minimizing or profit maximizing conditions. The use of such conditions for this purpose is in a way quite old since the estimation of the elasticities of a Cobb-Douglas production function on the basis of observed income shares may be considered as a simple example of this approach. It has, however, become particularly wide-spread since Arrow et al. (1961) regressed value added per worker on the wage rate in order to estimate the elasticity of substitution. The use of cost functions, which is of the same nature since such functions are based upon an assumption about cost minimization for each given output, has been much stimulated by the clarification in Shephard (1953) and later works of the duality relationship between cost functions and production functions. Cost functions are in this context considered as functions not only of output, but also of input prices.

Use of cost minimizing or profit maximizing conditions will of course also occur in various ways when the production function is considered in the context of a simultaneous equations model which is estimated with due regard to the simultaneity, but then it will of course not always turn out to be correct to go *from* estimation of parameters of relations expressing such conditions *to* parameters of the production functions. This will depend particularly upon the specification of exogenous variables.

We shall not go into these problems, but only pass a few remarks on the special problems in connection with the use of such indirect ways of estimating production functions on the basis of our technological assumptions.

The main point of taking such indirect routes to the production function is that one can utilize other types of data, viz. prices and costs, instead of or in addition to data on inputs and output, but one can relate this to the parameters of the production function only if one is willing to rely on certain assumptions concerning behaviour such as cost minimization under competitive conditions or under other specified types of market situations.

As has been touched upon already in another context the main difficulty with such approaches on the basis of our theoretical framework is that the connections between prices and producers' adaptations will now be of various sorts in that we have to distinguish between investment decisions and current operations on the basis of existing equipment.

Current operation decisions are determined by current prices only (on our strict assumptions). In our main case, with ex post Leontief functions for individual micro units, there is not much of interest to find out about short-run cost curves and factor demand functions. Micro studies, which are essentially interested in the micro level for its own sake, will of course often make less restrictive assumptions about the ex post micro production functions and then be able to find out something about this function on the basis of cost and price data. Time series data for individual enterprises with constant capital equipment would be the ideal thing to have, but such data are very rare.

Let us next consider the possibilities of estimation on the basis of cross section micro data. Price and wage variations could then be obtained mainly because of regional differences. With smooth ex post substitution possibilities we could then in a meaningful way estimate production function parameters via cost functions or profit maximum conditions such as the relation between value added per worker and the wage rate which is often used in estimating the elasticity of substitution in CES-functions. However, on the basis of our technological assumptions this would be much more dubious. The main problems are, firstly, that enterprises cannot in general be assumed to have chosen their techniques from the same ex ante function, and secondly that they cannot be assumed to have adapted to current prices only.

The first problem is encountered also when estimation is based upon input and output data and can under suitable circumstances be tackled either by stratifying the observations according to vintages or by introducing a parametric shift in the ex ante function with the passage of time as discussed in previous sections of this chapter, a shift which is transferred to cost functions and profit maximization conditions.

The second problem is particular to the indirect way of estimating production functions treated in this section. It follows from our technological assumptions that a rational investor should take into account future as well as current prices and wages in deciding about which one to choose from among the possibilities implied by the ex ante function.[36] Thus even if the

---

[36] See in this connection Johansen (1967).

first problem above were solved, e.g. by having a sample consisting only of newly established production units, we could in general not expect to find profit maximizing conditions holding between inputs, output and *observed* prices and wages. There seem to be four possible escapes from this difficulty:

(a) Prices and wages may in fact be constant over a longer period.

(b) Even if prices and wages are in fact changing, investors may have "static expectations" so that new production units are adapted to current prices.

(c) Investors have "non-static expectations", but expected future prices are related to current prices in a systematic way.

(d) We may use data on price expectations as well as observed prices.

Assumptions (a) and (b) are hardly realistic. Assumption (c) may be acceptable, but this may on the other hand be a somewhat treacherous case. The point is that it may give rise to high correlations, but nevertheless generate systematic biases when we try to infer something about the production function. A profit maximizing condition for the investment decision would now be e.g. that the marginal rate of substitution between labour and capital in the ex ante function should equal an expression in terms of capital goods price, interest rate and wages over the expected life of the production unit. By using a condition where the marginal rate of substitution is related to the current relative price between capital and labour we get a biased inference about the ex ante production function. If investors expect the wage rate to increase we will underrate the marginal productivity of labour in the ex ante function.

Case (d) above is hardly encountered in the literature, and it may be difficult to implement directly since data on price expectations are rarely available. It may point in the direction of an extended model where price expectations are only intermediate variables which are next replaced by some sort of distributed lag equations which explain how price expectations are formed on the basis of the development of prices over some past periods. Logically this seems to be perfectly all right, but as an approach to estimating production functions it is even more indirect and involves unknown parameters which are certainly not very stable. In some recent empirical investment behaviour studies an attempt has been made to test the putty-clay hypothesis along such lines as suggested above. Since the relevance of price expectations is very different in the putty-clay case from what it is in the pure neo-classical case, the lag structure in the relation between investments, labour hiring and price and wage development should reveal something about the degree of ex post substitution possibilities.[37] However, the test is rather weak because of the factors mentioned above. In fact, I think the best way to test the putty-clay hypothesis is simply to inspect production equipment and talk with engineers and technicians.

For studies based on aggregate data the conclusions are much the same as in the preceding sections, where we assumed data on inputs and output to form the basis for the estimations. There is a possibility that one might get something relevant for the long-run macro function from cross section data. The conditions are that enterprises in different regions are well adapted to current prices and wages in their respective regions (with all the problems which this involves as mentioned above), while there is sufficient variation in prices and wages as between regions. From aggregate time series data we are likely to get something which partly reflects short-run macro functions and partly reflects the long-run macro function, probably with a bias in the direction of underrating substitution possibilities as compared with those of the long-run macro function.

On the whole it seems that approaches based upon price and wage data and assumptions about the fulfillment of profit maximizing or cost minimizing conditions are less promising within our approach than in the pure neo-classical case.

A discussion of relevance for problems raised above is given by G. C. Harcourt (1966) and by R. Boddy in Brown (ed.) (1967), pp. 127–133. Some works on distributive shares in putty-clay growth models are also of interest, though more indirectly. For an explicit discussion of estimation problems related to those discussed in the text above, see Bardhan (1967, 1969). Bardhan's studies are of particular significance in that they, under certain assumptions, show the following result: Suppose that we have data from different countries which are all on long-run equilibrium growth paths. The technology is of the putty-clay type, with the same ex ante function in all countries. Now regress output per worker on the wage rate as done by Arrow et al. (1961) and many other recent studies. Then the regression coefficient will overestimate the elasticity of substitution of the ex ante function. The effect can be ascribed to the effect of the wage rate upon the useful life of capital. This result adds support to our previous suggestion to the effect that the putty-clay nature of the technology contributes to explaining

---

[37] See Rasche and Shapiro (1968), pp. 128–129.

why cross section studies tend to yield higher values of the elasticity of substitution than time series studies.[38]

8.6. *Input-output analysis*

The intention in this section is not to go deeply into input-output analysis, but only to point out the connection between our approach and a trend in recent research concerning changes in input-output coefficients.

Input-output analysis has mainly been concerned with short-run variation in production. On the background of our system of production functions the traditional assumption about constant input-output coefficients should then be judged in the light of our short-run macro function.

Constant input-output coefficients can be seen as an approximation to a short-run macro function which is established on the basis of a highly concentrated capacity distribution. The concentration of the distribution will (a) make the elasticity of substitution in the short-run macro function small since the standard deviations σ_1 and σ_2 in formula (4.48) will be small, (b) make the region of substitution narrow and concentrated along a ray from the origin as follows from the reasoning in Section 4.6, see particularly Figure 4.4, and (c) make the scale elasticity of the short-run macro function approach 1 (but being in fact <1 as long as the region of positive capacity has not collapsed completely), see particularly Figure 4.2. Taken together these effects mean that the short-run macro function can be approximated by constant input-output coefficients. But there will of course be a finite total capacity. The case shown in Figure 5.10 may be illustrative although the capacity distribution is not very concentrated in this case.

In general we should, however, expect some changes in average input coefficients even in the short run if there are significant changes in input prices, though less so the nearer we are to full capacity utilization. By varying total output we should expect average input coefficients to be higher at higher than at lower capacity utilization as a result of the fact that the scale elasticity is less than one. There may, however, also be systematic changes in input coefficients with output due to non-linear expansion paths which can easily be generated by suitable forms of the capacity distribution. In fact

---

[38] Bardhan's studies assume infinite physical durability of capital equipment. It is somewhat doubtful whether his results would stand up if physical durability could be chosen according to economic considerations in a trade-off against input requirements (assuming correct expectations about future wage rates as is done by Bardhan).

there will be at most one expansion path which is linear throughout since all expansion paths have to go from the origin to the point of full capacity utilization and at most one of these can be a straight line.

Such effects would, I think, be clearly revealed by good input-output data if it were not for the fact that our short-run macro theory rests on an assumption about short-run equilibrium, and this type of equilibrium will be only imperfectly realized in an economy subject to more or less continual changes – see the discussion in Section 6.6. We should therefore expect only imperfect reflections of these factors in changes in observed coefficients.[39]

The generalization discussed in Section 3.6 may be of some interest in this connection. We there assumed that the degree of utilization of a micro production unit was an increasing function of the rate of quasi rent earned, but not a step function jumping from zero to full capacity utilization at the point where we pass from negative to positive quasi rent. Such imperfections may come about simply because of inertia in adaptations, or because of restricted competition. We observed in Section 3.6 that this kind of imperfect adaptation tended to generate a short-run macro function which could be better approximated by a Leontief function (with limited capacity) – at least in the limit when quasi rents have no influence at all upon the decision whether to operate a production unit or not as shown by (3.50). Such effects as these may be partly responsible for the fact that empirical studies of input-output coefficients perhaps show less variation than one would expect on the basis of our concept of a short-run macro function.

In the longer run we should expect some more variation in input-output coefficients. This is of course entirely consistent with empirical findings. But it is hardly a confirmation of our theory since any alternative theory would probably also have the same implication. There is, however, a promising approach in the study of changes in input-output coefficients, which lends more specific support to our theory. I have in mind the approach where changes in input-coefficients of a sector are explained by the rate of gross investment in the sector, on the assumption that investments establish production units of the "best-practice" type which have input coefficients differing from those of the "average practice" type which are in existence. New input-output coefficients are formed as a weighted average of best-practice

---

[39] Input-output experiments with non-homogeneous input functions are of interest in connection with the scale effects mentioned above. Such studies are rare, but Ghosh (1964) reports an experiment which shows significant improvements in output projections for British manufacturing and trading industries by allowing for non-homogeneities in input functions.

coefficients and previous average practice coefficients, where the rate of investment then determines the weights.

This approach, which clearly rests on similar assumptions as ours about ex ante and ex post substitution possibilities, was suggested by Carter (1963) and pursued rather successfully in more recent research.[40] The same approach has found support by research in many countries such as France, England, Hungary and the U.S.S.R. In the same spirit is a recent paper by Forssell (1971) about changes in input-output coefficients in Finland around 1960. He found that changes in input coefficients particularly for labour and electric energy, but also for other inputs, were systematically related to an indicator of the "degree of mechanization". There were discernible effects of relative prices and product-mix, but the main conclusion arrived at by Forssell was that "mechanization of the production process was the factor most widely affecting input-output coefficients". This is exactly what we should expect on the basis of our theory.

In the study of changes in input-output coefficients prices should play a double role. In the first place they should induce substitution on the basis of the short-run macro function. In the second place they should influence the choice of new techniques from the ex ante function, i.e. work via the type and degree of mechanization chosen when investments take place. In the terminology suggested above we may say that prices should influence best-practice coefficients according to the scope for substitution in the ex ante function and influence the average practice coefficients according to the scope for substitution in the short-run macro function (the latter scope probably depending on the rate of capacity utilization). Carter (1970a, b, c) is near to such an approach when she faces explicitly, though in a very special way, the choice between some different processes in connection with increases in capacity and let this choice be determined by a programming procedure. There are also interesting suggestions in a recent study by Wigley (1970). But I know of no attempt at studying changes in input-output coefficients which is in full accordance with the theory presented in this book. Data problems would certainly be serious.

8.7. *Studies of productivity and industrial structure*

There are many types of empirical production studies which do not aim at

---

[40] See in particular Carter (1970a, b, c).

establishing production functions, but which nevertheless give empirical evidence of great interest in the context of our approach. In particular they may give information concerning the form of the capacity distribution. Such studies are usually found under the headings productivity studies or studies of the structure or structural change in a production sector.

Traditional productivity studies are mainly concerned with the development of average labour productivity. Such studies do not of course give much interesting information for our purpose. However, in recent years it has become customary to measure "best-practice" productivities on the basis of information from new plants and compare these with "average practice" productivities. In fact, the approach to explaining changes in input-output coefficients mentioned in the preceding section is a development from such productivity studies. Such studies are usually concerned with current inputs, and they accordingly give information which bears upon the form of the capacity distribution. In Figure 8.4 the shaded region is the region of positive

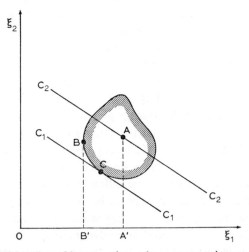

Fig. 8.4. Illustration of best practice and average practice productivities.

capacity in a ξ_1, ξ_2-plane where ξ_1 and ξ_2 are (as before) inputs per unit of output. In this figure point A represents average input coefficients, i.e. V_1/X and V_2/X, which are formed by averaging ξ_1 and ξ_2 over the whole region of positive capacity using the capacity distribution as a weight function. The inverse values are average productivities. Concerning best practice productivities there are (at least) two different concepts in use. The first type is concerned with one current input only, e.g. labour or some other dominant input such as fuel in power production. If input No. 1 is singled out as the input of greatest interest point B in Figure 8.4 would represent the best practice production unit since ξ_1 is here minimal. From productivity studies of the type under consideration we would then get productivity figures which can be translated into values for OB' and OA' in the figure, i.e. the values of ξ_1 at B and A respectively. A big difference indicates a wide region of positive capacity. The second type of productivity data are concerned with "total productivity" rather than productivity of one single input. Inputs are then aggregated by means of a set of prices, i.e. total current input is represented by operating costs. Best practice technique would then be represented by point C in the figure rather than B, and the difference between best practice and average practice would be revealed by the value of unit (operating) costs along the iso-unit-cost-lines C_1C_1 and C_2C_2. Again a large difference would indicate a wide region of positive capacity, but referring to the extension in another direction than in the first case. Such a wide region would generally suggest that we have a short-run macro function, where the scale elasticity coefficient falls considerably below 1 as capacity utilization increases, cf. the discussion in Section 4.4.

A rather early example of such a productivity study with a systematic discussion of some implications is by Maywald (1957); empirical evidence from various branches are found in Salter (1960) (particularly in the appendix to Ch. VII); a more recent example is Sporn (1969). Such studies do usually show that there is a considerable discrepancy between best practice and average practice productivities, whether they be of the one or the other type mentioned in connection with Figure 8.4. Usually there will be larger discrepancies in the case of labour productivities than e.g. in the productivity of fuel in producing electricity or in total unit costs since labour and capital are often easily substitutable in the ex ante function and wages increase rather strongly through time compared with most other prices. But, such studies show beyond doubt that there is usually a considerable extension of the region of positive capacity. It is not unusual that the best practice productivity is around twice as high as the average practice productivity in the case of labour. The full range is of course wider than the range between the best and the average. In Salter (1960) there are reported full ranges between best and "worst" practice labour productivities for some branches (here indicated by man-hours per unit of output) showing maximal labour requirements per unit of output as high as up to four times that of the minimum.

When time series are available for best practice and average practice productivities both will of course usually improve over time and one may observe the lag between the two. Average practice will often lag some 15–20 years behind best practice productivity. This lag will depend upon the rate of embodied technological progress, the rate of investment, changes in relative prices, particularly wages as compared with capital costs and other input prices, as well as several other factors. The figures indicate something about how the capacity distribution and thereby the short-run macro function move over time. This is a basic element of the dynamics of production as studied in Chapter 7.

An important limitation of such productivity studies as those discussed above is that they give information about the capacity distribution along one dimension only. Some studies of the structure of industrial branches do, however, provide more complete information. A very interesting example is Wohlin's study (1970) of the Swedish pulp and paper industry.

The statistical basis for Wohlin's study consists of returns to the official Swedish industry statistics, at the plant level. Total operating costs have been divided into wages, wood input and other current costs. (In some connections more detailed breakdowns are also presented.) In Figure 8.5 I reproduce, with the author's permission, a typical figure from his study, inspired by Salter (1960). This figure shows total operating costs per unit of output and components of costs in Swedish pulp factories 1964. The plants are grouped in 10 groups with approximately 10% of total capacity in each group. (Only plants not integrated in the paper industry are included.) Costs and cost components are given as proportions of product price 1964.

Total operating costs and particularly the wage component seem to vary

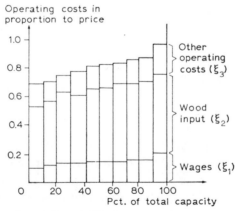

Fig. 8.5. Total operating costs per unit of output and components of cost in Swedish pulp plants 1964. Source: Wohlin (1970).

less among plants in this industry than in many other industries. What is particularly interesting, however, is to see the components of costs. On the basis of this information we can indicate roughly the capacity distribution in a three-dimensional ξ_1, ξ_2, ξ_3-space, where ξ_1, ξ_2, ξ_3 are simply the components as indicated in the figure; they are inputs per unit of output measured in the particular way indicated above. Instead of constructing a complicated three-dimensional figure I have, in Figure 8.6, plotted separately wood input per unit of output and "other operating costs" per unit of output against wages per unit of output.[41] There is clearly less variation in wood input per unit of output than in the two other input components. This is reasonable since technical progress as well as substitution possibilities in the ex ante function are not likely to affect wood input per unit of output *very* strongly.

In considering the degree of variation in Figure 8.6, one should remember that these 10 points represent average input coefficients for groups of plants. Each group has approximately the same total capacity. There are from 3 to 14 plants underlying each point in the figure; altogether there are 60 plants included. Each group is rather homogeneous with regard to total operating costs, since the plants are grouped on the basis of a ranking according to this criterion. But they need not be homogeneous with regard to the constituent components. Therefore a plotting based on individual plants rather than groups of plants would show some wider ranges of variation than the impression gained from Figure 8.6, particularly in the direction across rays from the origin – the "width dimension" to use an expression from Section 3.1.

Now the output of these plants is not quite homogeneous. Wohlin reports, however, that he has broken down the data according to types of pulp without this reducing the degree of variation significantly. Wohlin also gives data for paper production. Diagrams like Figure 8.6 for this case would show wider ranges of variation, but here output may be less homogeneous.[42]

Since I have here touched upon the wood processing industry I will report briefly on a small investigation which we carried out at the Institute of

---

[41] The points in the figure are actually plotted on the basis of Table 43 in Wohlin (1970), which underlies Figure 8.5. Points which coincide according to the figures are moved a little bit away from each other in our figure, in order to make them distinguishable.

[42] Before leaving Wohlin's study I should mention that his book contains many other theoretical as well as empirical observations which are very interesting in connection with our theoretical framework, but which it would take us too far to pursue here.

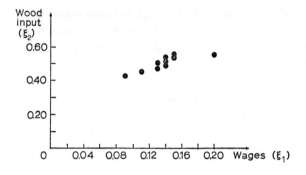

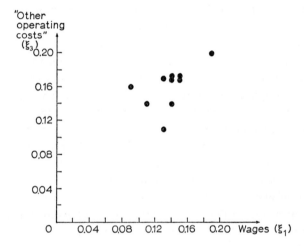

Fig. 8.6. Wood input per unit of output plotted against wages per unit of output (upper part) and "other operating costs" per unit of output plotted against wages per unit of output (lower part). Swedish pulp plants 1964. Based on Figure 8.5.

Economics at the University of Oslo.[43] The main purpose was to find out about the degree of variation in the capacity distribution in a typical manufacturing industry. We selected newsprint production so as to have a more homogeneous output than paper in general. Furthermore this branch is convenient for the purpose since the individual micro production units can be easily identified; they are simply the paper machines. There were 12 such machines included in the investigation, owned by a smaller number of companies. Through the kind cooperation of these companies we got data concerning capacity, actual output and the most important inputs such as la-

---

[43] Mr. Erling Eide was in charge of the work in collaboration with me.

bour, wood, pulp and electricity, as of 1967. In a few cases data were based on projected, but not yet installed machines. On this basis we calculated inputs per unit of output (ξ-coefficients) for each machine.[44] The overall impression gained was that there is a rather wide range of values of labour input per unit of output represented, being of the same order of magnitude as found in such productivity studies as were mentioned above. For electricity the range is also quite wide, but relatively narrower than in the case of labour. As is natural the range is most narrow in the case of wood and pulp input, but even here the variation is not negligible. Generally the distribution has a rather interesting form in that it is *not* the same machines which are most efficient with regard to all inputs, although there is of course a tendency for machines with large capacity to be relatively efficient in terms of inputs per unit of output.

We also had information concerning the year of installation of the machines and years of major reconstructions. Since newer machines are generally larger than older machines, it is statistically difficult to separate effects of technological progress from scale effects.

In general there was relatively more variation in the directions across rays from the origin (the width dimension) than in the direction along such rays (the length dimension) – more so than e.g. the impression gained from Figure 8.6.

This was clearly, to some extent, due to the fact that some of the older machines had been subjected to major reconstructions and improvements rather recently.

We shall not publish data on the individual machines, but the description given above is sufficient to draw the conclusion that the capacity distribution is not so narrowly concentrated as to be uninteresting, which was the main purpose of the investigation.

Before closing this section on studies of productivity and industrial structure I must draw the attention to a very important paper by Farrell (1957). This paper could have been treated previously in Sections 8.2 or 8.3. In fact Farrell's paper has to some extent influenced some of the works referred to in Sections 8.2 and 8.3, particularly those that employ the idea of fitting frontier functions. However, Farrell's main aim was not to estimate production functions, but rather to measure productive efficiency and components of this.

---

[44] There were some problems of comparability because of different degrees of integration of production processes. Some of the comparisons reported in the text were therefore carried out within subgroups of machines.

Farrell starts out from a description of a set of firms by plotting them according to inputs per unit of output for the various inputs – i.e. according to the ξ-coefficients in our notation. In order to get a standard for measuring the efficiency of the firms he fits a frontier function to the points (as a piece-wise linear function). Farrell calls this "the efficient production function". On our interpretation it would be the technique relation.

Next the efficiency of the various firms are measured by their location in the ξ-diagram relatively to the frontier curve.

Farrell introduces several efficiency concepts.

Technical efficiency is indicated by the nearness of the ξ-point of a firm to the frontier curve measured in the direction towards the origin.

Price efficiency is indicated by the degree of correctness in the adaptation of factor proportions to current input prices. Here the marginal rate of substitution as implied by the technique relation comes into play.

These two measures are such that a firm may be perfectly efficient in one sense without being so in the other sense.

Overall efficiency is a combination of the measures of technical efficiency and price efficiency; it indicates (inversely) the savings in costs which could be achieved if the firm were replaced by another which were perfectly efficient, both technically and in its adaptation of factor proportions to input prices.

These concepts refer to the efficiency of the individual firm. Farrell also introduces aggregate efficiency measures for the whole industry. This is called "*structural efficiency*" and indicates "the extent to which an industry keeps up with the performance of its own best firms". The structural efficiency is higher the more the capacity distribution is concentrated near to its frontier towards the origin in the ξ-space.

It is clear that empirical efficiency studies along the lines proposed by Farrell give much more interesting information than traditional types of productivity studies.

Farrell gives a careful discussion of the concepts and their interpretations. However, he is not quite explicit with regard to such aspects as we have emphasized in this study. I shall therefore add a few observations which seem to be in order if the underlying technological structure is as we have assumed.

We have on various occassions discussed factors which explain that there will usually be some extension of the region of positive capacity in all dimensions, i.e. factors which tend to produce apparent structural inefficiency in Farrell's sense. The two most important factors are:

(1) *Ex post rigidity of factor proportions*. This implies that factor proportions should, at the moment of investment, be adapted to some averages of

expected future input prices. If there are in fact changes in prices through time even a perfectly correct investment decision will give rise to a production unit which, according to Farrell's concept of price efficiency, will appear to be efficient only in a limited period of its useful life. In a dynamic economy there will thus be some optimal degree of price inefficiency, i.e. that amount of price inefficiency which will come about under correct price expectations and correct investment decisions. Inoptimal price inefficiency may result from incorrect price expectations or from wrong adaptations to correct expectations. This suggests that more complicated measures of price efficiency than Farrell's might be of interest if one should try to distinguish optimal from inoptimal adaptations and measure the loss by deviations from optimality.

(2) *Embodied technological progress.* To the extent that there is embodied technological progress we will always have firms that are technically inefficient in Farrell's sense. Like in the previous case this does not in itself indicate any deviations from optimality in a dynamic context. It is an interesting theoretical question to what extent expected embodied progress should induce postponement of investment, but it is clear that one will not always postpone all investments in order not to get tied up with a technology that will soon be outmoded.[45] This is not to deny that there will in practice be undesirable inefficiencies, but not all apparent technical inefficiency in Farrell's sense will indicate that there is something lost (as compared with *feasible* alternatives).

In Section 3.1 we listed a number of reasons why there will be a nondegenerate region of positive capacity in the ξ-space. Two of them were connected with changing input prices and with embodied technological progress. Many of the other points mentioned in Section 3.1 will give rise to such inefficiencies in Farrell's sense which indicate deviations from optimality.

Farrell is himself not unaware of the fact that inefficiency according to his measures does not necessarily indicate something undesirable, at least in the case of price inefficiency. He suggests (on p. 261) the role of future prices in investment decisions and says that his price efficiency will "provide a

---

[45] The apparent paradox which may lie here in the case of very fast and correctly foreseen embodied technological progress is resolved when we take into account the time profile of prices. If it, at constant prices, appears profitable always to postpone investments, then an expected time profile with declining output price may again make some immediate investments profitable, and such a profile will of course be plausible if many investments in a certain branch are postponed in expectancy of technological progress.

good measure of its [a firm's] efficiency in adapting to factor prices only in a completely static situation", whereas he seems to be less cautious in interpreting the measure of technical efficiency. However, since ex post rigidity of factor proportions and embodiedness of at least some amount of technological progress are essential elements in the theoretical structure of our study, we should be particularly careful not to attach undue normative significance to Farrell's measures of efficiency within our framework. His measures do, however, retain significance as interesting descriptive measures of certain characteristics of the capacity distribution and of growth potentials which can be realized by replacement investments.[46]

In most of the studies touched upon above labour is treated as one component, or sometimes split into production workers and administrative personnel. Some more detailed studies, e.g. in connection with problems of automation and employment, show that the degree of automation or mechanization may have considerable consequences for the skill and educational composition of the labour force. A study by Auerhan based on detailed information from Czechoslovakian industry[47] distinguishes between nine levels of mechanization and six skill levels and shows how the skill distribution shifts in the direction of higher skill levels as one moves towards higher levels of mechanization. Since the degree of mechanization is embodied in fixed equipment this suggests that our approach to production studies may be of some relevance also for the study of the development of demand for different skill or education categories of labour.

---

[46] For extensions and further discussions of Farrell's study, see Farrell and Fieldhouse (1962), Nerlove (1965), Chapter 5, and Seitz (1970). For a discussion more especially connected with the theoretical framework of the present study, see Førsund (1969).

[47] See Auerhan's contribution to Stieber (ed.) (1966).

CHAPTER 9

Empirical illustrations based on data for Norwegian tankers

9.1. Introduction

This chapter will illustrate some aspects of the theory outlined in previous chapters by means of data for Norwegian tankers. Not all aspects of the theory will be covered. We shall be particularly concerned with the capacity distribution and the construction of the short-run macro function which perhaps represent the more special features of our approach and which are therefore most in need of empirical illustration and verification.

A first question to be asked is whether the technology of tankers can be well represented by our standard model. According to specialized studies of tanker technology and economy the answer seems to be affirmative. As an example, let me refer to Goss (1968). In a chapter on "Economic Criteria for Optimal Ship Design" he first refers to the fact that "there are generally several different ways of designing a ship; ... Not only do we have many different types of engine and hull shapes to choose from, but any given flow of cargo can be carried in ships of different sizes and numbers, offering different service frequencies and, possibly, different sea speeds and turn-round times." Furthermore he refers to the choice of whether or not to use automatic devices for various purposes. It is clear that there are many aspects which give rise to considerable substitution possibilities ex ante. According to the author some of these substitution possibilities have been exploited to a high degree in recent years, mainly for the purpose of reducing the size of the crew.

Further on the author discusses how to allow for changing productivities of various inputs in economic calculations. In this connection he points out that "the effectiveness of a factor of production in, or around, a ship is largely determined by the design of that ship. Once you have built a ship intended to be operated by a given number of crew it is quite difficult to change either the number of men or the proportions of the various grades. Similarly, once the engine has been built it is quite difficult to improve its specific fuel consumption." This clearly indicates that there is not much scope for ex post substitution.

Several studies of supply conditions in the tanker freight market have explicitly or implicitly built on assumptions in at least approximate agreement with the technological and economic assumptions underlying our model. A classical study is by Koopmans (1939). Koopmans discusses various ways of increasing the performance of a given ship, but concludes that neither of these possibilities is "particularly important from a quantitative point of view". On this basis he constructs a supply curve for the tanker freight market by thinking of the vessels as ordered according to operation costs in a similar way as the pulp plants in connection with Figure 8.5; at any given freight rate those tankers which earn income over and above operation costs – i.e. earn a positive quasi rent – will be employed. This way of constructing a supply curve is in full agreement with the derivation of supply functions in Chapter 6 of this book. According to this construction one would expect the supply curve to be rather flat for low rates of capacity utilization, but becoming very steep when one approaches full capacity utilization. This expectation finds support in the data. Without having cost data concerning the individual tankers there are, however, statistical difficulties: time series studies suffer from the difficulty that the curve mentioned is a short-run supply function subject to frequent shifting as recognized by Koopmans.

Similar ideas about the supply curve in the tanker freight market are developed in Seland (1954), who also discusses the consequences of such supply conditions for the development of freight rates and the number of vessels laid up in the early post-world war period. The tonnage of ships laid up can of course be read off from a point on the supply curve when this is constructed as suggested above.

The conclusions suggested on the basis of these older studies are reinforced by a recent study, Hettena and Ruchlin (1969). These authors discuss carefully the cost function for individual tankers and come to the result that average operating costs decline sharply with increasing output level until "normal capacity" is reached. Then average costs increase between "normal capacity" and "maximum capacity", becoming a vertical curve at the latter point. The distance between "normal" and "maximum capacity" is, however, rather small. Thus "the cost/output relationship will always impel the tanker owner to operate at, or close to, full capacity or not to operate at all". The technical factors underlying these cost conditions are described in the following way: "A tanker cannot be 'used' more or less intensively except within exceedingly narrow limits. Only a very minor speed variation beyond normal output is possible, and the marginal cost of carrying additional cargo is virtually zero until the cargo load reaches maximum practical capacity. Since any reduction from maximum capacity produces no significant cost reduction, and since revenue is always proportional to the quantity of cargo carried, whenever a tanker operates, it will always do so at, or close to, 100 per cent of practical capacity."

For the total supply curve Hettena and Ruchlin give a description which fully accords with our approach, with contraction of tonnage supply through total shutdown of a part of the tanker fleet and short-run increases in supply by reactivation of laid-up vessels. In the longer run new construction expands capacity and moves the supply curve to the right, thus reducing reactivation chances of laid-up tonnage and accelerating scrapping of high-cost tankers already laid up.

Referring to our assumptions about technology the description quoted here perhaps conforms most directly with the case mentioned in Section 3.5, where "individual production units are of the sort that they can only be operated at zero level or at full capacity". As we noticed there our theoretical results are valid also for this case when there are so many micro units that a capacity distribution of the type we have used provides a reasonably good approximation.

Now a tanker can of course be operated through parts of a period of time – say, a year – and be laid up through the remainder of the period. If there were no costs associated with laying up a vessel and reactivating it, then the ex post micro production function could be thought of exactly as in our standard case. In fact such costs are not negligible. This creates some specific dynamic phenomena in the very short-run variations which are treated in the works referred to above. It may be profitable to keep a tanker in operation even at negative quasi rents if freight rates are expected to rise again in the near future, and it may be unprofitable to reactivate a tanker even at sufficiently high freight rates to yield positive quasi rents if the high level is expected to be of a short duration. At a given moment of time we should therefore expect some tankers in operation to yield lower quasi rents than those which some laid-up vessels (if there are any) would be able to earn if reactivated. This would be true even if all contracts were short-term contracts. In addition it is a fact that many tankers are on longer term charter contracts.

All this means that there are some features of short-run variations which are not well taken care of by our model, which is – as we have pointed out before – a short-run *equilibrium* model as far as the theory of the short-run macro production function is concerned.

9.2. *The data*

As has been indicated already the main purpose of the following study is to establish the capacity distribution and the corresponding short-run macro function for the Norwegian tanker fleet as of the beginning of 1967.

Not all details of the collection and processing of the data will be explained here. For details the reader is referred to a report by Eide (1969). Mr. Eide, in collaboration with me, was in charge of most of the empirical work presented in this and the three following sections.

The basic data are taken from the Norwegian ship register (Det norske Veritas) for 1967. This includes 377 tankers of more than 15,000 deadweight tons (DWT). Out of these there are 320 motor tankers and 57 turbine tankers. The choice between a motor tanker and a turbine tanker is part of the ex ante substitution possibility since these types of tankers have somewhat different input combinations.

Output will be considered as ton-mile transported per day. We shall consider two current inputs, No. 1: Fuel, and No. 2: Labour. We shall measure these inputs in values at prices and wages in given years.

Fuel and labour are the two most important current inputs. Other costs such as repair and maintenance (in addition to that done by the crew), insurance and administration are less directly connected with the operation of the ship. Port charges and other costs incurred by loading and discharging ought perhaps to be included, but would require more of a specialized study than we were prepared to carry out. Our aim has been to illustrate the general theory outlined in the previous chapters and not to contribute a specialized study in the economics of shipping. No doubt some of the observations and comments made in the sequel will appear somewhat amateurish to a shipping expert.

Referring to Sections 2.2 and 2.3 our task is first to establish, for each tanker, data for

$\bar{x}$ = output capacity in ton-miles per day;

$\bar{v}_1$ = fuel requirement per day (measured in 1968-prices);

$\bar{v}_2$ = labour requirement per day (measured in 1966-wages and -prices).

In the case of labour input we include some costs which are rather directly connected with labour such as provision etc.; that is why we measure labour input in 1966-wages *and -prices*.

The fact that we measure fuel in 1968-prices and labour costs in 1966-wages and -prices is a matter of convenience; these were the years for which data were most readily available. It is of no important consequence that we have different base years in the two cases; furthermore, the relevant fuel prices seem to have been almost the same in 1966 and 1968.

Figures for output $\bar{x}$ are based on the following information: gross dead-weight tonnage, bunker capacity, and speed of the ship. These data were in most cases almost directly available from the ship register, but some inter-polations had to be done for some (137) ships in the case of bunker capacity and for a few (27) ships in the case of speed. Details are given in Eide (1969); our impression is that the approximation found by the interpolations is satisfactory.

Fuel requirements are constructed on the basis of rather detailed tables given in R.S. Platou A/S: "Tanker Trip to T/C Conversion Tables on Net Return" (March 1968). These tables give normal fuel requirements per day for tankers of various sizes and speeds, for motor tankers and turbine tankers separately. Again some interpolations and extrapolations were nec-essary. Fuel prices as of March 1968 were taken from the same publication.

Labour requirements were calculated on the basis of detailed manning regulations according to Government Resolution of September 22, 1950, and later amendments. These regulations indicate the size of the crew for tankers classified according to motor/turbine, year of construction (mainly distin-guished by whether they are built before or after 1959), deadweight capacity, gross registered tonnage and indicated horse power. Except for some older turbine tankers we have assumed that these regulations are strictly adhered to. In practice some exemptions are granted for some ships built before 1959, so that these tankers have a somewhat smaller crew than is laid down in the regulations. This introduces a slight bias, but on the whole we think that the regulations are so closely observed that the constructed figures give a very good approximation to actual crew sizes.

We have calculated with average wages and average indirect labour costs as of 1966, based on statistics given in "Aktuelle Skipsfarts-spørsmål 1966" (Norsk Rederforbund). This is reasonable when we consider labour as homo-geneous, or if the composition of the crew were the same on all tankers. In fact the relative composition varies somewhat with the size. It would be possible to take account of this aspect by following the same approach as here, but with a distinction between types of labour. (Cf. the concluding remarks in Section 8.7.)

Having established $\bar{x}$, $\bar{v}_1$ and $\bar{v}_2$ for each tanker we calculate input coeffi-cients by

$$\xi_1 = \bar{v}_1/\bar{x}, \quad \xi_2 = \bar{v}_2/\bar{x}$$

as by (2.2).

TABLE 9.1

Exerpts of data for Norwegian tankers 1966. Source and further explanations given in the text. Numbers marked by * refer to turbine tankers

Year of construc-tion	No.	Size of ship in gross deadweight tonnage	Speed in miles per hour	Capacity in 1000 ton-miles per day $\bar{x}$	Fuel input per unit of output (in *kroner* per 1000 ton-miles) ξ_1	Labour input per unit of output (in *kroner* per 1000 ton-miles) ξ_2
1950	1	15 185	11½	3 854	0.444	0.947
	4	16 320	14	5 047	0.532	0.745
1951	5	16 345	14¼	5 180	0.550	0.726
	13	25 155	13	7 318	0.426	0.526
1952	14	15 625	12	4 195	0.460	0.897
	23	24 600	13	7 106	0.424	0.542
1953	24	15 775	14	4 890	0.538	0.757
	42	24 450	14	7 493	0.460	0.514
1954	43	15 610	14	4 855	0.531	0.793
	63	43 400	13½	13 073	0.363	0.295
1955	64	15 350	14½	4 881	0.562	0.789
	86	32 185	15½	11 061	0.434	0.348
1956	87	15 310	14¾	4 920	0.579	0.873
	105	35 425	14½	11 235	0.408	0.343
1957	106	15 350	14½	4 872	0.563	0.790
	130*	39 430	17½	14 840	0.616	0.232
1958	131	15 300	15	5 034	0.577	0.765
	172*	45 520	15¼	16 301	0.470	0.211
1959	173	15 704	13.8	4 892	0.527	0.696
	201	50 031	15½	17 508	0.330	0.200
1960	202	17 245	14½	5 621	0.536	0.606
	225*	49 102	16	17 050	0.518	0.208
1961	226	18 840	15	5 827	0.573	0.584
	249	52 268	16	18 424	0.352	0.190
1962	250	19 500	14	6 034	0.508	0.564
	266*	52 555	14½	17 002	0.451	0.208
1963	267	19 200	14	5 907	0.519	0.576
	289	91 375	16	32 880	0.255	0.112
1964	290	19 980	15	6 660	0.517	0.511
	323	92 420	16	35 489	0.237	0.104
1965	324	19 700	17	6 785	0.604	0.502
	355	98 310	15½	33 261	0.248	0.111
1966	356	48 100	16½	17 456	0.365	0.201
	377	149 556	16	54 311	0.185	0.069

The complete set of data thus obtained for the 377 vessels are given in Eide (1969). We have reproduced in Table 9.1 some of the data, so as to give a rough impression. We have for every year included the smallest and the largest vessel as measured by gross deadweight tonnage. The tankers are numbered from 1 to 377, starting with the smallest vessel (above 15,000 DWT) from 1950 and ending with the largest vessel, built in 1966. Numbers marked by * are turbine tankers, the others are motor tankers. Capacity $\bar{x}$ is given in 1000 ton-miles per day. Fuel and labour expenses are in *kroner* per day, and ξ_1 and ξ_2 accordingly in *kroner* per 1000 ton-miles.

The range of variation encompassed by the data is indicated by the following figures:

Year of build ranges from 1950 to 1966;

Size ranges from 15,000 to nearly 150,000 DWT;

Speed ranges from $11\frac{1}{2}$ to $17\frac{1}{2}$ miles per hour.

It is clear that such speed variations imply a considerable scope for substitution (ex ante, cf. the preceding section) between labour and fuel. Tankers Nos. 1 and 4 from 1950 in the table are illustrative. They are of approximately the same size. We see that the faster ship (No. 4) uses more fuel and less labour per unit of output.

However, the largest deviations in input requirements represented in the material is generated by the variation in size and the choice between motor and turbine tankers. This will be further illustrated in Section 9.3.

Before proceeding further it may be of interest to discuss the nature of manning regulations in relation to our model. Apparently these regulations tend to introduce a kind of institutional rigidity which has similar implications to the technological ex post rigidity which we assume elsewhere.

There is hardly any doubt that the existence of manning regulations which have to be fairly simple, thus not taking into account all feasible varieties of vessels that could be constructed, will tend to narrow down the range of actual choices from the ex ante function at any time. Thus the capacity distribution is probably somewhat more concentrated than it would have been without these regulations. At least this would have been so if the regulations had been the same all the time. But it is not quite clear when we take into account that the regulations were changed in 1959 in such a way as to widen the possibilities for exploiting labour-saving constructions. Some of the vessels constructed before 1959 may thus have been held "artificially" back and be more different from newer vessels than they would have been in a development unhampered by such regulations.

When it comes to the ex post technology there is a question of how to measure labour input. Suppose there were ex post fixed coefficients if labour input could somehow be measured in units of physical and mental effort. Then labour input measured by the size of the crew would not necessarily be related to output by a fixed proportion. The existence of manning regulations may serve to stabilize the proportion between labour as an amount of effort and labour measured by the size of the crew, and thus, from this point of view, perhaps be an advantage for our empirical investigation where we largely have to use the cruder measure of labour input.

9.3. *The capacity distribution*

The complete table underlying Table 9.1 gives a detailed description of the capacity distribution embodied in the Norwegian tanker fleet as of 1967 (restricted, however, to vessels above 15,000 DWT). Based on individual production units the distribution is given in discrete form, cf. the comments between Equations (3.1) and (3.2).

It is not easy, however, to get an impression of the form of the capacity distribution merely from the figures in such a table. In Figure 9.1 the distribution is visualized in a somewhat simplified form. The tankers are grouped in classes by intervals of 0.05 for ξ_1 (fuel) and ξ_2 (labour), and each class is represented by a rectangle in the figure with the centre placed in the centre of the ξ_1, ξ_2-box corresponding to the class. The sizes of the rectangles indicate roughly the amount of capacity in each class. The vessels are grouped by year of construction into three groups: 1950–55, 1956–61 and 1962–66.

It is seen that the capacity distribution has a rather peculiar form. There is a rather heavy concentration of new tankers in the south-western part of the distribution. The tankers constructed in 1956–61 branch out in two directions. The lower branch (relatively large fuel input, relatively small labour input) consists of turbine tankers, whereas the upper branch (smaller fuel input, larger labour input) represents motor tankers. The oldest tankers (1950–55) are largely found in the upper part of the motor tanker branch.

In the south-western part of the capacity distribution there are both motor tankers and turbine tankers. Also in this part the tendency for such a branching of the distribution can be found in the detailed data, but it is not so striking in this part.

The choice between motor and turbine tankers constitutes an important element of ex ante substitution possibilities. Other elements have to do with the speed as suggested before.

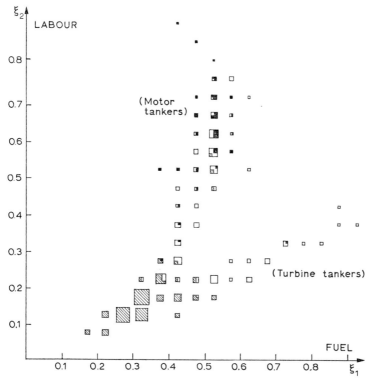

Fig. 9.1. Capacity distribution for Norwegian tankers 1967. Sources as for Table 9.1 Units of measurement as explained in connection with Table 9.1. Sizes of squares indicate amount of capacity: □ = 250 million ton-miles per day. Indication of year of construction: ▓: 1950–55, □: 1956–61, ▨: 1962–66.

A few further observations on the determinants of the form of the capacity distribution are offered in the following section.

9.4. Some further observations on the determinants of the form of the capacity distribution

The form of the capacity distribution shown in Section 9.3 is influenced by many factors. It is impossible to disentangle completely the effects of all these factors, but we shall try in this section to go at least some way in that direction.

It is clear already from Figure 9.1 that there is a marked vintage effect in the capacity distribution. Now it is equally clear from Table 9.1 that the vessels have tended to become bigger and bigger. An interesting question is

TABLE 9.2

Average input coefficients for tankers classified by year of construction and size

	15–20,000 DWT				20–24,000 DWT				24–30,000 DWT				30–40,000 DWT			
	m	$\bar{\xi}_1$	$\bar{\xi}_2$	$\bar{\xi}_3$	m	$\bar{\xi}_1$	$\bar{\xi}_2$	$\bar{\xi}_3$	m	$\bar{\xi}_1$	$\bar{\xi}_2$	$\bar{\xi}_3$	m	$\bar{\xi}_1$	$\bar{\xi}_2$	$\bar{\xi}$
1950–52	16	0.52	0.75	4.0	<5	0.43	0.55	3.7	6	0.44	0.52	3.3				
1953–55	45	0.53	0.69	4.1	9	0.63	0.57	3.9	<5	0.43	0.51	3.4	<5	0.52	0.41	3
1956–58	47	0.53	0.63	3.6	7	0.59	0.59	3.7	12	0.50	0.43	2.9	18	0.55	0.32	2
1959–61	30	0.53	0.56	3.7	<5	0.51	0.52	3.6	8	0.53	0.38	2.9	20	0.50	0.28	2
1962–64	8	0.52	0.53	3.9	<5	0.54	0.50	3.0	<5	0.83	0.35	2.7	<5	0.42	0.28	2
1965–66	<5	0.60	0.50	3.7												

	40–50,000 DWT				50–70,000 DWT				70–100,000 DWT				>100,000 DWT			
	m	$\bar{\xi}_1$	$\bar{\xi}_2$	$\bar{\xi}_3$	m	$\bar{\xi}_1$	$\bar{\xi}_2$	$\bar{\xi}_3$	m	$\bar{\xi}_1$	$\bar{\xi}_2$	$\bar{\xi}_3$	m	$\bar{\xi}_1$	$\bar{\xi}_2$	$\bar{\xi}$
1950–52																
1953–55	5	0.36	0.30	3.8												
1956–58	<5	0.55	0.23	2.4												
1959–61	13	0.50	0.23	2.6	<5	0.39	0.19	2.5								
1962–64	14	0.39	0.23	2.7	38	0.36	0.17	2.2	8	0.29	0.12	2.0				
1965–66	8	0.36	0.20	2.3	11	0.35	0.17	2.2	31	0.30	0.13	1.9	<5	0.21	0.07	1

m = number of vessels in the class. $\bar{\xi}_1$ = average fuel input coefficient. $\bar{\xi}_2$ = average labour input coefficient. $\bar{\xi}_3$ = average capital input coefficient.

whether there is still a vintage effect within size classes, i.e. if we eliminate the size effect. To find out about this we have calculated average input coefficients for the tankers cross-classified by year of construction and size class. The results are shown in Table 9.2.

Now the amount of capital invested per unit of capacity may also influence the input coefficients for current inputs. Here measurements are of course much more dubious, but an attempt has been made by Mr. Eide.

Out of the 377 tankers included in the material 251 have been imported. On the basis of data from the Central Bureau of Statistics of Norway Mr. Eide calculated average import prices per DWT for these imported tankers for each year in the period 1950–66 and for each size class. These prices were applied to each of the 251 imported tankers and to the 126 home-constructed tankers as well. Thus we have approximate values of the tankers when new, in current prices. Next a price index was constructed for the years 1950–66, with value 100 in 1964, as a weighted average of indices for each size class. The index rises from 55 in 1950 to 139 in 1961, and then declines to 97 in 1966. Using this index as a deflator we obtain the amount of capital invested in each tanker in constant prices.

On this basis capital per unit of output (capacity) has been calculated and the averages entered as $\bar{\xi}_3$ in Table 9.2 alongside average current input coefficients. The figures should at least give some rough indication of the tendencies, but they are clearly less reliable than the figures for current input coefficients.

Comparing size classes in Table 9.2 – i.e. reading the table horizontally – it is clear that larger vessels use very much less labour per unit of capacity than smaller vessels. In most cases they also use less fuel per unit of output, though this tendency is more modest than in the case of labour. Since the tendency through time has been in the direction of larger and larger vessels, this scale effect seems to explain a large part of the form of the capacity distribution shown in Figure 9.1.

According to our rough figures for capital invested per unit of capacity this economy in current inputs in larger vessels is not bought at the cost of larger investment per unit of output; the capital input coefficient is in fact declining with the size of the vessel in almost all cases.

It is thus rather clear that a large part of the wide range of current input coefficients in the capacity distribution in Figure 9.1 must be due to either an increasing exploitation of economies of scale in the ex ante function or embodied technological progress. It is, however, rather difficult to draw the line between these two effects. The crucial question is whether it would have been possible, on the basis of say 1950-technology, to build such large and efficient tankers as have become common more recently. The answer cannot be unambiguous. E.g., should we in expressing the ex ante function as of 1950 take into account the then existing types of shipyards, or should we think in ex ante terms to such a degree that we allow for the construction of new shipyards? In the first case the very large vessels would definitely not be encompassed by the 1950-ex ante function; in the latter case they *might* be so.

Another question is the external factors such as ports, canals, etc. There has been a development in these external factors which has tended to permit the use of the larger vessels. It is a matter of definition whether we include the limitation set by such factors in the ex ante function or not.

Now literature on tanker shipping does, however, suggest rather clearly that there are some elements of technological progress in the narrower sense behind the tendencies to build larger vessels in recent years such as improved strength of materials and constructions etc. We may therefore conclude that there is an element of technological progress in the development which is correlated with the tendency towards larger vessels.

Let us next read the table vertically, i.e. compare newer and older vessels within each given size class. There are clearly no such dramatic changes

TABLE 9.3

Input proportions $\bar{\xi}_1/\bar{\xi}_2$ and $\bar{\xi}_3/\bar{\xi}_2$. Based on Table 9.2

| | 15–20,000 DWT | | 20–24,000 DWT | | 24–30,000 DWT | | 30–40,000 DWT | |
	$\bar{\xi}_1/\bar{\xi}_2$	$\bar{\xi}_3/\bar{\xi}_2$	$\bar{\xi}_1/\bar{\xi}_2$	$\bar{\xi}_3/\bar{\xi}_2$	$\bar{\xi}_1/\bar{\xi}_2$	$\bar{\xi}_3/\bar{\xi}_2$	$\bar{\xi}_1/\bar{\xi}_2$	$\bar{\xi}_3/\bar{\xi}_2$
1950–52	0.69	5.33	0.78	6.73	0.85	6.35		
1953–55	0.77	5.94	1.11	6.84	0.84	6.67	1.27	7.56
1956–58	0.84	5.71	1.00	6.27	1.35	6.74	1.72	8.75
1959–61	0.95	6.61	0.98	6.92	1.39	7.63	1.79	9.64
1962–64	0.98	7.36	1.08	6.00	2.34	7.71	1.50	10.00
1965–66	1.20	7.40						

| | 40–50,000 DWT | | 50–70,000 DWT | | 70–100,000 DWT | | >100,000 DWT | |
	$\bar{\xi}_1/\bar{\xi}_2$	$\bar{\xi}_3/\bar{\xi}_2$	$\bar{\xi}_1/\bar{\xi}_2$	$\bar{\xi}_3/\bar{\xi}_2$	$\bar{\xi}_1/\bar{\xi}_2$	$\bar{\xi}_3/\bar{\xi}_2$	$\bar{\xi}_1/\bar{\xi}_2$	$\bar{\xi}_3/\bar{\xi}_2$
1950–52								
1953–55	1.20	12.67						
1956–58	2.39	10.43						
1959–61	2.17	11.30	2.05	13.16				
1962–64	1.70	11.74	2.12	12.94	2.42	16.67		
1965–66	1.80	11.50	2.06	12.94	2.31	14.62	3.00	21.43

within size classes as between size classes. But there is in most cases a very clear tendency towards lower labour input coefficients even within size classes. Generally there is also a tendency towards lower capital input, whereas there is no very clear tendency in the case of fuel input. This indicates that there is some embodied technological progress in addition to that element of progress which is associated with increasing size of vessels.

An interesting question is whether we can detect any substitution effects in the pattern of input coefficients shown in Table 9.2. In order to focus attention on this aspect, let us consider the input *proportions* as given by ξ_1/ξ_2 and ξ_3/ξ_2, i.e. we consider fuel and capital input in proportion to labour input. These proportions are given in Table 9.3 for the same classes as in Table 9.2. We see that there are considerable variations in factor proportions, also within size classes.

In order to see whether these variations can be explained at least to some extent as substitution responses to price changes we need price data for the various inputs. In Eide (1969) there are given rough indices for labour costs, fuel prices and capital costs for most of the years 1950–66. For the present purpose I recomputed these indices so as to be 100 in 1950, interpolated for the few missing years, formed the proportions between the price indices and finally calculated averages for the periods 1950–52, 1953–55, ..., 1965–66 corresponding to the age classification of the vessels. The results are given in Table 9.4. For sources for the basic indices from which Table 9.4 is

TABLE 9.4

Indices for relative input prices

	1950–52	1953–55	1956–58	1959–61	1962–64	1965–66
Index for fuel costs in proportion to labour costs	104	86	97	60	43	32
Index for capital costs in proportion to labour costs	129	175	259	244	174	111

computed I refer to Eide (1969). I shall here only explain a little bit more about "capital costs". The index for capital costs is partly based on the purchase prices mentioned before. The index for this component rises from 1950 to 1961 and then declines. The other component of capital costs is the interest rate. Here an average interest rate is formed for each year on the basis of typical interest rates charged by the most important suppliers of ships to Norway, i.e. Sweden, United Kingdom and Japan besides Norway. This index is rather constant through 1950–54, then rises to 1957 and remains at the higher level with rather modest variations throughout the remainder of the period.

The index for capital costs used in Table 9.4 is formed by taking the product of the price index and the average interest rate.

It is clear that such an index can only give a very rough indication of the development of capital costs, but since it shows such a marked pattern of change over the period we may perhaps attach some importance to it.

The labour cost index, which is used as the common deflator in forming the indices for relative prices in Table 9.4, rises monotonically from 1950 to 1966.

Let us first consider the input proportion ξ_1/ξ_2 in relation to the fuel/labour cost index. The relative price of fuel to labour declines throughout the period apart from a temporary peak in 1956–58 which is of course related to the Suez crisis. We should accordingly expect the input proportion ξ_1/ξ_2 to show an increasing tendency. This tendency is very clear in the size classes 15–20,000 DWT and 24–30,000 DWT, and traces of it may perhaps also be found in some other instances. A clear tendency in the reverse direction is not seen in any of the size classes. There are no visible effects of the peak in the fuel/labour price in 1956–58. This is, however, reasonable since with ex post freezing of factor proportions the expected factor prices over a longer period should decide the choice of factor proportions, and the price proportions in 1956–58 were hardly expected to continue.

It is a clear pattern that the fuel/labour input proportion on average increases with the size of the vessel. The gradual shifting in the direction of ever larger vessels is therefore also consistent with the development of the fuel/labour relative price development.

Next consider the capital/labour input proportion. In this case the relative price first increases and then declines. We find few movements in the ξ_3/ξ_2-proportion in Table 9.3, which can be explained as a response to this development of relative prices. In fact the capital/labour proportion remains rather stable within size classes.[1]

There may be several explanations of the failure to find any clear responses to price changes in this case. First of all data on this aspect are very rough and unreliable. Secondly, the manning regulations have imposed restrictions which may have suppressed responses which would otherwise have appeared. We see a reflection of the manning regulations in the increased capital/labour proportions from 1956/58 to 1959/61. The changes in manning regulations from 1959 opened for a limited change in labour input which was consistent with the capital/labour price development from 1959 shown in Table 9.4.[2]

From Table 9.3 it is clear that the capital/labour proportion is generally higher for larger than for smaller vessels. The fact that the changeover to really big vessels has taken place particularly in the latter half of the period considered is thus consistent also with the development of the capital/labour relative price.

In principle we should consider all inputs and all prices simultaneously rather than by such pair-wise discussions as we have presented above. However, the data do not seem to warrant any more refined analysis.

Summarizing the discussion we may say that there has clearly been considerable technological progress taking place – partly correlated with the increase in average size, but also within size classes. There are rather clear reflections within size classes of the development of the fuel/labour input price proportion, but not of the development of the capital/labour price proportion. The increase in size of vessels is not neutral with respect to input proportions, but reduces labour input in proportion to both other inputs. The development in the direction of larger vessels, particularly in the

---

[1] Mr. Eide (1969) found some systematic tendencies in the changes in capital/labour proportions for narrower size classes, but the evidence is not very strong.

[2] The manning regulations should of course also affect the fuel/labour proportion. However, the scope for substitution which is implied by the turbine/motor tanker choice and by the choice of speed is not restricted by the manning rules to the same extent as various types of automation which might make for capital-labour substitution.

latter half of the period considered, is consistent with the development of the relative input prices in this period, but it is hard to say to what extent the development is motivated by these price developments and to what extent it is stimulated by technological development regardless of prices.

9.5. *The short-run macro function*

On the basis of the data on the capacity distribution as presented in Table 9.1 and Figure 9.1 one may establish the short-run macro production function for the Norwegian tanker fleet as of 1967. Since the data are in discrete form and since the form of the capacity distribution does not lend itself easily to a nice, smooth representation in the form of a continuous distribution function, we have to use summation rather than integration. The simplest way to proceed seems to be as follows.

Select a pair of input prices Q_1, Q_2. For each tanker, calculate its operating costs (on fuel and labour) by

$$Q_1 \xi_1^i + Q_2 \xi_2^i = C^i, \tag{9.1}$$

where ξ_1^i, ξ_2^i are input coefficients for tanker No. i, for $i = 1, 2, \ldots, 377$ (377 being the number of tankers included in the data). Next order the tankers according to increasing values of C^i. Let the new numbering be indicated by (j).

We now want a point on the isoquant corresponding to a total output X. We then determine which tankers should be operated by determining a number n_X by

$$\sum_{j=1}^{n_X-1} \bar{x}^{(j)} < X \le \sum_{j=1}^{n_X} \bar{x}^{(j)}, \tag{9.2}$$

where $\bar{x}^{(j)}$ is the capacity of tanker No. (j), i.e. when they are ordered according to increasing values of operating costs. Then clearly all tankers $j = 1, \ldots, n_X-1$ should be fully utilized while No. $j = n_X$ is the marginal tanker which should be idle a proportion

$$u = \frac{\sum\limits_{j=1}^{n_X} \bar{x}^{(j)} - X}{\bar{x}^{(n_X)}} \tag{9.3}$$

of the time.

Corresponding to this determination of vessels to be operated we have the total input requirements

$$
V_1 = \sum_{j=1}^{nx} \bar{v}_1^{(j)} - u\bar{v}_1^{(nx)}
$$

$$
V_2 = \sum_{j=1}^{nx} \bar{v}_2^{(j)} - u\bar{v}_2^{(nx)},
$$

(9.4)

where $\bar{v}_1^{(j)}$ and $\bar{v}_2^{(j)}$ are input requirements for tanker No.(j) when operated at full capacity, i.e. $\bar{v}_1^{(j)} = \xi_1^{(j)} \bar{x}^{(j)}$ and $\bar{v}_2^{(j)} = \xi_2^{(j)} \bar{x}^{(j)}$, cf. (2.2). By (9.4) total inputs are calculated by summation over all operated tankers, with a correction for the unutilized proportion for the marginal one.

By this we obtain the coordinates V_1, V_2, X of a point on the macro function with a given output X and a given slope of the isoquant represented by $-Q_1/Q_2$.

By carrying out such calculations for various values of total output X and for various pairs Q_1, Q_2 we obtain sufficient information to get an impression of the short-run macro function. We carried out the calculations for $X = 200,000$, $400,000$, $600,000$, $\ldots$, $4,400,000$, $4,600,000$ and for $X = 4,797,000$, which is total capacity of all vessels taken together (in 1000 ton-miles per day), and for the following pairs of values of Q_1 and Q_2 with the corresponding slopes $-Q_1/Q_2$:

Q_1	Q_2	$-Q_1/Q_2$
0	1	0
1	2	-0.5
1	1	-1.0
2	1	-2.0
4	1	-4.0
1	0	∞

The case $Q_1 = 0$, $Q_2 = 1$ generates the right boundary of the region of substitution, while the case $Q_1 = 1$, $Q_2 = 0$ generates the upper boundary (cf. Section 4.6).

The results of these calculations are given in Table 9.5. On this basis the isoquant map is drawn in Figure 9.2. (More details are given in Eide 1969.) The isoquants should of course in principle be drawn as piece-wise linear curves, but with 377 micro units the smooth approximations give a good indication of the forms.

In the figure we have also indicated the region of positive capacity so that

TABLE 9.5

Points on the short-run macro production function for Norwegian tankers 1967. X = output in 1000 ton-miles per day; V_1 = fuel input in 1000 kroner per day; V_2 = labour input in 1000 kroner per day

X	$Q_1=0, Q_2=1$		$Q_1=1, Q_2=2$		$Q_1=1, Q_2=1$		$Q_1=2, Q_2=1$		$Q_1=4, Q_2=1$		$Q_1=1, Q_2=0$	
	V_1	V_2	V_1	V_2	V_1	V_2	V_1	V_2	V_1	V_2	V_1	V_2
200,000	43.4	15.9	43.2	16.0	43.2	16.0	43.2	16.0	43.2	16.0	43.2	16.0
400,000	102.3	37.5	94.5	38.1	94.2	38.3	94.2	38.3	94.2	38.3	94.2	38.3
600,000	158.4	60.5	155.5	60.8	152.1	63.1	151.8	63.7	151.6	64.2	151.6	64.2
800,000	220.0	85.4	214.3	86.8	213.7	87.4	211.2	90.6	211.2	90.7	211.0	92.1
1,000,000	278.9	112.4	274.8	113.9	273.7	114.6	271.2	118.6	271.2	118.6	271.1	119.8
1,200,000	338.5	140.4	334.9	142.0	333.9	142.8	333.5	143.4	333.2	144.4	333.2	144.4
1,400,000	403.3	169.3	399.7	169.8	399.7	169.8	399.7	169.8	398.4	173.5	398.2	175.4
1,600,000	474.8	201.6	465.5	202.7	465.5	202.7	465.4	203.0	465.3	203.1	464.3	210.7
1,800,000	545.4	234.9	532.0	236.4	531.7	236.7	531.7	236.7	531.6	237.0	530.8	242.5
2,000,000	613.9	268.9	600.0	271.3	598.7	272.0	598.7	272.0	598.6	272.5	598.5	273.6
2,200,000	684.3	304.9	671.9	308.1	668.8	310.7	668.8	310.7	668.8	310.7	668.8	310.7
2,400,000	765.3	343.5	752.0	344.4	748.3	347.1	745.3	351.1	744.0	355.0	744.0	355.9
2,600,000	848.9	384.2	830.8	388.0	829.1	389.0	826.8	392.4	825.3	395.5	824.3	405.0
2,800,000	936.8	428.6	920.5	431.4	915.1	435.3	910.9	441.0	910.1	443.2	908.7	466.4
3,000,000	1037.1	477.3	1012.0	481.3	1006.9	485.3	1000.8	493.3	996.9	504.3	985.5	522.2
3,200,000	1131.7	532.5	1010.0	537.5	1099.9	543.5	1094.7	551.1	1089.7	565.3	1085.9	598.1
3,400,000	1246.0	595.3	1215.0	601.2	1203.9	608.9	1189.3	630.4	1187.2	636.3	1182.8	682.0
3,600,000	1350.3	670.4	1334.9	673.8	1309.4	692.0	1300.3	705.1	1288.2	738.5	1284.7	790.1
3,800,000	1462.3	767.7	1435.9	772.6	1425.5	780.5	1406.6	807.0	1393.0	845.7	1388.7	894.1
4,000,000	1561.7	874.5	1546.8	877.8	1536.2	884.9	1514.1	915.8	1499.6	957.5	1493.9	1010.2
4,200,000	1666.0	993.8	1652.9	997.0	1639.8	1006.4	1622.1	1033.7	1609.1	1069.7	1600.8	1131.1
4,400,000	1770.7	1120.8	1758.4	1124.8	1748.0	1133.0	1732.3	1158.5	1719.2	1197.2	1710.8	1251.9
4,600,000	1876.6	1258.2	1868.6	1261.7	1864.5	1264.1	1847.2	1288.4	1837.6	1314.8	1836.8	1319.0
4,797,000	1954.3	1370.2	1954.3	1370.2	1954.3	1370.2	1954.3	1370.2	1954.3	1370.2	1954.3	1370.2

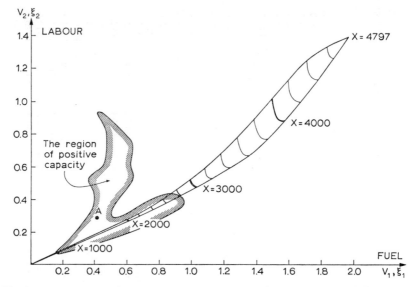

Fig. 9.2. Isoquant map for the short-run macro production function, Norwegian tankers 1967, together with the region of positive capacity.

the whole figure corresponds to Figure 4.4 in the theoretical part of the study. In Figure 9.2 we have measured X, V_1 and V_2 in millions (rather than thousands) of ton-miles and *kroner* per day. Then the same axes are suitable both for measuring ξ_1 and ξ_2 for the capacity distribution and V_1 and V_2 for the macro production function.

It would be a simple matter to draw expansion curves in Figure 9.2, but their form is obvious so that it would not add much of information.

It is seen that the scope for substitution is rather narrow, particularly for low total output values. This is because the new and efficient vessels are rather concentrated in the capacity distribution. As output increases the split in the capacity distribution causes a wider range of substitution, which has, however, to narrow down again when we approach full capacity utilization.

The form of the region of substitution can be understood on the basis of the reasoning presented in connection with Figure 4.3. First think of the upper boundary of the region of substitution in Figure 9.2. This is formed by letting a vertical line move through the capacity distribution as illustrated in Figure 4.3 – in the calculations described above by having $Q_1 = 1$, $Q_2 = 0$. The moving of the line corresponds to letting the critical value of C defined by (9.1) increase. (We may put $q_1 = Q_1/C$, $q_2 = Q_2/C$.) The slope of the upper boundary is equal to the slope of the ray from the origin to the average point along the vertical line (the angle α in Figure 4.3). In Figure 9.2 this slope will largely increase until we have exhausted most of the upper branch (the motor tanker branch) of the capacity distribution. For the further expansion we have to exploit the lower branch (the turbine tanker branch) of the capacity distribution, and the slope of the upper boundary of the region of substitution falls off. This happens at a total output around $X = 4400$ million ton-miles per day. For the right boundary of the region of substitution we have a similar effect. Here we have to think of a horizontal line moving through the capacity distribution and observe the slope of the ray from the origin to the average point on this line. There will be a marked change in the slope when we have exhausted most of the lower branch of the capacity distribution. This happens at a total output between 3400 and 3800 million ton-miles per day.

These effects give the region of substitution a bent shape which makes the macro function deviate in an interesting way from the form of a fixed coefficient function.

The elasticity of substitution will of course have to undergo some changes corresponding more or less to the width of the region of substitution as we increase output, since the isoquants are vertical at the upper and horizontal at the right boundary of the region of substitution. The relevant formulas are given in Section 4.5, e.g. by (4.48'). The standard deviations σ_1 and σ_2 are clearly relatively small for small values of X; this contributes to a low value of the elasticity of substitution s_{12} for this part of the function. For larger output X, when the branching out of the capacity distribution becomes relevant, the standard deviations contribute more to the elasticity of substitution (although $\tilde{\xi}_1$ and $\tilde{\xi}_2$ in the formula also increase). Also the scale elasticity ε is smaller in this part, making the factor $1/\varepsilon$ in Equation (4.48') larger. On the other hand the term $J/(2X)$ is clearly tending to make s_{12} smaller – compare the interpretation in connection with Equation (4.50) with Figure 9.1.[3]

The macro function does of course also deviate from a fixed coefficient

---

[3] The special form of the capacity distribution will give a rather complicated form to the changes in the elasticity of substitution *along* an isoquant. If we, for a large value of X, rotate the zero quasi rent line so as to generate an isoquant, then we will at one extreme have rather small values of σ_1 and σ_2 because the line passes through only one of the branches of the capacity distribution. The same will hold at the other extreme position. At intermediate positions the line will pass through both branches and σ_1 and σ_2 will be larger. Thus s_{12} should be greater in the interior than nearer to the borders of the region of substitution. I think this effect can be seen particularly near the right boundary.

function in that there are decreasing returns. This is clearly seen by comparing the distances between the isoquants. (Notice that we have drawn first the isoquants for $X = 1000$ and $X = 2000$, and from there on for every 200 million ton-miles per day.) An expression for the scale elasticity is given in connection with Figure 4.2.

The average input coefficients for all capacity are $\xi_1 = 0.41$, $\xi_2 = 0.29$. This is represented by point A in Figure 9.2. If we think of the position of the zero quasi rent line so that one is very near to utilizing all capacity, and so that the line passes through both branches of the capacity distribution, then the scale elasticity ε is a little above $\frac{1}{2}$ according to the expression given in connection with Figure 4.2. Thus, for intermediate positions on the isoquants it is suggested that the value of the scale elasticity ε declines from 1 towards a little more than $\frac{1}{2}$ with increasing output. (The decline is rather sharp towards the end and does not show up clearly in Figure 9.2; more densely spaced isoquants would be needed.) But ε is not constant along an isoquant. Because of the special form of the capacity distribution it would, for rather high values of output, tend to be lower near the boundaries of the region of substitution than in central parts of it.[4]

As already suggested the form of the macro function arrived at above is not easily captured by a mathematical formula. If we should compare with some of the mathematical cases used as illustrations in Chapter 5, the "classical" Houthakker-Pareto-Cobb-Douglas case would not be the most relevant case. It would rather be the very simple case studied in Section 5.3, i.e. the case of capacity being distributed along a right-angled curve; however, we would have to use the modified case where the distribution is truncated by means of the parameters k_1 and k_2 so that the region of substitution would be as given by $OQ_1Q_2Q_3O$ in Figure 5.2. Some of the features shown in Figure 5.2 are present also in Figure 9.2. But the form is of course distorted by the high concentration towards the south-western corner of the capacity distribution, and by the fact that there is more capacity along the upper branch than along the lower branch of the capacity distribution in Figures 9.1 and 9.2.

9.6. Some observations on laying-up and sales of Norwegian tankers

It is part of our theory of the short-run macro production function that

---

[4] This again influences the elasticity of substitution and further complicates the effects discussed in the preceding footnote.

current decisions about whether or not to utilize a micro unit of production are taken on the basis of obtainable quasi rents at current prices.

In the case of ships there are several reasons why we cannot in practice expect full conformity with this hypothesis.

First there are special technological differences between the tankers which are suppressed in our treatment; e.g., not all vessels can be used in all trades because of size, port conditions, etc.

Next there are some aspects of the market systems which prevent a full adherence to our theory. In particular fairly long-term charter contracts are quite common, and there are costs of laying up and reactivating a ship as mentioned before which bring in economic considerations in addition to quasi rents even in the case of short-term contracts. These effects of market conditions reflect the discrepancy between short-run equilibrium and actual observations which will in most cases reflect some degree of disequilibrium, as we have pointed out before.

In spite of these factors we would of course expect some tendency for high cost vessels to be more frequently laid up than efficient, low cost vessels.

A special feature in this sector is that a micro unit – the ship – can easily be sold and transferred abroad, unlike fixed equipment in many other branches of production. Rather than having a ship laid up for a very long time it might be more profitable to sell it. Again we should expect some correlation between costs or obtainable quasi rents and the likelihood that a ship be sold, but perhaps not exactly corresponding to the case of laying up. In the case of Norway there are relatively high wages as compared with many other shipping nations. A vessel which, because of a high labour input coefficient, is not able to earn positive quasi rents at the Norwegian wage level might be able to do so when transferred to other countries. On the other hand, fuel prices are much more similar regardless of where the ship belongs. As a result of this we should expect the sales of tankers to be more concentrated among vessels with particularly high labour input coefficients, as compared with laid-up vessels which should be found among high cost vessels regardless of whether the high costs are due to high labour input, high fuel input, or both. But again we could not expect an absolutely clear pattern, since there are of course many factors – financial, organizational and personal – which influence decisions about whether or not to sell a ship. In any case it is clear that expectations about future prices and wages are of prime importance in connection with such decisions, and they are not necessarily similar and determined by current prices and wages.

Some investigations into these problems have been made by Mr. Tor

Hersoug in collaboration with me. Details are given in Hersoug (1969a).

In 1966 no Norwegian tanker (above 15,000 DWT) was laid up, and in the years before 1966 only a few were laid up. To get a rough picture with more than a few observations of ships laid up, we collected data for all vessels included in our data (i.e. tankers above 15,000 DWT which have been built in the period 1950–66) which have been laid up at least once during the period 1955–66. (Layup for maintenance and repair was not taken into account.) The same was done for sales of tankers.

Altogether 48 vessels (above 15,000 DWT) had been laid up once or more during 1950–66, because of the freight market conditions, without having been sold from Norway before the end of 1966. These 48 vessels are thus among the 377 vessels contained in the data used in the previous sections of this chapter. In the same period 223 vessels were sold from Norway, either for use by the new owner or for demolition (the latter applies only to very few of the vessels). These 223 vessels are of course not among the 377 treated previously. For these 223 vessels capacities and input coefficients had to be calculated. This was done so as to make the figures as much as possible comparable to the figures for the 377 vessels.

Figure 9.3 shows the distribution of the 48 vessels that have been laid up

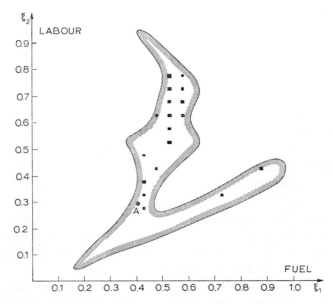

Fig. 9.3. The distribution of tankers which have been laid up (black rectangles) in relation to the 1967 region of positive capacity.

some time during the period 1950–66. The black rectangles represent capacity (but the scale is not the same as in Figure 9.1). The region of positive capacity is suggested by the shaded border-line in the figure, and we have indicated the average point of the 1967 capacity distribution as in Figure 9.2. It is apparent that the vessels that have been laid up are largely found among those with high operating costs, as we should expect.[5]

In Figure 9.4 is shown in a similar way the distribution of vessels sold in

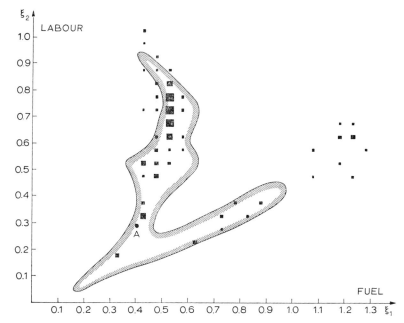

Fig. 9.4. The distribution of sold tanker capacity (black rectangles) in relation to the 1967 region of positive capacity.

the period 1950–66. Some of the vessels sold are of course located outside the 1967 border of the region of positive capacity. It is seen that some rather efficient ships have been sold, but the bulk of sold capacity is located somewhat farther out in the inefficient direction than the capacity that has been idle but not sold. This is natural since chances are lower for a profitable

---

[5] A warning should perhaps be given in interpreting this observation, so as not to attach excessive importance to it. Since older vessels have been under observation for a longer period than newer vessels, and since older vessels are not found in the south-west part of the capacity distribution, some effect similar to the one observed might result also if a random sample of vessels were laid up every year.

reactivation of a very inefficient than for a somewhat less inefficient ship, and accordingly the chances of the very inefficient ship being sold are bigger.

Comparing Figures 9.3 and 9.4 it is hard to find any indication of different roles of labour and fuel input coefficients in the case of layup and the case of sales as discussed above.

For further comparisons of the distribution of vessels laid up and sold vessels one may eliminate one dimension by considering total current costs. The sum $\xi_1 + \xi_2$ for each vessel will give total fuel and manpower costs per unit of output at around 1966 prices (see Section 9.2). We now group all vessels in the 1967 fleet, all vessels that have been laid up and all sold vessels in classes according to the value of $\xi_1 + \xi_2$; let us call these groups "cost groups".

We next calculate the proportion of total capacity in each cost group that has been laid up some time during the period. The result is illustrated by the lower curve in Figure 9.5. It is clear that the proportion is largely higher the higher are the costs. (In the highest cost group there are very few vessels so that the sample from which we could observe layups is here very small.)

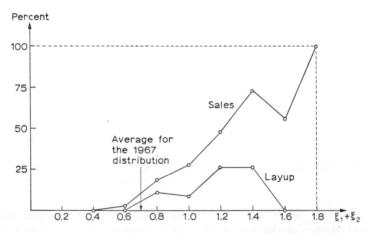

Fig. 9.5. The proportion of tanker capacity which has been laid up some time during 1950–66 (lower curve) and the proportion of sold capacity to the sum of sold and still remaining capacity as of 1967 (upper curve). Grouping according to fuel+labour costs per unit of output.

For the vessels that have been sold it is more appropriate to calculate slightly different proportions, viz. the proportions of sold capacity to the sum of sold and still remaining capacity as of 1967 in each cost group. This proportion is shown by the upper curve in Figure 9.5. This curve is increasing almost monotonically with costs $\xi_1 + \xi_2$ and of course goes up to 100% at cost levels above those represented in the 1967 fleet.

The distribution of the full capacity existing as of 1967 ranges from $\xi_1 + \xi_2$-values near to 0.25 to around 1.5, as is seen from Figure 9.1, with the average at 0.70.

In the period 1950–66, from which the observations underlying Figure 9.5 are drawn, input prices were not as in 1966 throughout the period. Through much of the period the relative price of fuel to labour was higher than around 1966 as shown by Table 9.4. Total fuel and labour costs per unit of output as calculated by $\xi_1 + \xi_2$ do therefore not represent the relevant input prices for the whole period. Taking account of this would however not change the general impression significantly.

It is tempting to compare the curves in Figure 9.5 with the generalization of the construction of the short-run macro function discussed in Section 3.6. We there assumed that the degree of utilization was an increasing function – but not necessarily a step function – of quasi rents per unit of output. Corresponding to this the proportion of vessels laid up should be an increasing function of operating costs per unit of output.[6] This is roughly what is suggested by our observations of vessels laid up, although the impression is perhaps not quite conclusive. In this connection it should be remembered that we have no data on layups among vessels that have been sold during the period, i.e. vessels that have been laid up before they were sold. If these had been observed they would probably add to the right part of the layup curve in Figure 9.5. Furthermore, if sales of ships had not been possible, then we would probably have had many more vessels laid up, and again mainly towards the right in the figure. Thus we would get a picture where operating costs – and thereby quasi rents – would seem to be more decisive than according to the layup curve in Figure 9.5. A final point is that we have only registered whether or not vessels have been laid up. If we had taken into account the frequency and duration of layups, then the dependence of the rate of layup upon costs would probably prove to be sharper.

It may be concluded that the evidence and discussion in this section lend some support to the generalization in Section 3.6, when there is a question of describing actual behaviour by means of a short-run macro function. This does of course not contradict the construction of our standard short-run

---

[6] Notice that it is of no special significance to compare operating costs as indicated by $\xi_1 + \xi_2$ with the value 1. This would be of interest only if input prices had been deflated by output price.

macro function when this is conceived as a function giving *maximum* output for given total inputs. What it means is that this maximum is not necessarily achieved in practice; or, in other words – as suggested several times before – our standard short-run macro function represents short-run *equilibrium* positions whereas actual observations usually represent some degree of deviation from equilibrium.

Bibliography

Aigner, D.J. and S.F. Chu (1968), On estimating the industry production function. *The American Economic Review.*

Allen, R.G.D. (1967), *Mathematical analysis for economists.* London, MacMillan.

Arrow, K.J. et al. (1961), Capital-labour substitution and economic efficiency. *The Review of Economics and Statistics.*

Atkinson, A.B. and J.E. Stiglitz (1969), A new view of technological change. *The Economic Journal.*

Bardhan, P.K. (1967), On estimation of production functions from international cross-section data. *The Economic Journal.*

Bardhan, P.K. (1969), Equilibrium growth in a model with economic obsolescence of machines. *The Quarterly Journal of Economics.*

Belinfante, A.E.E. (1969), *Technical change in the steam electric power generating industry.* Ph.D. dissertation, University of California, Berkeley, Calif.

Bentzel, R. and Ø. Johansson (1959), Om homogenitet i produktionsfunksjoner. *Ekonomisk Tidskrift.*

Bjøntegård, E. (1970), En analyse av aggregerte produktfunksjoner ved imperfekt optimalisering. *Memorandum from the Institute of Economics,* University of Oslo, 7 October 1970.

Bliss, C.J. (1968), On putty-clay. *Review of Economic Studies.*

Brown, M. (1966), *On the theory and measurement of technical change.* Cambridge, University Press.

Brown, M. (ed.) (1967), *The theory and empirical analysis of production.* New York, NBER and Columbia University Press.

Carter, Anne P. (1963), Incremental flow coefficients for a dynamic input-output model with changing technology. In: *Structural interdependence and economic development,* edited by T. Barna. London, MacMillan.

Carter, Anne P. (1970a), *Structural change in the American economy.* Cambridge (Mass.), Harvard University Press.

Carter, Anne P. (1970b), Technological forecasting and input-output analysis. *Technological Forecasting.*

Carter, Anne P. (1970c), A linear programming system analyzing embodied technological change. In: *Contributions to input-output analysis (published in honor of W. Leontief),* edited by A.P. Carter and A. Brody. Amsterdam, North-Holland Publishing Company.

Chenery, H.B. (1949), Engineering production functions. *Quarterly Journal of Economics.*

Chenery, H.B. (1953), Process and production functions from engineering data, In: Leontief et al. (1953).

Cramér, H. (1946), *Mathematical methods of statistics.* Princeton, N.J., Princeton University Press.

Danø, S. (1966), *Industrial production models.* Wien-New York, Springer-Verlag.

DeSalvo, J.S. (1969), A process function for rail linehaul operations. *Journal of Transport Economics and Policy.*

Eide, E. (1969), En metode for konstruksjon av aggregerte korttids produktfunksjoner illustrert med data for den Norske tankflåte. *Memorandum from the Institute of Economics*, University of Oslo, 6 May 1969.

Eisner, R. (1970), Tax policy and investment behaviour: further comment. *American Economic Review*.

Fair, R.C. (1969), *The short-run demand for workers and hours*. Contributions to Economic Analysis 59. Amsterdam, North-Holland Publishing Company.

Farrell, M.J. (1957), The measurement of productive efficiency. *Journal of the Royal Statistical Society*, Series A, Part III.

Farrell, M.J. (1959), The convexity assumption in the theory of competitive markets. *The Journal of Political Economy*.

Farrell, M.J. and M. Fieldhouse (1962), Estimating efficient production functions under increasing returns to scale. *Journal of the Royal Statistical Society*, Series A, Part II.

Forssell, O. (1971), Explaining changes in input-output coefficients for Finland. Paper presented at *The Fifth International Conference on Input-Output Techniques* in Geneva, January 1971.

Førsund, F.R. (1969), Mål for produksjonsenheters effektivitet. *Memorandum from the Institute of Economics*, University of Oslo, 4 March 1969.

Førsund, F.R. (1970), A note on the technically optimal scale curve in inhomogeneous production functions. *Memorandum from the Institute of Economics*, University of Oslo, 20 June 1970.

Frisch, R. (1935), The principle of substitution. An example of its application in the chocolate industry. *Nordisk Tidsskrift for Teknisk Økonomi*.

Frisch, R. (1965), *Theory of production*. Dordrecht-Holland, Reidel.

Furubotn, E.G. (1965), Engineering data and the production function. *The American Economic Review*.

Galatin, M. (1968), *Economics of scale and technological change in thermal power generation*. Amsterdam, North-Holland Publishing Company.

Ghosh, A. (1964), *Experiments with input-output models*. Cambridge, University Press.

Gort, M. and R. Boddy (1967), Vintage effects and the time path of investment in production relations. In: M. Brown (ed.) (1967).

Goss, R.O. (1968), *Studies in maritime economics*. Cambridge, University Press.

Haavelmo, T. (1960), *A study in the theory of investment*. Chicago, University of Chicago Press.

Hanoch, G. (1969), Homotheticity, Homogeneity and Separability. *Discussion Paper No. 98, Harvard Institute of Economic Research*, Harvard University.

Harcourt, G.C. (1966), Biases in empirical estimates of the elasticities of substitution of C.E.S. production functions. *Review of Economic Studies*.

Hersoug, T. (1969a), Den relative effektivitet av Norske tankskip som er solgt til utlandet eller har ligget i opplag i perioden 1950–66. *Memorandum from the Institute of Economics*, University of Oslo, 10 May 1969.

Hersoug, T. (1969b), Om Slutsky-sammenhenger i produksjonsteorien. *Memorandum from the Institute of Economics*, University of Oslo, 12 June 1969.

Hettena, R. and H.S. Ruchlin (1969), The U.S. tanker industry: a structural and behavioral analysis. *The Journal of Industrial Economics*.

Hildebrand, G.H. and T.-C. Liu (1965), *Manufacturing production functions in the United States*, 1957. Ithaca, N.Y., New York State School of Industrial and Labor Relations, Cornell University.

Hildenbrand, W. (1968), The core of an economy with a measure space of economic agents. *The Review of Economic Studies*.

Hildenbrand, W. (1969), Pareto optimality for a measure space of economic agents. *International Economic Review*.

Houthakker, H.S. (1955–56), The Pareto distribution and the Cobb-Douglas production function in activity analysis. *The Review of Economic Studies*.

Hu, S.C. (1970), On ex post factor substitution. *Journal of Economic Theory.*

Johansen, L. (1959), Substitution versus fixed production coefficients in the theory of economic growth: a synthesis. *Econometrica.*

Johansen, L. (1960), Investeringsrate og vekstrate. *Ekonomiska Samfundets Tidskrift.*

Johansen, L. (1967), Some problems of pricing and optimal choice of factor proportions in a dynamic setting. *Economica.*

Johansen, L. (1968), Production functions and the concept of capacity. In: *Recherches récentes sur la fonction de production.* Namur, Centre d'Etudes et de la Recherche Universitaire de Namur.

Johansen, L. (1969), Outline of an approach to production studies. *Memorandum from the Institute of Economics,* University of Oslo, 28 April 1969.

Johansen, L. and T. Hersoug (1969), Derivation of macro production functions from distributions of micro units with respect to input coefficients. Some mathematical illustrations. *Memorandum from the Institute of Economics,* University of Oslo, 18 October 1969.

Johansen, L. and Å. Sørsveen (1967), Notes on the measurement of real capital in relation to economic planning models. *The Review of Income and Wealth.*

Katz, J.M. (1969), *Production functions, foreign investment and growth.* Amsterdam, North-Holland Publishing Company.

Komiya, R. (1962), Technological progress and the production function in the United States steam power industry. *The Review of Economics and Statistics.*

Koopmans, T. (1939), *Tanker freight rates and tankship building.* London, Netherlands Economic Institute and P.S. King & Son.

Kurz, M. and A.S. Manne (1963), Engineering estimates of capital-labor substitution in metal machining. *The American Economic Review.*

Lave, L.B. (1966) Engineering production functions and capital-labor substitution in metal machining: comment. *The American Economic Review.*

Lehmann, E.L. (1959), *Testing statistical hypotheses,* New York, John Wiley & Sons.

Leontief, W. et al. (1953), *Studies in the structure of the American economy.* New York, Oxford University Press.

Levhari, D. (1968), A note on Houthakker's aggregate production function in a multifirm industry. *Econometrica.*

Liviatan, N. (1966), The concept of capital in professor Solow's Model. *Econometrica.*

Lundberg, E. (1961), *Produktivitet och räntabilitet.* Stockholm, Studieförbundet Näringsliv och Samhälle.

MacAvoy, P.W. (1969), *Economic strategy for developing nuclear breeder reactors.* Cambridge, Mass., The M.I.T. Press.

Mayor, T.H. (1969), Some theoretical difficulties in the estimation of the elasticity of substitution from cross-section data. *Western Economic Journal.*

Maywald, K. (1957), The best and the average in productivity studies and in long-term forecasting. *The Productivity Measurement Review, No. 9. (Reprint Series* No. 132, University of Cambridge, Department of Applied Economics.)

McFadden, D. (1967), Review of Hildebrand and Liu (1965). *The Journal of the American Statistical Association.*

Nerlove, M. (1963), Returns to scale in electricity supply. In: *Measurement in economics: studies in mathematical economics and econometrics in memory of Yehuda Grunfeld,* edited by C.F. Christ et al., Stanford, Calif., Stanford University Press.

Nerlove, M. (1965), *Estimation and identification of Cobb-Douglas production functions.* Amsterdam, North-Holland Publishing Company.

Nerlove, M. (1967), Recent empirical studies of the CES and related production functions. In: M. Brown (ed.) (1967).

Newman, P. (1969), Some properties of concave functions. *Journal of Economic Theory.*

Park, S.Y. (1966), Bounded substitution, fixed proportions, and economic growth. *Yale Economic Essays.*

Puu, T. (1966), Les effets de substitution et d'expansion dans la théorie de la production. *Revue d'Economie Politique.*

Puu, T. (1968), Complementarity, substitutivity and regressivity in the theory of production. In: *Recherches récentes sur la fonction de production.* Namur, Centre d'Etudes et de la Recherche Universitaire de Namur.

Puu, T. and S. Skogh (1968), An analytical production function with variable returns to scale. Mimeographed. Institute of Economics, University of Uppsala.

Rasche, R.H. and H.T. Shapiro (1968), The F.R.B.-M.I.T. econometric model: its special features. *The American Economic Review, Papers and Proceedings* of the Eightieth Annual Meeting of the American Economic Association.

Ringstad, V. (1967), Econometric analyses based on a production function with neutrally variable scale-elasticity. *The Swedish Journal of Economics.*

Rothenberg, J. (1960), Non-convexity, aggregation, and Pareto-optimality. *The Journal of Political Economy.*

Salter, W.E.G. (1960), *Productivity and technical change.* London, Cambridge University Press.

Samuelson, P.A. (1967), The monopolistic competition revolution. In: *Monopolistic competition theory; studies in impact* (essays in honor of E.H. Chamberlin), edited by R.E. Kuenne. New York, John Wiley & Sons.

Sanyal, S.K. (1967), On Houthakker's relation between the Pareto distribution and the Cobb-Douglas production function with special reference to jute industry in India. *The National Sample Survey, Technical Paper Series*, Technical Paper No. 11. Calcutta, Indian Statistical Institute.

Scheper, W. (1968), Ein neoklassisches Wachstumsmodell mit unterschiedlichen ex ante- und ex post-Substitutionselastizitäten. In: *Recherches récentes sur la fonction de production.* Namur, Centre d'Etudes et de la Recherche Universitaire de Namur.

Seitz, W.D. (1970), The measurement of efficiency relative to a frontier production function. *American Journal of Agricultural Economics.*

Seland, J. (1954), Fraktmarkedet, skipsoppleggene og deres bakgrunn. *Statistiske Meldinger*, No. 11. Oslo, Central Bureau of Statistics of Norway.

Shephard, R.W. (1953), *Cost and production functions*, Princeton, N.J., Princeton University Press.

Smith, V.L. (1961), *Investment and production.* Cambridge, Mass., Harvard University Press.

Solow, R.M. (1960), Investment and technical progress. In: *Mathematical methods in the social sciences*, edited by K.J. Arrow, S. Karlin and P. Suppes. Stanford, Calif., Stanford University Press.

Solow, R.M. (1962), Substitution and fixed proportions in the theory of capital. *The Review of Economic Studies.*

Solow, R.M. (1963), Heterogeneous capital and smooth production functions: an experimental study. *Econometrica.*

Solow, R.M. (1967), Some recent developments in the theory of production. In: M. Brown (ed.) (1967).

Solow, R.M., J. Tobin, C.C. von Weizsäcker and M. Yaari (1966), Neoclassical growth with fixed factor proportions. *The Review of Economic Studies.*

Sporn, P. (1969), *Technology, engineering, and economics.* Cambridge Mass., The MIT Press.

Stieber, J. (ed.) (1966), *Employment problems of automation and advanced technology.* London, MacMillan.

Svennilson, I. (1964), Economic growth and technical progress. In: *The residual factor and economic growth*. Paris, OECD.

Thãnh, P.C. (1966), Production processes with heterogeneous capital. *The Economic Record*.

Walters, A.A. (1963), Production and cost functions: an econometric study. *Econometrica*.

Walters, A.A. (1968), *An introduction to econometrics*. London, MacMillan.

Whitaker, J.K. (1965), Vintage capital models and econometric production functions. *The Review of Economic Studies*.

Wigley, K.J. (1970), Production models and time trends of input-output coefficients. In: *Input-output in the United Kingdom*, edited by W.F. Gossling. London, Frank Cass & Co.

Wohlin, L. (1970), *Skogsindustrins strukturomvandling och expansionsmöjligheter*. [Forest-Based Industries: Structural Change and Growth Potentials, in Swedish with English summary]. Stockholm, Industriens Utredningsinstitut.

Index